SketchUp for Site Design

SketchUp for Site Design

A Guide to Modeling Site Plans, Terrain, and Architecture

Second Edition

Daniel Tal, ASLA

Cover image: Daniel Tal

Cover design: Wiley

This book is printed on acid-free paper. ∞

Copyright © 2016 by John Wiley and Sons, Inc. All rights reserved

Published by John Wiley & Sons, Inc., Hoboken, New Jersey

Published simultaneously in Canada

For general information about our other products and services, please contact our Customer Care Department within the United States at (800) 762-2974, outside the United States at (317) 572-3993 or fax (317) 572-4002.

Wiley publishes in a variety of print and electronic formats and by print-on-demand. Some material included with standard print versions of this book may not be included in e-books or in print-on-demand. If this book refers to media such as a CD or DVD that is not included in the version you purchased, you may download this material at http://booksupport.wiley.com. For more information about Wiley products, visit www.wiley.com.

ISBN 978-1-118-98507-6 (paperback)—ISBN 978-1-118-98504-5 (pdf)—
ISBN 978-1-118-98506-9 (epub)—ISBN 978-1-118-98503-8 (O-book)

Printed in the United States of America

10 9 8 7 6 5 4 3 2 1

To my wife, Jenn (with gratitude for her contributions as both writer and editor), and our daughter, Anina Sofia

Contents

Introduction to SketchUp

How to Use
This Book

Welcome to the second edition of *SketchUp for Site Design*. This book describes SketchUp Process Modeling, a methodology for working with SketchUp. This approach provides a step-by-step road map that will show you how to use the tools and functions to construct expressive models of exterior spaces and architecture.

The process addresses three main areas of instruction: drafting, modeling order, and organization. Mastering these skills will allow you to create models that are highly detailed and articulate, easy to work with, optimized for computer performance, and organized.

Figs. 1-1 through 1-3 and Figs. 1-8 through 1-13 are examples of site plans and architectural projects created using SketchUp Process Modeling.

Fig. 1-1: Model of park overlook (SketchUp model rendered in Lumion)

Fig. 1-2: Cherry Hills residence, Colorado (SketchUp model rendered in Lumion)

Fig. 1-3: Cherry Hills residence bridge crossing (SketchUp model rendered in Lumion)

The book contents and tutorials were designed to work with all versions of SketchUp. Readers are strongly encouraged to download the free version of SketchUp, called SketchUp Make, from SketchUp's website (www.sketchup.com).

What's New in the Second Edition?

SketchUp has undergone a number of changes since the first edition of *SketchUp for Site Design* was published in August of 2009. Mainly, Trimble purchased SketchUp from Google. The new ownership has proven a positive outcome for SketchUp with a boost to staff and development resources. As a result, SketchUp has added a number of new features and improved performance.

SketchUp for Site Design has aged well with SketchUp. The original manuscript was written to focus on processes and methods over tools and menus. The processes are still valid, as are the many tutorials found in this book. In this regard, the second edition has remained unchanged.

However, given the changes to the software, *SketchUp for Site Design* contains updated content and includes two new chapters:

Chapter 5, "Ruby Scripts," has been retitled "SketchUp Extensions." This completely rewritten chapter provides a concise and clear overview of must-use custom apps (tools) for SketchUp.

Chapter 15, "Sandbox Architecture," has been replaced with "Digital Elevation Modeling." This chapter reviews how to generate and model on imported terrain and contour files, and it fits with the natural progression of Part 3, "Terrain Modeling."

Updated tool tips and processes are included throughout the various tutorials. Primarily, the updates focus on how to use extensions or apps as part of the grading, terrain, and CAD-to-SketchUp workflow.

www.danieltal.com

There is a subscription website that includes free resources (and free sign-up) to accompany this book. This book stands on its own; however, the resources available at www.danieltal.com are an excellent supplement. You do not need to become a member at DanielTal.com to learn and apply the skills and processes.

The website is mentioned in several chapters, usually to indicate where additional tutorials can be found that expand on the book's content. The website includes a link to the author's second book, *Rendering in SketchUp,* and downloadable component models. DanielTal.com has tutorial topics on site modeling, animations, extensions, terrain modeling, and more.

Who Can Use This Book?

Both beginners and advanced SketchUp users can benefit from this book. It is partitioned into four parts, starting with a basic explanation of SketchUp tools and functions. It transitions into more complex and detailed methods that incorporate terrain, AutoCAD, and the creation of complex forms. This provides a holistic approach for all levels of SketchUp users.

Even if you are a proficient SketchUp modeler, the methods and tips discussed here will help you better organize your models, use more sophisticated tools (**extensions**), and represent your ideas. Every tutorial in this book was vetted by two independent landscape architects: Carol McClanahan and Natalie Vaughn. Both professionals used the tutorials to learn SketchUp; neither of them had any prior experience using the software. In the course of their review, they discovered common user errors and software problems. Based on their comments, tutorials were clarified, added, or removed.

This book focuses on the tools and functions used to model site plans, outdoor areas, and architecture. The material includes sections devoted to modeling terrain and integrating AutoCAD and SketchUp. This book is devoted to achieving specific modeling results; however, it does not cover everything that SketchUp is capable of doing.

Learning Tutorials

SketchUp Process Modeling is best learned by doing. Step-by-step tutorials are included to illustrate how concepts work. The tutorials allow you to check your progress by comparing your results with those in the book. Completing these tutorials more than once will make it easier for you to master the presented concepts as they guide you along a gradual learning curve.

Downloadable Tutorial Models

Free downloadable SketchUp models are provided for you to use in tandem with the tutorials. The available models are listed at the beginning of each tutorial. To perform some of the tutorials, you will need to download the models. Some available model names will be provided in an image caption unrelated to a tutorial. Viewing the models in tandem with this book will help you understand the concepts being discussed. Part 1 of the book (Chapters 1 through 5) has no downloadable models.

To download the chapter tutorials or caption models, use the following procedure:

1. Open up SketchUp and select File ➤ 3D Warehouse ➤ Get Models.

2. The 3D Warehouse browser will open in SketchUp (see Fig. 1-4).

3. Search for the models in the browser and insert them directly into SketchUp.

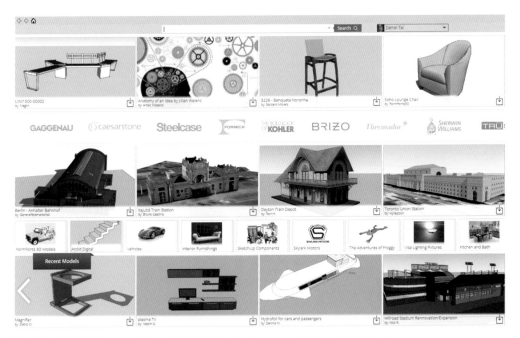

Fig. 1-4: 3D Warehouse contains all the tutorial and reference models found in this book.

The models for this book are part of 3D Warehouse Collections. The model collections correspond to the various parts (Part 2, Part 3, and Part 4) of the book.

You can find the tutorial and caption models by performing a search on the 3D Warehouse home page (Fig. 1-5). Directly to the left of the Search button, select the pull-down menu by clicking the downward arrow. From the menu, select Search For Collections. To find a model for a particular chapter, search by the part number of the appropriate chapter, as shown in Table 1-1.

Table 1-1: Search Terms for Models	
Search Term	**Will Bring All the Models For**
SPM Part 2	Chapters in Part 2
SPM Part 3	Chapters in Part 3
SPM Part 4	Chapters in Part 4

Fig. 1-5: To find the tutorial models, use the Search bar with Collections selected.

The models are further organized by their names. The chapter number will appear at the start of the model name, and the model names correspond to the model titles given in this book for any given tutorial (Fig. 1-6, Fig. 1-7).

If needed, you can search 3D Warehouse using the author's name, Daniel Tal, and all the book models will be displayed.

Two types of models are provided for this book at 3D Warehouse. The first type includes models to be used as part of a tutorial. Most (but not all) of these are for Part 3, "Terrain Modeling." The other models are "check" models. You can compare your results or caption models to these "checks" after you complete the corresponding tutorial in the text.

Save the models to your hard drive for easy access. If needed, you can redo any of the tutorials.

Downloadable Pre-Made Components

In addition to the tutorial models, you will need the SketchUp models called components. Chapter 3, "Components and Groups," provides detailed instructions on how to download and use these models, which are found on 3D Warehouse and at www.danieltal.com.

The Four Parts

The book is divided into four parts and ordered in a linear progression; each part and chapter builds on the previous sections.

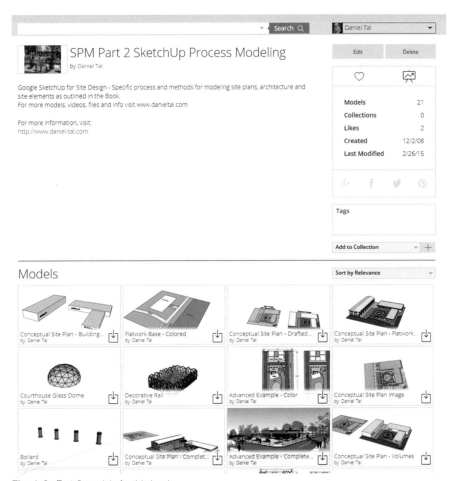

Fig. 1-6: Part 2 models for this book

No matter what your level of expertise, you should follow this linear progression. If you are an advanced user, you may want to skim the material, but you'll need to become familiar with the terminology and procedures outlined for SketchUp Process Modeling. You'll need to understand them for later parts of the book.

Part 1: Introduction to SketchUp

Chapter 2, "SketchUp Basics," reviews how SketchUp works and introduces its basic tools and functions. Chapter 3, "Components and Groups," introduces components and groups. Chapter 4, "Problem Solving," discusses how to best use SketchUp to problem-solve models and how to best problem-solve SketchUp when it performs in unexpected ways. Chapter 5, "SketchUp Extensions," introduces readers to Extensions, custom tools that make working with SketchUp easier.

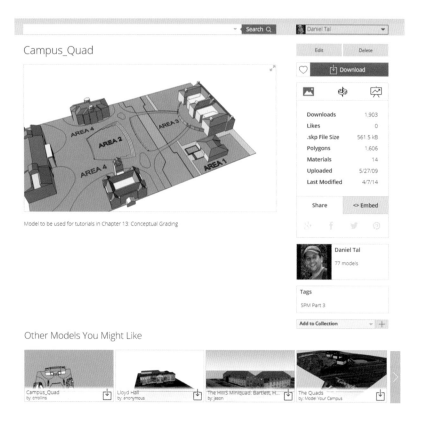

Model to be used for tutorials in Chapter 13: Conceptual Grading

Other Models You Might Like

Fig. 1-7: 3D Warehouse view of Conceptual 3D Grading tutorial model for Chapter 13

Fig. 1-8: Rain garden model completed in SketchUp

Fig. 1-9: Bridge and site model (SketchUp model rendered in Lumion)

Part 2: Introduction to SketchUp Process Modeling

SketchUp Process Modeling provides a road map for how best to accomplish specific goals in SketchUp. Chapter 6, "Introduction to SketchUp Process Modeling," introduces SketchUp Process Modeling through a tutorial modeling a site plan that includes a building, walks, trees, lawns, and trails.

Chapter 7, "Detailed Site Plan Modeling," applies the method as a modeling exercise utilizing a scanned and imported hand-drawn site plan. Chapter 8, "Custom Site Furnishings," provides a series of tutorials to create custom site objects. Chapter 9, "Custom Architecture," reviews how to model basic buildings and building elements such as windows and doors.

Chapter 10, "Arranging and Presenting the Model," unifies Chapters 7, 8, and 9 and shows users how to combine all the elements into a single model. Chapter 11, "Architectural Tutorial," completes SketchUp Process Modeling with a tutorial of a detailed and complex building model.

Part 3: Terrain Modeling

The Sandbox and terrain extensions are powerful and easy-to-use tools that can create complex and organic forms. Chapter 12, "Introduction to the Terrain Tools," introduces readers to the Sandbox tools and associated extensions in a series of simple diagrams.

Chapter 13, "SketchUp Conceptual Grading," demonstrates how the Sandbox tools can create conceptual terrain and grading. Chapter 14, "Complex Canopies," utilizes the Sandbox tools to create complex canopies and tensile structures. Chapter 15, "Digital Elevation Modeling," reveals how to apply the terrain tools to a complete terrain site model.

Fig. 1-10: Complete streets concept and park plaza (SketchUp model rendered in Lumion)

Fig. 1-11: River walk, Cedar Rapids, Iowa (SketchUp model rendered in Lumion)

Part 4: AutoCAD to SketchUp

Many SketchUp users, depending on their professions, utilize Computer Aided Design (CAD) software when drawing site plans and buildings. Part 4 details a specific method for efficiently and quickly converting an AutoCAD file into a 3D model.

Chapter 16, "Overview of AutoCAD to SketchUp," is an overview of the general AutoCAD-to-SketchUp conversion method. Chapter 17, "Organizing AutoCAD," provides a detailed procedure for organizing AutoCAD files for import into SketchUp.

Fig. 1-12: Model of Denver Justice Center plaza and building (Model courtesy of studioINSITE)

Fig. 1-13: Neighborhood revitalization concept model

Chapter 18, "Modeling the AutoCAD Flatwork Base," details how to model the organized AutoCAD information from Chapter 17. Chapter 19, "Arranging the Model," adds detail and final touches to the SketchUp model that started in AutoCAD.

SketchUp Basics

To effectively use SketchUp Process Modeling, you'll need to have a basic understanding of the SketchUp concepts described in this chapter. This includes knowing the SketchUp terminology and understanding how SketchUp displays models, how some tools function, and how to work in the SketchUp environment.

Geometry

SketchUp displays models through geometry. It digitally generates lines and surfaces that when combined create shapes, forms, and objects. For this book, the term *geometry* refers collectively to edges and faces, as described in the following section.

Simple Geometry

SketchUp constructs models using faces and edges. *Edges* are single lines that can be connected, moved, and adjusted. Connecting three or more edges in a closed loop can create a face. The words *line* and *lines* are used interchangeably with *edge* and *edges* throughout this book.

A *face* is composed of connected edges and resembles a single, infinitely thin surface (Fig. 2-1). Faces can resemble many shapes and forms.

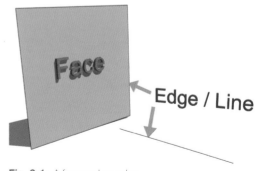

Fig. 2-1: A face and an edge

Deleting edges that compose a face will delete the face. Adjusting edges that compose a face will affect and adjust the face. Faces can be given *volume* to make them three-dimensional.

Complex Geometry

By connecting geometry in a particular order, you can create surfaces and objects. A curved or round surface is composed of a series of faceted flat faces that are connected to create the illusion of curvature. A simple 3D cube object is composed of six connected faces and their associated edges (Fig. 2-2).

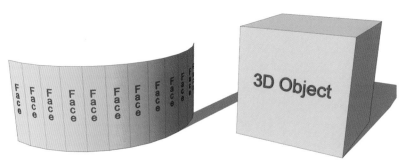

Fig. 2-2: A surface composed of faces (left) and a cube/object (right)

The 3D cube has volume; it has a varying length, width, and depth. This cube volume is hollow, as opposed to being seemingly solid. Deleting a face will reveal the interior of the cube. All 3D objects in SketchUp have volume and are hollow (Fig. 2-3). The term *volume* is used regularly in this book to describe geometry that has length, width, and depth.

Healing Faces

The term *healing faces* refers to using Draw or other tools to generate face geometry from edges. The simplest way to *heal a face* is by using the Line tool to create edges that will generate a face (Fig. 2-4).

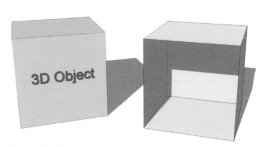

Fig. 2-3: Three-dimensional objects in SketchUp are hollow.

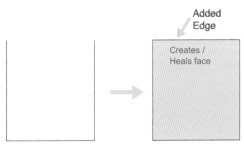

Fig. 2-4: The Line tool and edges are used to heal/create faces.

Subdividing Faces

Subdividing is a term used throughout this book. It refers to using geometry, typically edges, to further divide a face into multiple faces. There are many instances where you will be asked to use the SketchUp drawing tools to partition or subdivide a face into multiple faces (Fig. 2-5).

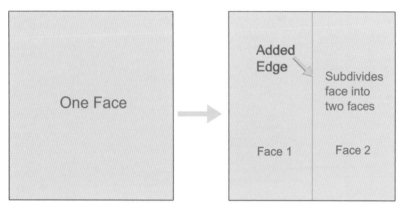

Fig. 2-5: Edges can subdivide a single face into two or more faces.

Sticky Geometry

Edges and faces in SketchUp are "sticky" relative to other geometry to which they are connected. Moving, rotating, or editing an edge or face will affect all the connected geometry. This "stickiness" is very useful when you're working with SketchUp's inference system (see "Navigation and 3D Inference System," p. 21). However, "sticky geometry" can sometimes get in the way (Fig. 2-6, Fig. 2-7). You can deal with this by using components and groups (see Chapter 3).

Fig. 2-6: All of the geometry is attached (touching).   **Fig. 2-7:** Moving the front face of the cube will stretch/move all of the connected adjacent geometry.

Face Count

The term *face count* refers to how many faces compose a model or object. A *high face count* indicates that a model or object is composed of many faces. High face-count objects typically have more detail, which makes them more desirable—for example, 3D trees compared to 2D trees (Fig. 2-8).

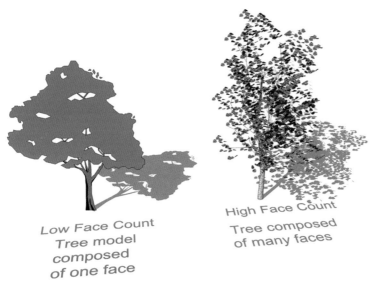

Fig. 2-8: A low face-count object (left) versus a high face-count object (right)

A high face-count model or a model filled with many high face-count objects can affect and possibly slow down computer performance. The process described in this book directly addresses this problem with strategies to use high face-count objects while preserving computer performance.

Basic SketchUp Tools

SketchUp tools operate by using the Click+release technique. After a tool is activated, click and release the left mouse button to draw edges, move items, or perform some other function. Do not click and hold to perform functions; this is known as Click+drag.

To practice the Click+release technique, activate a tool, select the first point, and release the mouse button. Do not click and drag. Depending on the tool, further input is typically required, usually clicking the left mouse button to complete an action. Practice the Click+release technique when you work with the following tutorials (Fig. 2-9, Fig. 2-10).

Fig. 2-9: SketchUp tools use the Click+release technique.

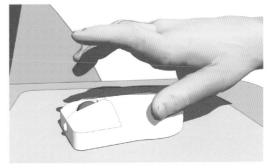

Fig. 2-10: Activate a tool, click the geometry to select, and release the mouse button to perform actions.

Drawing and Modification Tools

SketchUp uses a series of drawing tools to construct edges and faces. Most of these tools can be accessed from the top menu bar by selecting View ➤ Toolbars. Then select the Large Tool Set to activate SketchUp's primary tool palette. Hover your cursor over the tool icons of the Large Tool Set to identify the tools. To illustrate how most tools work, the next section provides a detailed overview of the Line and Select tools. Additional tools are described in short tutorials and summaries.

The Line Tool

The Line tool is used to draw edges that can subdivide or heal faces. Select the Line tool from the Large Tool Set. Draw a line by selecting (left-click) the first point, releasing the mouse, and then selecting a second point. You should notice that the Line tool is still active or "elastic," meaning SketchUp is waiting for you to draw additional edges. Draw a second line, trying to keep it "flat" on the drawing surface. Draw a third line connecting to the open end of the first line. If drawn correctly, SketchUp will generate a face between all the lines (Fig. 2-11).

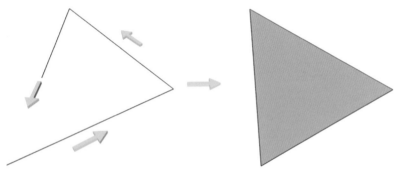

Fig. 2-11: The Line tool can create/heal a single face with three drawn edges.

The Select Tool

Choose the Select tool (arrow) from the Large Tool Set. This tool will be used often. The Select tool does as its name implies; it selects edges and faces. There are several ways to select geometry.

Single Clicking To select geometry, simply click on an edge or face with the Select tool.

Add/Subtract Geometry Holding the Shift key down while using the Select tool (referred to as Shift+click) will select multiple edges, faces, and geometry. If the selected geometry is clicked on again while holding Shift+click, geometry will be subtracted or deselected from the selection set.

Additive Method Ctrl+click is identical to Shift+click except that it will not subtract or deselect geometry already selected.

Using a Selection Box Clicking and dragging the Select tool (Click+hold and drag) will create a *selection box*. The direction of the selection box provides two options:

Dragging from left to right creates a selection box that will select only geometry that is entirely within the box (Fig. 2-12, Fig. 2-13).

Dragging from right to left creates a selection box that selects anything the box touches, including the geometry inside.

Shift+click and Ctrl+click work when the selection box is used.

The Click and Select Method Clicking on an object or face will select that geometry. Double-clicking on a face will select the face and the edges that compose that face. Triple-clicking on a face will cause all connected geometry to be selected.

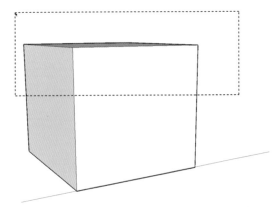

Fig. 2-12: A selection box is used to select the geometry of the 3D cube/object.

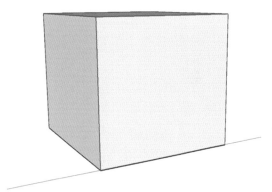

Additional Tools

Fig. 2-13: The selected object

The following tools are basic SketchUp tools used to draw, modify, or adjust face and edge geometry. Many of these tools are used extensively with the various tutorials. You should become familiar with how they function. Additional tools are reviewed throughout the book.

The Arc Tools There are several arc tools in SketchUp. The tool to focus on for this book is the Two-Point Arc. Experiment with the Arc tools as needed. The Two-Point Arc requires three points to be inputted. The first and second points define the length, and the third point provides a radius or bulge for the arc (Fig. 2-14).

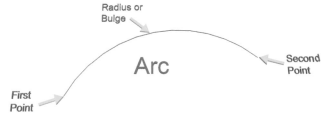

Fig. 2-14: The Arc tool requires three points to define an arc.

Rectangle The Rectangle tool creates a rectangular face. Activate the Rectangle tool and select the first rectangle point. The tool will remain active and require a second input that will help define the width and length of the rectangle (Fig. 2-15).

Move/Copy Selected geometry can be relocated or copied. Selected geometry can be moved by simply clicking on a point with the Move tool and moving it to the desired location.

To create a copy, select the geometry and, with Move/Copy active, Ctrl+click, release the mouse button, and move the cursor away from the original. The copied geometry will move when it is dragged (Fig. 2-16).

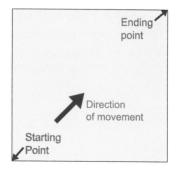

Fig. 2-15: The Rectangle tool

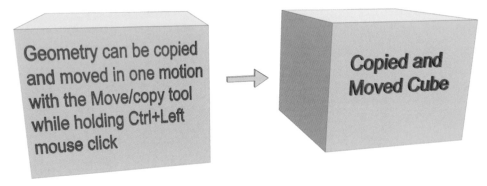

Fig. 2-16: Selecting an object and then holding Ctrl with the Move/Copy tool will create a copy of that object.

Eraser and Hidden Geometry Dragging the Eraser tool over edges or faces will delete them. Holding the Shift key while using the Eraser tool on geometry will hide it from view. You can see the hidden geometry by turning on View ➢ Hidden Geometry.

Offset The Offset tool creates a copy of selected geometry parallel to the original selection. Using Offset on a selected face will create a copy of all the edges that compose that face and will either expand the face (offset outward) or further subdivide the face (offset inward) (Fig. 2-17). Selecting and offsetting edges will create copies of the selected edge.

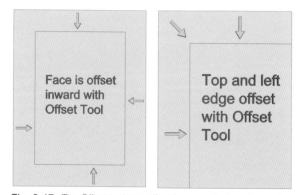

Fig. 2-17: The Offset tool can offset faces and edges to create parallel elements.

Push/Pull The Push/Pull tool allows users to add volume to a face. Activate the tool and hover the cursor over a flat face. The face will become highlighted. Click and release on the face. Push the cursor upward. This will add volume to the face by generating additional geometry (Fig. 2-18).

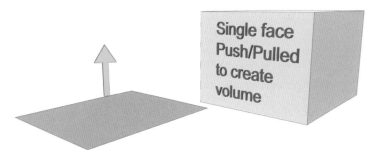

Fig. 2-18: The Push/Pull tool creates 3D volumes from faces.

The Measurement Window

The Measurement window, located at the bottom-right corner of the screen, allows users to accurately portray dimensions and achieve precision while modeling. Inputting specific numerical values provides lengths, widths, heights, rotation angles, and other dimensions for the geometry (Fig. 2-19). SketchUp must be maximized to view the Measurement window.

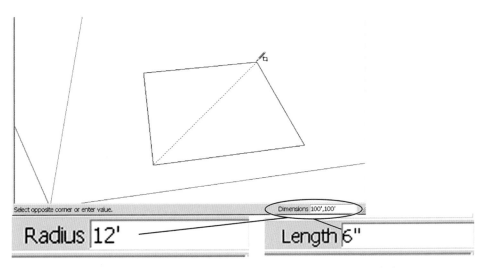

Fig. 2-19: The Measurement window allows users to enter exact lengths, widths, and other dimensions to create precision geometry.

To enter a value, you do not need to select the Measurement window. When a tool is active, simply type the desired value into the Measurement window. Press the Enter key to apply that value.

Example: Select the Rectangle tool and pick the first point. Then type **100',100'** (the rectangle dimension) and press Enter. SketchUp will create a flat rectangular surface that is 100 feet in length and width.

Styles

SketchUp lets you adjust how geometry and the SketchUp environment appear. They can be adjusted through the Styles menu (Window ➢ Default Tray ➢ Styles). The Styles menu has many options, and it takes some practice to realize the full potential of this menu. For now, the focus is on edges and the SketchUp environment.

Edge Settings

On the Styles menu, select the Edit tab. Five icons that control many SketchUp settings will appear. Select the Edge settings (first from the left). By default, Display Edges and Profiles are both checked. Unselecting both options will make all the edges in the model invisible.

The Profile line adds thickness to SketchUp lines that form the perimeter edges of faces. Profile lines also indicate when edges are subdividing a face; the lines will lose their thick profile and become thin when they properly subdivide a face (Fig. 2-20, Fig. 2-21).

The downside to keeping Profiles checked is that it makes perimeter edges appear very thick in comparison to other edges. Practice working with Profiles unchecked. You can then determine for yourself whether or not you want to use them.

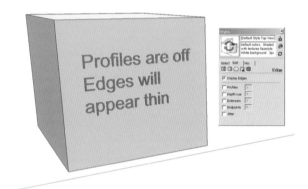

Fig. 2-20: Profiles are unchecked, displaying thin edges.

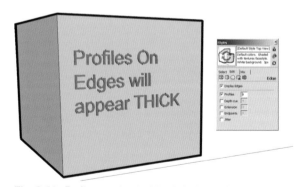

Fig. 2-21: Profiles are checked "on," displaying thicker edges.

Background Settings

In the Styles menu, the background options are in the middle under the Edit tab. There are several options: Background Color, Sky, and Ground.

For now, focus on the background. The default background color is beige. You will probably want to adjust the background color to white. This will make the edges and faces easier to see. Double-click on the background color swatch. A color menu will appear. Adjust the value to make the background white.

Checking the Sky or Ground tab will add a faded simulated sky or ground to the model environment. For now, keep both options unchecked (Fig. 2-22).

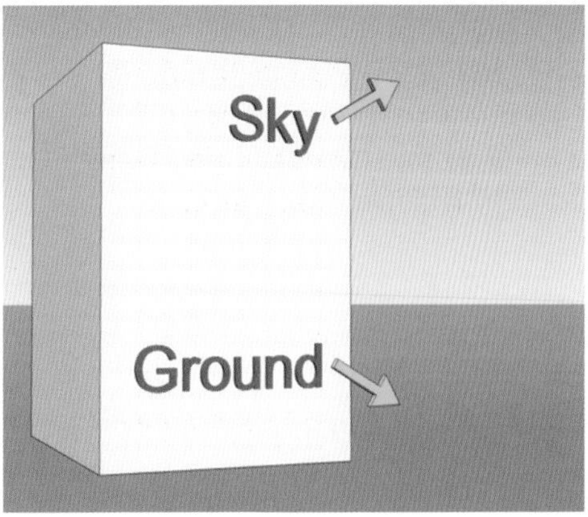

Fig. 2-22: The Background setting for Sky and Ground is turned on in a SketchUp model.

Navigation and 3D Inference System

SketchUp is a two-dimensional interface allowing for movement in a three-dimensional environment. Without a reference system, it would be difficult to orient your projects. SketchUp's inference system helps you find your position in 3D space and ensure precision. The inference system is comprised of drawing axes, point inferences, and linear inferences.

Navigation

You need to understand how to move around the SketchUp environment. The basic controls are

Middle Mouse Button (MMB) The middle mouse button allows you to zoom in and out.

Holding the Middle Mouse Button Holding the middle mouse button and moving the mouse will cause SketchUp to orbit.

Holding Shift+Middle Mouse Button Holding the Shift+middle mouse button (Shift+MMB) will cause a little hand to appear as the mouse pointer, allowing you to pan around the model.

SketchUp requires geometry to be present to easily move in 3D space. If you try to zoom in on an "empty" space, the Zoom function may be slow or unresponsive. If you zoom in and out when the cursor is aligned over any geometry, the Zoom function will respond. The same is true for orbiting; make sure the cursor is aligned over geometry and then orbit. This will cause SketchUp to orbit around the geometry the cursor is referencing.

Inference System

SketchUp utilizes specific visual cues to help you find your relative position within the model environment. This is called the inference system and is comprised of the following:

Drawing on Axes The *drawing axes* are composed of three lines: red, green, and blue. These lines represent directions in 3D space. Green and red represent horizontal space. The blue axis represents the vertical dimension (Fig. 2-23).

Point Inference *Point inference* helps connect and attach geometry in 3D space. The Point Inference system appears as little colored boxes on edges and faces. Because you can identify the connection points, the inference system allows you to connect lines and surfaces with accuracy and precision. Geometry can be "snapped" to specified connection points (Fig. 2-24).

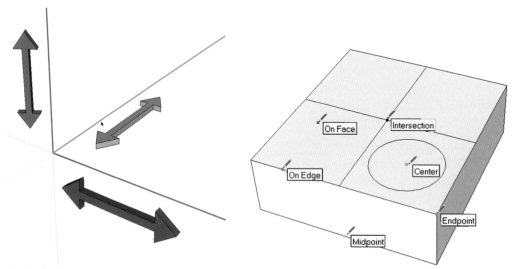

Fig. 2-23: Drawing axes

Fig. 2-24: The point inference system

Example: Draw a simple 2D line with the Line tool. Next, hover the Line tool at either end of the drawn line. A little green box appears at the endpoints. Move the Line tool over the drawn line and find some of the other colored points listed in Table 2-1. Do the same thing with a single face.

Table 2-1: Inference Box Colors	
Inference	**Color**
Endpoint	Green
Midpoint	Cyan
Intersection	Red "x"
On Edge	Red
Center (of circle)	Green
On Face	Blue

Linear Inferences When drawing lines, or moving or copying objects, SketchUp will indicate the direction of movement by displaying a dashed-colored line that is green, red, or blue; each line represents a drawing axis. This is SketchUp's way of indicating the axis on which the geometry is being drawn, moved, or copied (Fig. 2-25 through Fig. 2-28).

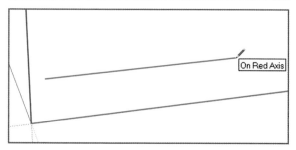

Fig. 2-25: The Line tool drawing on an axis indicated by linear inference

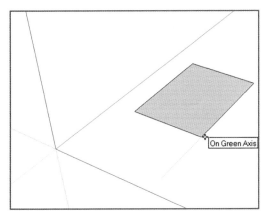

Fig. 2-26: Moving geometry along the green axis

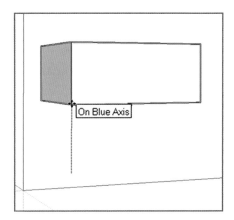

Fig. 2-27: Moving an object "up" the blue axis

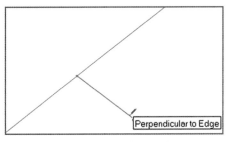

Fig. 2-28: Drawing perpendicular edges

Drafting with Edges

Using already-drawn edges is a useful method of drafting geometry. When trying to further subdivide a face, you can move or copy edges to subdivide faces as follows:

1. Draw a 50′ × 50′ rectangle.

2. Select an edge with the Move/Copy tool.

3. Copy and move the edge 20′ inward on the face.

4. Make sure the copied edge stays parallel/perpendicular to the other edges.

Once placed, the copied edge will have further subdivided the rectangle's face (Fig. 2-29).

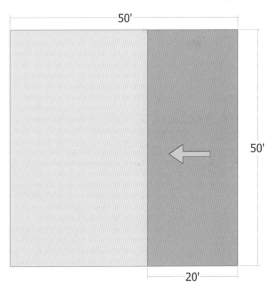

Fig. 2-29: The right edge of this face is selected and copied 20′ over. The copied edge will subdivide the single face into two faces.

Similarly, a face can be further subdivided or have details added by using tools such as Rectangle and Circle. Using the Rectangle tool on the surface will not create two faces on top of each other. Rather, the edges from the Rectangle tool will subdivide the face on which they are placed (Fig. 2-30).

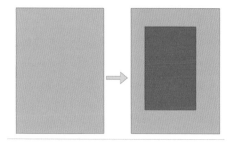

Fig. 2-30: A rectangle added to a face will further subdivide that face.

In many instances, it is useful to move geometry by using other edges for reference. One example is using the various points of an edge, such as endpoints and midpoints, to help place other geometry. This is done by selecting the geometry that is being moved or copied and using adjacent geometry for reference. This allows for simple and accurate placement (Fig. 2-31).

Another example is using the length of an edge to move or copy geometry. This is a common method when working with buildings.

Example: Draw a 30′ × 30′ rectangle. Using the Push/Pull tool, pull the face upward 25′ (Fig. 2-32). Next, with the Select tool, select the four edges that compose the top surface of the cube. With the edges selected, copy a set of four edges directly downward along the vertical axis.

Use one of the vertical edges that compose the volume for reference—meaning, hover the Move/Copy tool over the edge and move the tool down. Move/Copy will reference the edge. The copied edges can be moved a specific distance by entering that distance into the Measurement window. Move/Copy the edges 5′ down (Fig. 2-33).

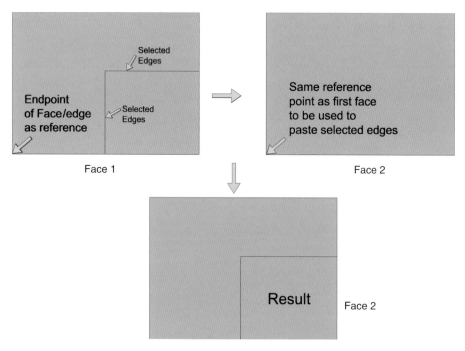

Fig. 2-31: Use edges for reference to move or copy other geometry to specific and precise locations. The edges in Face 1 are copied to Face 2.

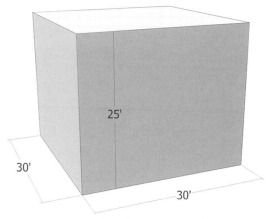

Fig. 2-32: Draw a 30′ × 30′ rectangle. Push/Pull the face 25′ in height.

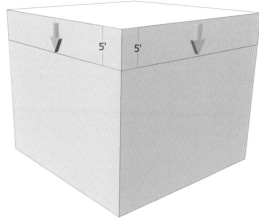

Fig. 2-33: Select the top edges of the cube and copy them downward 5′, using the vertical edges of the cube for reference.

The copied edges have further subdivided all four faces of the volume. The subdivided faces can be further manipulated; Push/Pull can be applied to move the faces in or out (Fig. 2-34).

Model Organization

Two very important and synergistic systems are used to organize model geometry. The Components and Groups system is described in detail in the next chapter; it helps consolidate geometry into *bundles*. These bundles can then be placed on the second system, called *layers*, providing users with the ability to toggle the visibility (on/off) of the bundles.

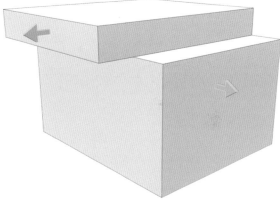

Fig. 2-34: The resulting subdivision in faces can be Push/Pulled in any direction.

Layers

Layers (Window ➢ Default Tray ➢ Layers) are the most important organizational tool in SketchUp. Using layers correctly is essential to efficient modeling; layers affect the modeling process and computer performance.

Specifically, layers control the visibility of SketchUp geometry. Turning off a layer will make the geometry on the layer invisible. Alternatively, toggling on a layer makes the geometry on that layer visible.

SketchUp models can contain loads of geometry. The more visible geometry there is, the more likely it is that computer performance will be slowed, thereby hindering work production. Furthermore, having a lot of visible objects can impede your ability to navigate within the SketchUp 3D environment because the geometry starts to get in the way.

By placing edges and faces on layers and using those layers properly, you can minimize or eliminate the challenges created by abundant geometry.

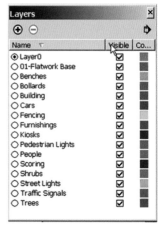

Layer 0

Layer 0 is the default layer in SketchUp (Fig. 2-35). Whenever a face, line, or edge is drawn in SketchUp, it should be drawn on Layer 0. (Make sure the Layer dialog box has a little black dot "on" to the left of Layer 0.) Modeling on Layer 0 will prevent drawn faces and edges from ending up on other layers and from conflicting with geometry as more detail is added.

Fig. 2-35: A typical site model layer list

CHAPTER 3

Components and Groups

SketchUp has a unique way of organizing edges and faces into easy-to-manage bundles of geometry. Two or more edges or faces can be made into a *component* or *group*. These combined edges and faces become a single item that can be easily replicated and edited. Creating components and groups allows for greater flexibility when you work with geometry.

The Importance of Components and Groups

Components and groups are the mainstays of constructing and organizing geometry. Completed and detailed site and building models are filled with them. You should become very familiar with how they work.

The advantages of using components and groups include the following:

▶ They can be edited, copied, moved, rotated, or deleted.

▶ They can be moved away from adjacent geometry. (Ungrouped or noncomponent edges and faces stick to other geometry. Components and groups are self-contained and not sticky.)

▶ They can be placed on their own layer easily. (Layers are discussed later in this chapter.)

Components and groups are almost identical. However, they have one important difference: Editing or altering a component affects every instance of that component. Although multiple copies of a group are identical, editing one group has no effect on other copies of that group.

Using Components

There are millions of already made components that you do not need to create but can use to add significant levels of detail to your models. Understanding how to use them and where to find them is important.

Tutorial: With the Rectangle tool, create a face that is 10′ × 10′. Use Push/Pull to add volume by extruding it 10′ in height (Fig. 3-1). With the Select tool, select all the geometry (edges and faces) that composes the cube. Hover over the selection and right-click. This

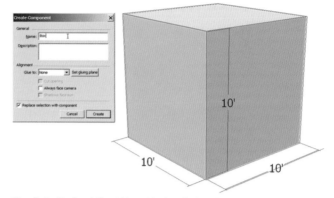

Fig. 3-1: Draft a 10′ × 10′ × 10′ cube. Select the entire object and right-click. From the menu, select Make Component. Name the new component **Box**.

will bring up a context menu. Select Make Component. Enter a name in the dialog box (**Box**, for example) and select OK. Make sure that the Replace Selection with Component option is checked. A blue outline will appear around the cube. It is now a component (Fig. 3-1).

Using the Move/Copy tool, make five copies of the cube and place them in a row next to the original (Fig. 3-2, Fig. 3-3).

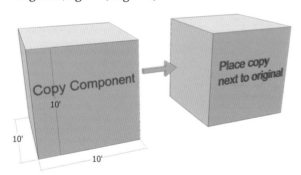

Fig. 3-2: With the Move/Copy tool, make a copy of the component and place it next to the original.

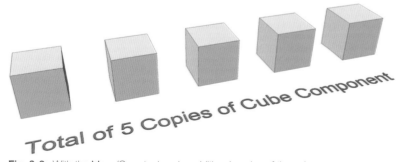

Fig. 3-3: With the Move/Copy tool, make additional copies of the cube.

Component Instances

Select a copied component, right-click, and select Edit Component from the context menu—or simply double-click on the component object. When you are editing a component or group, this is called *working within the component or group instance*; only the geometry comprising the component or group is accessible (Fig. 3-4).

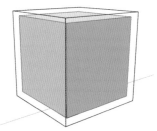

Fig. 3-4: Edit the copied component by entering the component instance. Notice the outline around the object. You should become very familiar with working within a component instance.

 Many of the tutorials in this book require you to work within a component or group instance. Failure to work within the instance will cause objects and operations to function improperly.

Editing Components

While still working in the copied component instance, draw another rectangle on one of the faces. Select and snap to a corner of the face (Fig. 3-5). The rectangle should subdivide the face of the cube. Push/Pull the subdivided (smaller) face inward (Fig. 3-6).

Notice that all the Cube components are altered in the same manner as the edited component (Fig. 3-7, Fig. 3-8). This is how components work. However, if the original cube had been a group, editing a copy of the group would not have affected any other iteration of that group.

Clicking outside of the instance will return you to the general modeling space. Practice going back and forth between the model and the component instance.

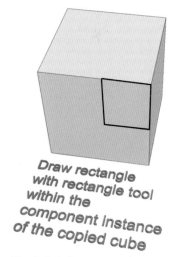

Draw rectangle with rectangle tool within the component instance of the copied cube

Fig. 3-5: In the component instance, draw a rectangle on the cube face as indicated.

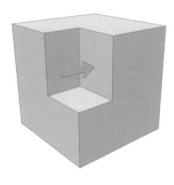

Fig. 3-6: With the Push/Pull tool, push in the face you created with the Rectangle tool.

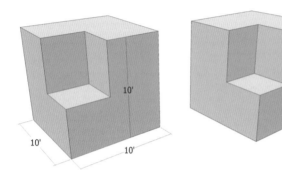

Fig. 3-7: Editing one component will edit all iterations of that component throughout a model.

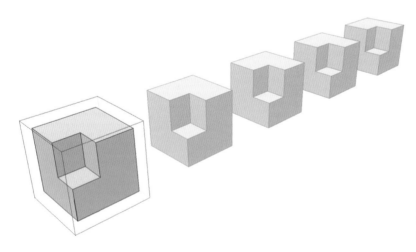

Fig. 3-8: All versions of the Cube component are adjusted.

Adjusting the Component/Group View

The way users view a component or group instance can be adjusted in SketchUp. By adjusting the view settings of the components and groups, you will gain a better understanding of what it means to work within a component or group instance.

To help demonstrate this point, next to the previously made Cube components, create another component: Using the Circle tool, draw a 10′-diameter circle on the ground. Next, using Push/Pull, add a 10′ volume to the circle, creating a cylinder:

Select the entire cylinder, right-click, and select Make Component. Name the component **Cylinder** (Fig. 3-9). Make two copies of the Cylinder component and place them near the cubes (Fig. 3-10).

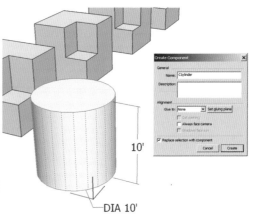

Fig. 3-9: Create a Cylinder component adjacent to the cubes. Make the cylinder 10′ in diameter and 10′ tall.

Next, select one of the Cube components, right-click, and select Edit Component—or just double-click on the component. Either method will place the view context into the component instance.

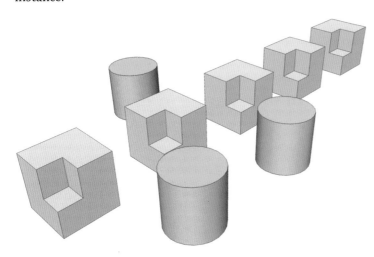

Fig. 3-10: Make two copies of the Cylinder component and place them near the Cube components.

As previously stated, the dashed line appears around the Cube component that is being edited. This indicates which version of the component is being worked on (Fig. 3-11).

All the other Cube components are screened back, but they are more vivid or clear than the Cylinder components. When a component instance is entered, similar components won't have as much contrast as the rest of the model, indicating which components are the same (Fig. 3-11).

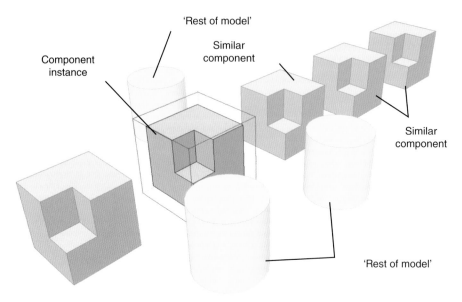

'Rest of model'

Similar
component

Component
instance

Similar
component

'Rest of model'

Fig. 3-11: The model view changes in a component instance. Similar components are slightly faded, while the rest of the model (in this case, the cylinders) becomes almost invisible.

The Cylinder components (or rest of the model) have more contrast to distinguish between the specific component instances and the rest of the model geometry. If there were any other unrelated model faces and edges, they would be just as faded.

You can adjust these view settings. Go to the Window menu and select Model Info. From the Model Info menu box, select Components. The settings found under this tab allow you to adjust the contrast of similar components (or the rest of the model) when you are working within a component instance (Fig. 3-12).

You can adjust the slider under Fade Similar to decrease or increase how vivid the similar components will appear when you are in that specific component instance (Fig. 3-13). The Fade Rest of Model slider works similarly: adjusting it will make the rest of the model less or more vivid when you enter a component instance (Fig. 3-14).

Next to each slider is a check box that says Hide. When this box is checked, all similar components or the rest of the model will be hidden when you enter a component instance.

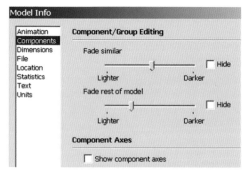

Fig. 3-12: The Model Info Components tab is used to adjust the way a model appears when its components are edited.

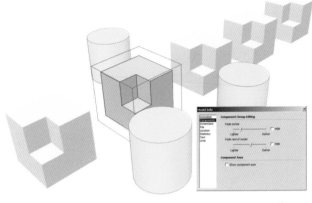

Fig. 3-13: The Component view settings are adjusted, and the rest of the model is made more visible.

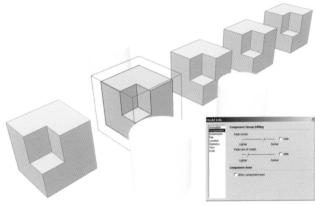

Fig. 3-14: The Component view settings are adjusted. Similar components become more vivid, while the rest of model is faded even more.

You need to know when you're working in a component or group instance instead of the rest of the model. Entering a component or group instance is easy. It is so easy that you can do it accidentally by double-clicking on a component or group. The difference in contrast and the clarity of objects are your important clues. Make sure you are familiar with these important indicators of component instances.

Components within Components

Components and groups can be located, pasted, or created within other components.

Example: Enter the group instance of one of the cubes. Next, select two of the smaller adjacent faces, right-click, and select Make Component. Name the faces **Cube Faces** and select OK. The two faces are now a separate component within the Cube component (Fig. 3-15).

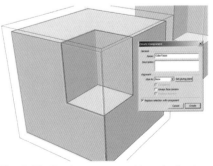

Fig. 3-15: Create a component by selecting two faces within the Cube component instance.

Because they are the same component, every version of the cube will have this new component created within its instance (Fig. 3-16). Exit the cube instance.

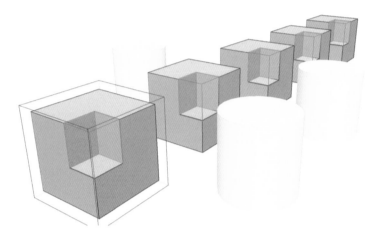

Fig. 3-16: The Cube Faces component is created in all instances of the Cube component.

Select the Cylinder component, and select Copy from the Edit menu (or press Ctrl+C) (Fig. 3-17). Reenter any of the Cube instances, select the Cube Faces component, and enter that component instance.

To ensure the model view is in the correct component instance, simply compare the contrasted model geometry as mentioned previously. While in the Cube Faces instance, go to Edit and select Paste (or Ctrl+V) (Fig. 3-18). This will paste a version of the Cylinder component within the Cube Faces instances.

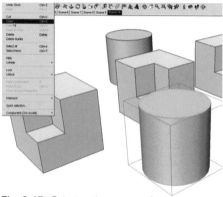

Fig. 3-17: Select and copy one of the Cylinder components.

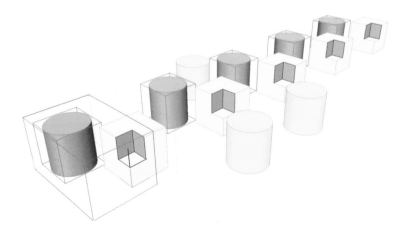

Fig. 3-18: Enter the Cube instance and then enter the Cube Faces instance. Paste the cylinder into the Cube Faces component. The Cylinder will be pasted into all instances of the Cube and Cube Faces components.

This example illustrates how a component can be within a component within a component. These steps can be repeated endlessly and are important to understand; many objects in SketchUp are components constructed from other components. This makes the ability to navigate between component instances very important.

Once you can navigate between them, you can easily edit components within components.

1. Exit the Cube Faces and Cube component instance and return to the general model workspace.

2. Select the Cylinder component, right-click, and select Edit Component (or double-click on the component). Notice that the Cylinder components within the Cube Faces component instance have the same vivid appearance.

3. Push/Pull the top of the Cylinder another 5′. All versions of the Cylinder component will be adjusted (Fig. 3-19). Exit the component instance and return to the general modeling space.

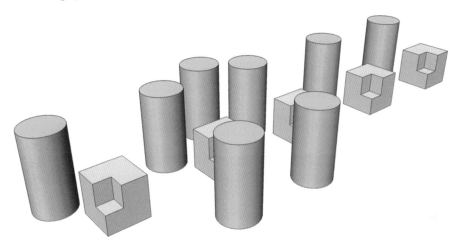

Fig. 3-19: Editing the Cylinder component will edit all similar components, regardless of the instance in which they are located.

Components and Layers

In the previous chapter, you were introduced to SketchUp layers and their importance in organizing geometry within a model. Components and groups can easily be placed on layers. Using layers provides a powerful way to maintain model organization and maintain computer performance; intensive components, such as trees, are easier to control within a model.

Using the previous Cube components, the following exercise demonstrates this technique.

1. From the Window menu, select Layers. Create a new layer called Cubes.

2. Select all component versions of the cube by using the selection arrow and holding down the Shift key (Add Select). Once all the Cube components are selected, right-click while hovering over one of the cubes, and from the context menu, select Entity Info.

3. The Entity Info menu box will appear. The Layers window indicates the layer on which the selected objects reside—currently Layer 0. Selecting the pull-down arrow to the right of layers will provide a list of all the layers in the model (Fig. 3-20). By selecting a layer from the list, you can place all selected geometry onto that layer. With the Cube components still selected, select the Cubes layer.

4. In the Layers menu, toggle the Cubes layer off to make all the cubes disappear. Toggling the layers on will make them reappear.

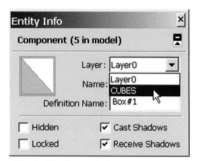

Fig. 3-20: The Entity Info menu lets you place geometry on specific layers.

This technique (placing components on layers) is utilized heavily in this book and when modeling. Practice organizing components onto layers, so that you become proficient.

Pre-Made Components

Many objects in the built environment can be added to a model as components. Although you can create custom components, the fastest and most convenient way to populate a model with objects is to use pre-made components.

Components can include benches, cars, people, pedestrian lights, trash receptacles, signs, traffic signals, buildings, various furnishings, trees, shrubs, flowers, windows, doors, trains, and bridges. The list is endless. Most models incorporate a large variety of components. Virtually any object found in the real world is available in some pre-made composition. You can find these pre-made components in a variety of places, some of which are listed in the following sections.

Understanding the basics of working with components and groups is important. By knowing how they function within a model, you'll be prepared to work, create, and adjust them as you explore the rest of this book.

Component Library

Compiling and organizing a component library made of both pre-made and custom components (Fig. 3-21) is important. Organize your components by category types (for example, trees, benches, buildings). The Components menu (Window ➤ Default Tray ➤ Components) can be linked to a user component library for easy access (Fig. 3-22).

In this section, you will learn about various online locations where you can download a variety of component types. Consider keeping an organized library as you work on projects and download and research new types of components.

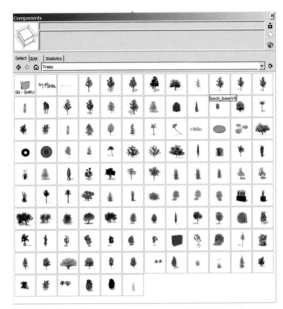

Fig. 3-21: Tree component library compiled from various websites

Fig. 3-22: Organize your components into a coherent component library for easy access and use.

3D Warehouse

3D Warehouse is a great source for free 3D models. The Warehouse is the single best location to obtain and download models (Fig. 3-23). It's the single largest repository of 3D models on the Web. SketchUp users, companies, and institutions upload and download over a billion models a year.

Fig. 3-23: The 3D Warehouse browser in SketchUp allows you to download models directly into your model.

As briefly described in Chapter 1, 3D Warehouse is accessed through a browser in SketchUp. To access it, go to File ➢ 3D Warehouse ➢ Get Models. Notice that you can select Share Models as well, permitting you to upload your models to 3D Warehouse for others to view and use (Fig. 3-24).

3D Warehouse allows users to download almost any kind of object, from high-quality buildings and vegetation, vendor-created, and specific models, to interiors and amenities.

In addition to downloading the tutorial models, experiment with downloading from the Warehouse different types of objects suitable for your projects.

Fig. 3-24: The option to open and download or upload models is found under File ➢ 3D Warehouse, Get Models or Share Models.

DanielTal.com

DanielTal.com offers access to high-quality components. Signing up for free provides you access to the component pack. It includes over 2,500 components spanning multiple industries, including architecture, interior design, and site design. Using this website is the best way to jump-start your own component library (Fig. 3-25).

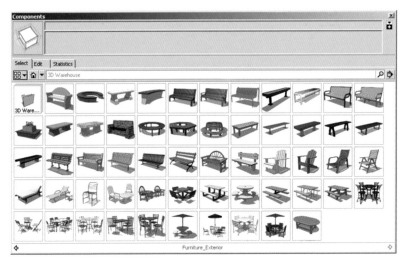

Fig. 3-25: At DanielTal.com, you can sign up for free and gain access to thousands of high-quality pre-made components.

FormFonts

FormFonts (www.formfonts.com) is a subscription site that offers a lot of high-quality components. The subscription is affordable, and the available models are very useful.

A subscription is a valuable way to download the exact models you need for a project without having to search 3D Warehouse—and FormFonts offers thousands of model types not found at the Warehouse.

You can download a free sampling of FormFont models from 3D Warehouse. Search for **FormFonts3D** using the Collections Option (Fig. 3-26).

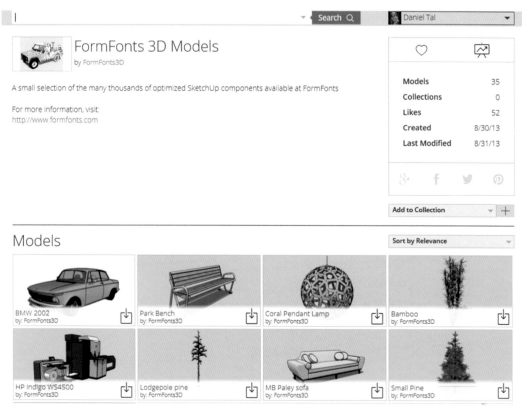

Fig. 3-26: FormFonts offers thousands of high-quality pre-made components.

DynaSCAPE Sketch3D

DynaSCAPE SketchUp 3D (http://sketch3d.dynascape.com) offers thousands of unique high-quality plant and outdoor amenity models specific for SketchUp (Fig. 3-27). Although using it requires a subscription, the available models are unparalleled for vegetation models that include grasses, ornamentals, deciduous trees, evergreens, and considerably more.

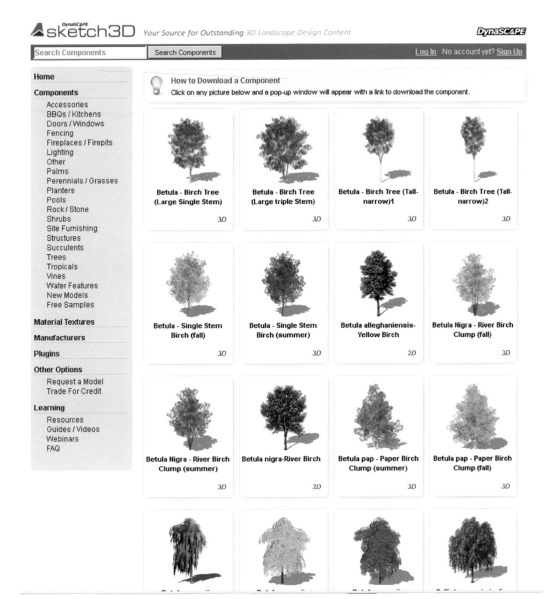

Fig. 3-27: Sketch3D by DynaSCAPE offers a unique plant library for SketchUp.

From the 3D Warehouse, you can download a sampling of Sketch3D plants. Perform a search for models (not collections) in 3D Warehouse for DynaSCAPE (Fig. 3-28).

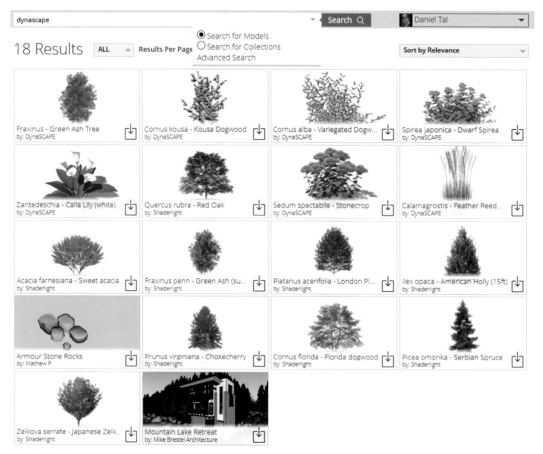

Fig. 3-28: Searching for DynaSCAPE on 3D Warehouse provides access to a Sketch3D component sampling.

Problem Solving

SketchUp is a problem-solving tool. Hobbyists and designers use it to help generate objects that best represent ideas. There is usually more than one way to accomplish a task in SketchUp. By mastering SketchUp, you open up a wealth of possibilities for accomplishing whatever goals you can imagine.

SketchUp Process Modeling offers a template you can apply to modeling. In order to problem solve, you need to envision what your completed model will look like and what it will accomplish. Although this notion seems to be abstract, with practice you will come to understand what is required to create a model, what it will look like, and what parts will take the longest to complete. The specifics vary from model to model, but the process to create the models is the same.

As you work with SketchUp, you will soon discover that it does not always operate as intended. Sometimes, tools and operations will yield unexpected results, and you will need to problem solve to accomplish a task.

According to the Global Development Research Center (www.gdrc.org), problem solving consists of several general steps:

1. Defining the problem
2. Analyzing the problem
3. Generating possible solutions
4. Analyzing the solutions
5. Choosing the best solution(s)
6. Planning the next course of action (next steps)

Problem solving with SketchUp entails these same basic steps. If SketchUp fails to perform as desired, find another solution; there is more than one way to reach your modeling goals.

The simple mantra of "keep moving forward" is very relevant to working with SketchUp. This is where learning and understanding what SketchUp tools can accomplish comes in handy. Some SketchUp tools can accomplish the same task as others, but they do so by using different steps and processes. With use and practice, you will come to understand these differences. This chapter discusses some common SketchUp problems and how to work around them.

Problem-Solving Tutorials

The exercises and tutorials in this book are meant to show you how to use SketchUp. Invariably, you will run into problems, errors, and mishaps when the tutorials do not produce the desired results. These mishaps can be frustrating; however, don't be disheartened. Evaluate the problem to see if the error was due to a misunderstanding or a misstep of the instructions. In some instances, the errors might be a problem with SketchUp itself. In either case, you will learn by doing, and problem solving will help you master SketchUp.

As you are working with the tutorials, keep the following points in mind:

▶ If your exercise's outcome differs from the book's, make sure you didn't skip or misinterpret any steps.

▶ Make sure you are working within the correct component instance. If you are working in the wrong instance, start the tutorial over from the beginning. Working within the correct component instance is particularly important for the tutorials in Chapters 7 through 10.

▶ If the tools or geometry do not work correctly or produce the wrong results, keep going and see if you can complete the tutorial. Sometimes SketchUp will not perform in a consistent manner. Some of these imprecise results are reviewed in the next section.

▶ If a problem persists or it is impossible to get the results as indicated in the tutorial, restart the exercise from the beginning. A fresh start will usually address any problems encountered.

As suggested previously, try to work through a tutorial more than once. The detailed nature and complexity of the instructions make the tutorials worth repeating. Repetition will help you learn the nuances involved with SketchUp. This is especially true when you run into problems or get stuck in an exercise.

Typical SketchUp Problems

The following discussion is by no means comprehensive; however, it does cover some of the most common problems and possible solutions.

Different Results on Different Computers

Not all computers behave equally with SketchUp. Unlike Photoshop, AutoCAD, and other 2D programs, SketchUp has some higher requirements.

In short, the type of hardware your computer utilizes does affect SketchUp's performance. This is especially true when you are working with very detailed and rich models.

Computers that use video gaming cards, such as NVIDIA and ATI Radeon cards, will perform better than Intel integrated or lesser cards. Furthermore, the better the processor and the more RAM, the better the computer will function. Laptops are specifically challenged on these fronts. However, there are some dedicated "gaming" and "media" laptops that can handle almost any SketchUp model.

SketchUp Freezes

SketchUp sometimes *seems* to freeze when you run an operation (for example, when you turn on Shadows or try to pan around a model). However, SketchUp *rarely* freezes. That is not to say that it does not crash. You will know when SketchUp crashes because the custom Bug Splat window will appear, telling you that a crash has occurred.

When SketchUp seems to be frozen, you need to dig deep and come up with a reserve of patience. SketchUp is still functioning. Just wait for SketchUp to complete its task.

PC users can check the Task Manager to see if SketchUp is frozen. To open the Task Manager, press Ctrl+Alt+Delete. When you're working with SketchUp, keep Task Manager open and minimized on the Desktop. When it's minimized, a small green performance bar will appear at the bottom right of the Desktop. When SketchUp is processing, the performance bar will be either half or completely full of green bars.

Auto Save

SketchUp has an automated Save feature (Window ➤ Preferences ➤ General) that is set to save your work every 5 minutes. When checked, the setting saves the model and SketchUp may seem to be frozen. If this is problematic, you can change the Auto Save to a longer interval—but don't turn it off.

Subdivide

In some instances, SketchUp may not subdivide a face. This usually happens when you draw edges (line or arcs) on a face to create multiple surfaces.

There is no easy solution to this problem. SketchUp has fixed many instances of this occurrence, but not all of them. The easiest solution is using the Rectangle tool instead of drawing a single edge to accomplish the same task.

1. Place a rectangle on the face that needs to be subdivided.

2. Make sure the rectangle does *not* snap to any adjacent edges.

3. Draw edges from the rectangle endpoints to the adjacent edges to create the desired outline. Delete any extra edges, keeping the lines that subdivide the face into the required surface.

In most cases, the Rectangle tool edges will subdivide a face. In general, the rectangle edges are used to help define the outline of the surfaces that are being subdivided from the original face, using edges to help further "sculpt" the face to the desired form.

Resources

Here are some helpful online resources if you get stuck:

- ▶ The DanielTal.com website (www.danieltal.com) includes free resources and models. In addition, the tutorials review many ways to problem solve some of the issues mentioned above.

- ▶ Many advanced users live on the SketchUcation forums (www.sketchucation.com). This must-visit website is an excellent resource to get help, download custom Ruby Scripts, and learn about current SketchUp trends. I strongly recommend signing up for free.

- ▶ Mike Brightman authored *The SketchUp Workflow for Architects* (Wiley, 2013), which is a useful resource for all disciplines. It shows you how to use the LayOut program that accompanies SketchUp Pro. He also offers tutorials and additional resources. Perform a Google search on Mike Brightman.

CHAPTER 5

SketchUp Extensions

Extensions are the backbone of SketchUp and should be included in any introduction of the program to new users. In this chapter, you'll find explanations and procedures for using them. I want to credit Chris Dizon for inspiring the approach to material covered in this chapter.

Using SketchUp

Out-of-the-box SketchUp is loaded with a simple set of menus. (Fig. 5-1). Similar to a smartphone, it's not preloaded with very many apps or tools (Fig. 5-2). Also like a smartphone, SketchUp can be customized for specific tasks or functions (Fig. 5-3).

Assembling the correct Extensions for the task is the key to unlocking SketchUp's ability to model quickly and accurately.

If you are using SketchUp for the very first time and starting to get the sense of basic modeling, start using extensions. If you're an intermediate or advanced user, extensions should be a fundamental part of your workflow.

Extensions were formerly called plugins, scripts, and Ruby Scripts. The terms have all been officially consolidated into the term *extensions* by the SketchUp team. However, these terms are still found on many external extension websites.

On www.danieltal.com, members have access to a series of videos on Extensions. This includes detailed instructions on searching for, installing and demonstrating extensions. The tutorials cover more specific material and review extensions in various workflows.

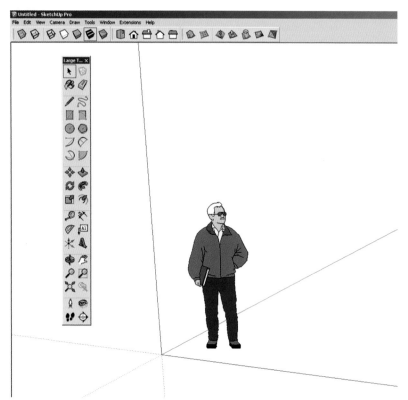

Figure 5-1: SketchUp comes with a simple toolset. Shown is the Large Tool Set, which contains most of the primary modeling tools.

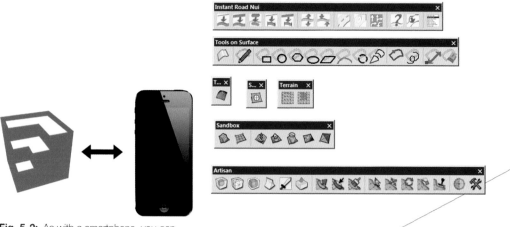

Fig. 5-2: As with a smartphone, you can customize your SketchUp toolsets.

Fig. 5-3: Extension terrain tools

Extension Warehouse

Smartphones have app stores, and SketchUp has the Extensions Warehouse (Fig. 5-4). The Extension Warehouse allows you to search and install Extensions. Each Extension is vetted, tested, and updated for future SketchUp versions. Many, if not most, are free.

Fig. 5-4: The SketchUp Extension Warehouse is similar to a smartphone apps store.

Many of the extensions on the Extension Warehouse website are developed by independent companies and individuals. These developers are referred to as authors, and you can search for extensions by author. Most authors have external websites where you can download additional extensions not found on the Extension Warehouse.

Installing Weld

The following tutorial will walk you through the process of accessing the Extension Warehouse and then searching for, installing, and using the Weld extension. Weld is authored by the website Smustard (reviewed later in this chapter).

1. Go to Window ➤ Install Extension Warehouse.
2. This will launch the Extension Warehouse browser (Fig. 5-5).
3. At the top of the screen, sign in. This requires a Google account.
4. In the Extension Warehouse Search box at the top of the screen, type **Weld**.

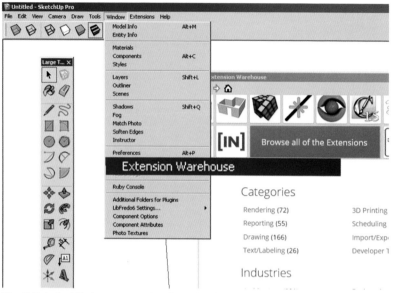

Fig. 5-5: In the Window menu, select Extension Warehouse to open the Extension Warehouse browser.

5. The search results will show Weld and PathCopy as the top two extensions (Fig. 5-6). (PathCopy is reviewed in Chapter 6.)

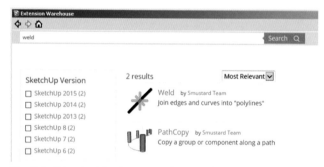

Fig. 5-6: Extension Warehouse search results for Weld

6. Select Weld. This will take you to the Weld installation page (Fig. 5-7).

7. Each extension has its own page. Make sure to review the extension pages carefully. In many instances, they contain important information about how to use and install the extension.

8. At the top right, select Download. SketchUp will ask for permission to install the extension on your system. Click Yes through the options.

9. SketchUp will indicate the extensions is active.

10. A new extensions menu line will appear at the top of the screen.

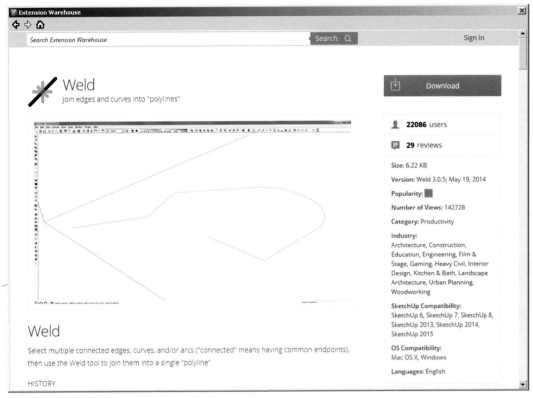

Fig. 5-7: The Weld page on the Extension Warehouse

Using Weld

The following instructions demonstrate how to use the Weld extension.

1. With the Arc tool, draw two connected arcs (Fig. 5-8).

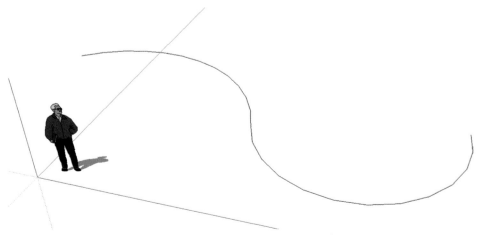

Fig. 5-8: Draw two connected arcs.

2. Select both arcs.

3. Go to the Extensions menu option at the top of the screen.

4. Select Weld (Fig. 5-9).

The two arcs are now joined as a single selectable entity.

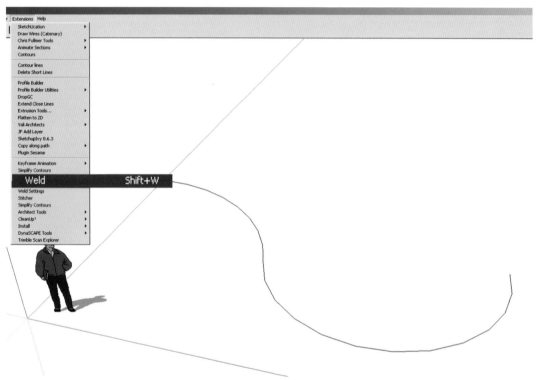

Fig. 5-9: With the arcs selected, choose Weld from the Extensions menu.

Weld has many uses where multiple edges and arcs are welded together. There are many advantages to welded edges, including making it easier to offset lines.

Extension Websites

As noted, many authors have created extensions for SketchUp. The two main websites where you can find their extensions are reviewed later in this chapter. Collectively, SketchUcation and Smustard provide access to hundreds of extensions, most of which are not available on the Extension Warehouse.

Installing Extensions

There are three ways to install extensions.

▶ By accessing the Extension Warehouse as demonstrated previously

▶ By selecting SketchUp Preferences ➤ Extensions (Fig. 5-10)

▶ By manually installing through Windows or Mac file folders

When you access a given site, make sure you read their specific instructions for how to install their extensions. The general process is usually the same, but the specific steps may vary slightly.

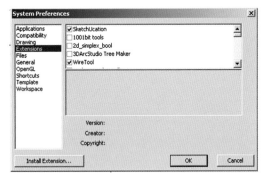

Fig. 5-10: You can install some extensions by selecting Preferences ➤ Extensions.

SketchUcation Plugin Store

The SketchUcation Plugin Store is an essential extension. The more powerful terrain tools can be found only on SketchUcation. Like the Extension Warehouse, the Plugin Store is a browser that allows you to search and install extensions directly into SketchUp from the SketchUcation website.

To install the SketchUcation Plugin Store extension, simply follow these steps:

1. Perform a Google search to locate the SketchUcation Plugin Store.

2. Select the Plugin Store link.

3. Register for a free account.

4. Download and save the SketchUcation Tools file to your computer.

5. Open SketchUp and select Window ➤ Preference.

6. Select the Extensions tab.

7. Select Install Extension.

8. Navigate to the download location.

9. Select the SketchUcation Tools file and click OK.

10. Close and restart SketchUp.

11. Go to Extensions and select SketchUcation.

12. Select SketchUp Plugin Store from the list.

This will open the browser where you can search and install extensions (Fig. 5-11).

Fig. 5-11: The SketchUcation Plugin Store browser in SketchUp

Smustard

Smustard.com has many powerful scripts (Fig. 5-12), including Profile Builder Pro (discussed in Chapter 8) and the AutoCAD Cleanup scripts (discussed in Part 4). Smustard also has two free scripts on the Extension Warehouse: Weld, discussed previously, and PathCopy.

Smustard.com ™
the Companion to SketchUp™

Search for a script

Home   Products   Forum   FAQ   About   Contact

Smustard Scripts

2015-Click-Change	free	This plugin offers a large number of products to finalize your kitchen projects. Each component is dynamic and can of change appearance with a simple click !	more info
2ptCircle	$6.00	Create a 2D circle by specifying the diameter end points. The circle will directly face the Camera.	more info
2ptPerspective	$6.00	Quickly change the Camera setting, via 3 options, to obtain a 2 point perspective	more info
3DTextTool	$12.00	Create 3D Text without ever leaving SketchUp! Just type the Text string you want, pick your Font, click OK. Edit capability too. Now works with Pro and Google SketchUp!	more info
3ptCircle	$6.00	3ptCircle will create a circle through triangulation. After you choose three points, the circle will be created to fit those points.	more info
AddConstructionPoint	$4.00	Add Construction points anywhere by left clicking.	more info
AddPages	free	Add pages orthographically	more info
AnimatedClock	$4.00	Impress your coworkers with an Animated Clock! (It keeps accurate time too!)	more info
ApplyTo	free	Apply a component definition to selected component instances.	more info
ArrayTo	free	Utility script to convert array elements to numbers. Used by other scripts.	more info
AttribReporter	free	Creates BOM Reports To Spreadsheet	more info
Attributes	free	Creates and reads obiect attributes	more

Fig. 5-12: The Smustard extensions website

Recommended Extensions

Table 5-1 lists some useful extensions and where to find them. Take some time to explore the tools mentioned here and learn how to apply them to your workflow. You'll find a treasure trove of ideas and your time will be well spent.

Table 5-1: SketchUp Extensions	
Name	**Where to Find**
Artisan	Extension Warehouse
CAD Clean-Up tools*	Extension Warehouse
CAD Import Clean-Up*	DynaSCAPE Sketch3D
CLF Repeat Copy	Extension Warehouse
CLF Scale and Rotate Multiple*	Extension Warehouse
CLF tools	Extension Warehouse
Close Open Line Segments*	Smustard
Delete Short Line*	Smustard
Extend Close Line*	Smustard
Flatten	Smustard
Fredo 6 Tools	SketchUcation
Instant Road Nui	Extension Warehouse Vali Architects
Instant Roof Nui	Extension Warehouse Vali Architects
Key Frame	Extension Warehouse
Land F/X	Extension Warehouse Land F/X
Layer Panel	Extension Warehouse
LibFredo6	Extension Warehouse SketchUcation
JointPushPull*	SketchUcation
Make Faces*	Smustard
PathCopy*	Smustard
Profile Builder Pro*	Extension Warehouse
Repaint Face	Extension Warehouse
Rotate Rectangle	Extension Warehouse
Round Corner	SketchUcation
Selection Memory	Extension Warehouse
Selection Toys	Extension Warehouse
Shortcut (beta)	SketchUcation

Table 5-1 *(continued)*	
Name	**Where to Find**
Soap Skin Bubble*	Extension Warehouse
Super Drape	SketchUcation
TIG Tools	SketchUcation
Tools on Surface*	SketchUcation
Topo Shaper	SketchUcation
Weld*	Extension Warehouse Smustard

*Indicates that the extension is reviewed in this book

SketchUp
Process
Modeling

You can find the models for Part 2 at 3D Warehouse. To go to 3D Warehouse, use the Google search engine and search for 3D Warehouse. Use the search term **SPM Part 2** and check Collections.

Introduction to SketchUp Process Modeling

SketchUp is a three-dimensional modeling program you can use to construct rich and expressive environments. Because SketchUp was developed as a 3D modeling tool for everyone, its power is derived from its easy-to-use tools and an intuitive 3D work environment. Using a streamlined modeling process is the secret to creating efficient and detailed SketchUp models. The SketchUp Process Modeling method used in this book includes

- ▶ Constructing a model in a logical order
- ▶ Adding detail by using available resources
- ▶ Organizing a model to maintain computer performance and a clean 3D workspace

Whether you're a beginner or an advanced SketchUp user, you'll need to understand the SketchUp Process Modeling method to fully utilize this book. The following chapters employ the process as a base upon which to develop more advanced modeling techniques. Whether you are modeling from your imagination, hand-drawn plans, Computer Aided Design (AutoCAD), or Digital Elevation Models (DEMs), the process itself is identical.

The Built Environment

As a modeler, you'll use SketchUp to portray the built environment. The phrase *built environment* refers to the surroundings that provide the settings for human activity, ranging from large public spaces to small intimate gardens.

SketchUp Process Modeling divides the built environment into two categories:

- ▶ Surfaces that define areas
- ▶ Objects that sit on surfaces

These terms directly relate to the descriptions provided for the geometry (edges and faces) outlined in Part 1.

Surfaces

Surfaces define the physical planes and edges composing the built world—roads, sidewalks, streams, trails, terrain, lawns, curbs, parkways, open spaces, driveways, parking areas, lakes, etc. (Fig. 6-1). Surfaces are composed of materials such as asphalt and concrete, grass and flowers, soil and gravel, and water and sand.

SketchUp Process Modeling combines the surfaces that form the model's base as the *Flatwork Base*. The first step of the modeling process is to construct the Flatwork Base.

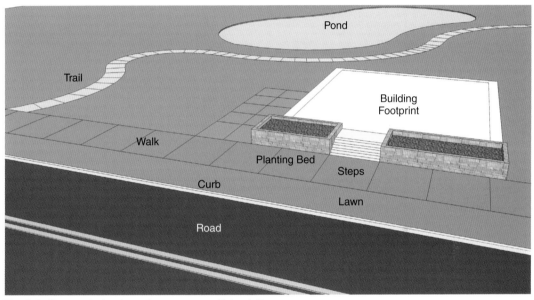

Fig. 6-1: Some typical surfaces that compose a Flatwork Base

Objects

Surfaces are populated with objects that simulate the built environment. *Objects* are items that are placed on the Flatwork Base—buildings and structures, fences, monuments, trees, cars, streetlights, outdoor furnishings, traffic signals, shrubs, planters, ramps, etc. (Fig. 6-2).

The second step in SketchUp Process Modeling is to place the objects. Once all the objects are placed on the surfaces, the model is complete (Fig. 6-3).

Fig. 6-2: Buildings, trees, and lights are typical objects.

Fig. 6-3: Surfaces and objects compose the built environment.

The 2D = 3D Method

When you are using SketchUp modeling to create surfaces and objects, the 2D = 3D method of problem solving is an important one to understand. If you can imagine and draw something two-dimensional in SketchUp, you can translate the 2D drawing into 3D (Fig. 6-4).

Throughout this book, you'll see 2D drafted edges subdividing a face that is then given volume using various tools. This book focuses on drafting a 2D representative base and articulating that base into a 3D model (Fig. 6-5, Fig. 6-6).

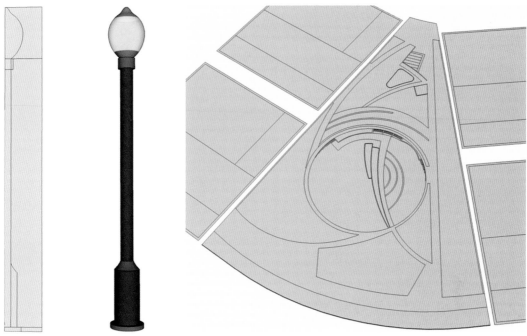

Fig. 6-4: This 2D drafted face of a light was modeled into 3D.

Fig. 6-5: A 2D site plan ready to be made 3D

Fig. 6-6: A 2D site plan modeled into a 3D site plan

Drafting the Flatwork Base

The term *Flatwork Base* is used throughout the book. It refers to the basic modeling area composed of surfaces.

Let's begin by modeling a built environment from scratch. The following exercise will:

▶ Introduce the typical composition of a Flatwork Base. In it, you will carve up a rectangular 3D face to create individual surfaces that define the built environment—a road, sidewalk, tree lawn, curving trail, building footprint, steps, and walls.

▶ Familiarize yourself with the process of drafting the Flatwork Base, including organizing and using the drawing tools and layers. Later in this chapter, you'll learn how to add objects to the Flatwork Base.

Drawing the Base

Using the Draw tools to draft a simple Flatwork Base, follow these steps:

1. Draw the base (Fig. 6-7).

   a. Open Layers (Window ➤ Layers) and make sure Layer 0 is current (it should be). Select the Rectangle tool.

   b. Draw a 100′ × 100′ rectangular surface by selecting the first rectangle draw point, typing **100′, 100′**, and pressing the Enter key.

   The generated rectangular face will be used to compose the Flatwork Base. The Draw tools will be used to subdivide the face into smaller individual faces.

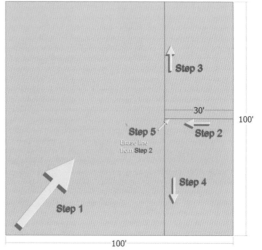

Fig. 6-7: Drafting the Flatwork Base and defining the road

2. Define the road (Fig. 6-7).

   a. Using the Line tool, find the midpoint (cyan box) of the right edge of the rectangle. Snap to the midpoint and draw toward the center of the rectangle, perpendicular to the drawing edge

   b. Enter the value **30'** (in the Measurement window). This will draw a 30′ line perpendicular to the right edge.

3. Continue to define the road.

   a. Continue to draw a perpendicular line from the endpoint of the 30′ line to the top edge of the rectangle. This will create the first subdivided face on the surface.

   b. Using the Select tool (black arrow), select the smaller surface area. The surface is its own subdivided face. Deselect the face by pressing Ctrl+T. This command allows you to deselect any selected geometry.

4. Continue to define the road.

   a. From the endpoint of the first line, draw another line to the bottom edge of the rectangle.

5. Continue to define the road.

   a. Use the Eraser tool and erase the first drawn line (from step 2). This combines the smaller surfaces into a single surface.

   The subdivided surface represents the road.

6. Define the sidewalk and tree lawn (Fig. 6-8).

   a. With the Select tool, select the line drawn in the previous section.

   b. With the line selected, select the Move/Copy tool (View ➤ Toolbars ➤ Modification menu ➤ Move/Copy).

   c. With Move/Copy active, select the bottom endpoint of the line. Hold Ctrl and Click+drag the mouse to the left, using the bottom edge for reference. Type **8′** (in the Measurement window) and press Enter.

   A copy of the line is created 8′ from the edge. The narrow area between the two lines should be its own selectable face.

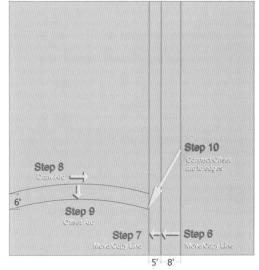

Fig. 6-8: Drafting the walks and trails

7. Continue to define the sidewalk and tree lawn:

   a. Select the newly copied line and Move/Copy the line 5′ to the left, by repeating step 6.

   The two narrow surface areas represent the tree lawn and concrete walk.

8. Add a curved trail (Fig. 6-8).

   a. Select the Arc tool. Approximately a quarter of the way up from the bottom-left corner of the initial rectangle, start to draw an arc, snapping to the left edge and moving to the right, perpendicular to the left edge.

   b. Snap the second arc point to the copied line generated in step 7.

   c. Select the third point to define the radius of the arc (the bulge). Make sure to snap to the On Face inference point. Give the arc a gentle curve, as shown in Fig. 6-8.

9. Duplicate the arc to define the trail (Fig. 6-8).

   a. Using the Offset tool (View ➤ Toolbars ➤ Modification menu ➤ Offset), create a duplicate of the drawn arc. Select the arc and offset the arc line 6′ going "south" on the surface.

Notice that the endpoints of the offset arc do not touch or connect to either of the adjacent edges. This will prevent the area defined for the trail (between the two arcs) from being subdivided.

10. Define the curved trail.

    a. Zoom into both ends of the offset arc and use the Line tool to draw an edge from the endpoint of the arc to the adjacent line.

    b. Check to see that the added edges now subdivide the area between the arc into a separate surface. This surface will be the trail.

11. Build a building footprint (Fig. 6-9).

    a. Starting from the top-left corner, draw a 50′ × 25′ rectangle that is 13′-6″ from the far left edge and 13′-6″ down from the top edge.

    b. The Rectangle tool has subdivided the large area. This smaller surface represents the footprint of the building.

12. Add a building entry path (Fig. 6-9).

    a. Starting 25′ down from the top-right corner of the building footprint drawn in step 11, draw a perpendicular line to the right. Connect the line to the "walk" edge from step 7.

13. Continue adding a building entry path.

    a. With Move/Copy, make the walk 6′ wide by copying and moving the line drawn in step 12.

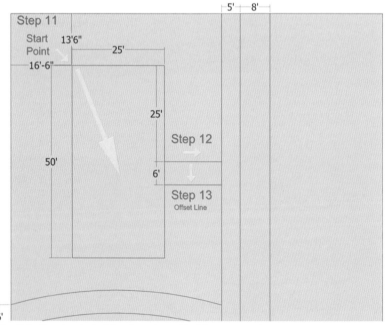

Fig. 6-9: Drawing the building footprint and building entry path

14. Copy and paste edges to define stairs adjacent to the building footprint (Fig. 6-10).

   a. With Move/Copy, create a series of steps using the building footprint line.

   When the two entry lines were drawn adjacent to the building, defining the entry walk, the edge composing the building footprint was further divided. The linework for the building located between the two entry lines is now its own selectable line.

   b. Select this line between the two edges from the previous step and Move/Copy to create three steps, each 1′ apart. These are the steps leading to the building.

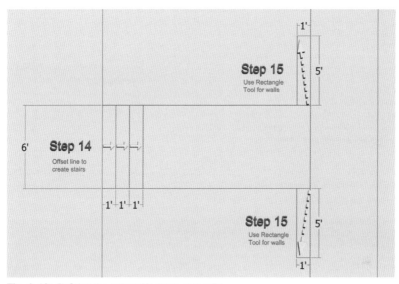

Fig. 6-10: Defining the entry with steps and walls

15. Draft the entry walls (Fig. 6-10).

   a. With the Rectangle tool, select the endpoint at the intersection of the entry walk and sidewalk, drawn in step 9. Enter a value of **5′,1′**. Make sure the drawn rectangle's length is parallel to the sidewalk.

   b. Repeat this step for the other side of the walk. These surfaces will be used to generate walls.

Reviewing the Drawing

The previous exercise drew, copied, and moved line work on a single surface. By subdividing the single surface into smaller areas, you drew footprints that signified specific surfaces. Now that you've finished drafting the Flatwork Base surfaces (Fig. 6-11), you need to associate colors with these surfaces to convey more meaning.

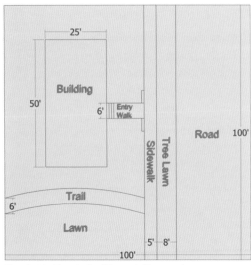

Fig. 6-11: The drafted Flatwork Base surfaces

Applying Material and Color

The next phase is to apply colors to the faces to give meaning to the *surfaces*. Select the Paint Bucket from the Large Tool Set to open the Materials menu. The Materials menu provides a wide-ranging set of colors and textures that can be applied to faces.

For this exercise, choose colors that best represent each surface (Fig. 6-12):

- ▶ Dark gray for the road
- ▶ Light gray for the sidewalk and steps
- ▶ Dark brown for walls
- ▶ White for the building area
- ▶ Beige or brown for the trail
- ▶ Light green for the tree lawn and lawn surfaces around the building

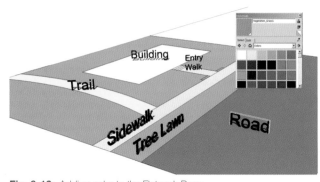

Fig. 6-12: Adding color to the Flatwork Base

Once you've selected a color from the Materials menu, simply click on a surface with the applicator (the Paint Bucket). This will apply the color to the surface.

Apply your colors to a 2D surface when you can. Once a 2D surface is Push/Pulled to add volume, the color will automatically be applied to the volume as a whole. Applying color now saves you time because you don't have to reapply colors to newly generated surfaces created by the Push/Pull tool (Fig. 6-13).

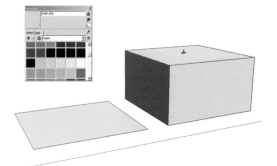

Fig. 6-13: Any color on a face will automatically be applied to the volume when Push/Pulled.

Organizing Models

Make the colored and completed Flatwork Base into a group. Using the Select tool, draw a selection box around all the faces and edges that compose the Flatwork Base. Right-click over the base and select Make Group (Fig. 6-14).

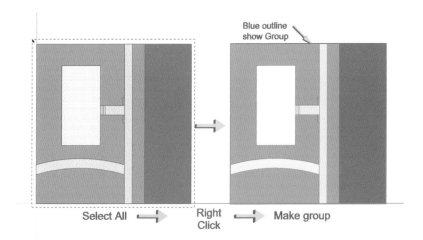

Fig. 6-14: Turn the Flatwork Base into a group.

The grouped Flatwork Base provides the first opportunity to apply layer organization. In the Layers menu (Window ➤ Default Tray ➤ Layers), create a new layer by selecting the Add Layer button (+) at top of the menu bar. A new layer called Layer 1 will be created.

Layers can be displayed in alphabetical/numerical order. Double-click on the new layer name. Rename the layer **01-Flatwork**. Applying 01 to the Flatwork Base layer ensures that the Flatwork Base will always be the top layer displayed, which makes it easier to locate as more layers are added.

The next step is to move the Flatwork Base group onto the 01-Flatwork layer. To do this, select the Flatwork Base group, right-click to bring up the context menu, and at the very top, select Entity Info.

The Entity Info menu provides information, including an object's layer location, about selected objects. It also allows the selected objects to be relocated to a different layer. Currently, the Flatwork Base group is located on Layer 0.

Relocate the group to the newly created 01-Flatwork layer. In Entity Info, select the Layers pull-down menu. Check to make sure the Flatwork Base group is still selected. Then select 01-Flatwork Layer. The Flatwork group is now located on the 01-Flatwork layer (Fig. 6-15).

Turning off this layer will make the group invisible; toggling it back on will make it visible.

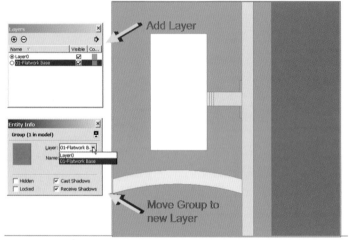

Fig. 6-15: Create a new layer for the Flatwork Base group. Relocate the Flatwork Base group onto the new layer.

Adding Volumes

The easy-to-use Push/Pull tool (View ➤ Toolbars ➤ Modification menu ➤ Push/Pull) adds 3D volume to 2D faces. Select the Push/Pull tool and enter the Flatwork Base Group instance. Next, hover over a surface. Click and push the mouse forward. Push/Pull will convert the flat 2D surface into a 3D volume.

As with many SketchUp tools, Push/Pull allows the user to input specific values and dimensions. Select a 2D surface. Then enter a value dimension (in the Measurement window) and press Enter. Push/Pull will create a volume height based on the entered value.

You can use the same method to define the road, steps, walls, and the building. Push/Pulling surfaces is the last step in generating the Flatwork Base.

Lowering the Road

The roadway is one of the first surface areas you should define with volume. Even adding a small amount of volume helps provide scale and definition to all adjacent surface areas.

1. Enter the Flatwork Base group instance.

2. Select the Push/Pull tool. Hover over the area designated as road. Push/Pull downward: Click and drag the cursor down. Immediately type the value **6″**. SketchUp will do one of two things (Fig. 6-16):

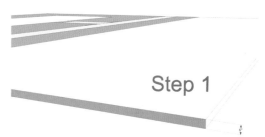

> ▶ SketchUp will create a 6″ thick volume.

Fig. 6-16: Push/Pull the road surface downward 6″.

> ▶ SketchUp will lower the top surface 6″, and the road surface will have 6″ walls surrounding it.

Depending on the situation, you should clean up the road surface by doing one of the following:

> ▶ If SketchUp created a 6″ volume, delete the top surface and the adjacent "walls."

> ▶ If SketchUp lowered the top surface, simply delete the adjacent walls (Fig. 6-17).

Fig. 6-17: Delete the excess faces and lines around the lowered road.

In either case, do not delete the geometry that defines the 6″ curb adjacent to the tree lawn and walks.

Creating the Building

Push/Pull the surface area designated as the building. Push/Pull the building footprint to a volume of 13′ height (Fig. 6-18).

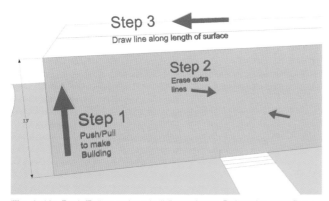

Fig. 6-18: Push/Pull to make a building volume. Delete the extra lines on the face. Draw a line along the top length of the volume.

On the building volume face, two vertical lines were created where the entry walk edges met the building. These lines will get in the way when you create the roof in the next section. Delete these lines using the Eraser tool. Do not delete the face (Fig. 6-18).

Making a Roof

Draw a line along the length of the top surface of the building volume. Draw the line from midpoint to midpoint (Fig. 6-18).

Select the drawn line and use the Move/Copy tool to lift the line upward along the (blue) vertical axis. Use a vertical building edge as reference. Immediately enter a value of **5′** (Fig. 6-19).

This will cause the top surface to fold with the line, simulating a roof.

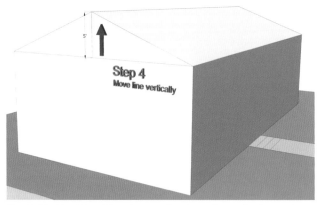

Fig. 6-19: Use Move/Copy to move the drawn line on the top surface along the vertical axis to fold the top face to make a roof.

Push/Pulling the Steps

Starting with the step furthest from the building, Push/Pull upward and enter the value **6″**. This will create a step with a 6″ riser (Fig. 6-20).

Hover over the next step with Push/Pull and double-click. Push/Pull will automatically repeat the last command entered. The two steps are now the same height. Double-click again. This will Push/Pull the face another 6″ above the first step (Fig. 6-21).

Repeat this step for the other stair surfaces until they are all 6″ above the adjacent steps, ascending toward the building.

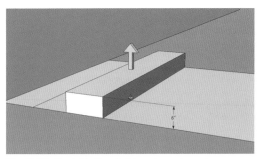

Fig. 6-20: Push/Pull the first face to make a step 6″ high.

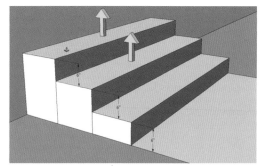

Fig. 6-21: Repeat Push/Pull on the other steps.

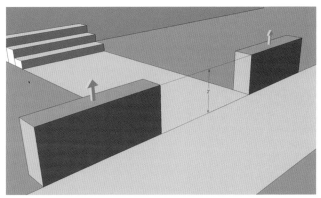

Fig. 6-22: Push/Pull the wall faces to a 2′ height.

Push/Pulling the Walls

Use the Push/Pull tool to raise both surfaces designated as walls to a 2′ height. The entry walk to the building should be flanked by two volumes representing walls (Fig. 6-22).

Adding Objects to the Flatwork Base

Now that the Flatwork Base is complete with surface geometry, color, and volumes (Fig. 6-23), the next step is to incorporate and arrange objects onto the base. As noted, the most efficient way to populate the Flatwork Base is to use pre-made components.

This exercise will focus on populating the Flatwork Base with pre-made components (objects) such as trees, pedestrian lights, benches, cars, people, and shrubs. You can experiment and incorporate other objects as you like.

As previously discussed, you can download pre-made components at a number of sources. At minimum, make sure to download the free components from 3D Warehouse.

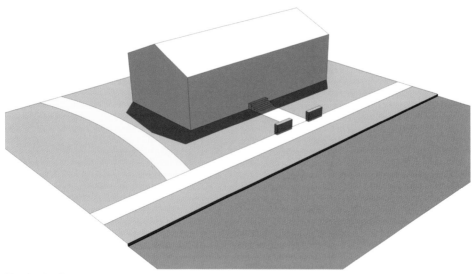

Fig. 6-23: Completed volumes

Organizing Components

Components need to be imported, organized, and placed on layers for two reasons:

▶ Some components, such as 3D trees and shrubs, are composed of many edges and faces. Copying them in mass can significantly hinder computer performance.

▶ The ability to turn off components will allow you to better navigate the SketchUp workspace. The less geometry visible, the more smoothly SketchUp will operate.

An example of a final layer list for a composed and detailed model might look like Fig. 6-24.

Creating Component Layers

Prior to importing a component into SketchUp, create a specific layer for that particular component type. For example, if the component is a 2D tree, use the Layers menu (Window ➤ Default Tray ➤ Layers) to create a layer named 2D Trees (Fig. 6-24). Make this layer active.

The next step is to import the component. There are two options:

▶ Under File ➤ Import, set the file extension to .skp, and navigate to the component location. Select the desired component.

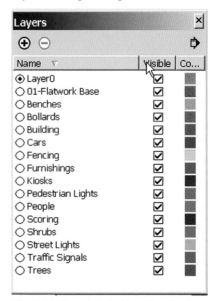

Fig. 6-24: A model's final layer list after the addition of component layers

▶ Use the Components menu (Window ➢ Default Tray ➢ Components) to navigate to the desired component folder and select the component.

The selected component will appear in the model and on the new layer. When a component is copied, it will stay on the same layer.

Component Tools

There are many tools that affect the placement, copies, rotation, and scale of components. The following list is a quick overview of some tools:

Move/Copy Like many of SketchUp's tools, Move/Copy has multiple functions. Ctrl+Alt+click and drag to create a copy of the selected component/geometry. Entering a value (distance) in the Measurement window will locate the copied component the specified distance away from the original.

Move/Copy Array – Linear Move/Copy has the ability to create multiple copies in a row.

Example: To copy a component 10′ in any direction, enter **5X** in the Measurement window. Four copies will be generated along the same axis of movement, each 10′ apart (Fig. 6-25).

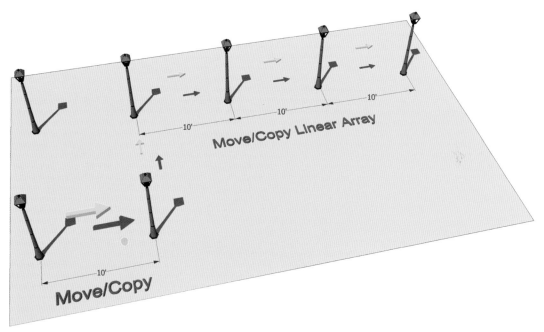

Fig. 6-25: A Move/Copy linear array

You can change the distance and value in this example as needed. Move/Copy will always create a set number of copies (the value entered minus 1) equidistant from each other.

Move/Copy Array – Division Copy and place a component 40′ from the original. Enter **5/** (divide symbol). Four copies will be created, equally spaced between the two components (Fig. 6-26). As with Array – Linear, the distance and value can be changed as needed.

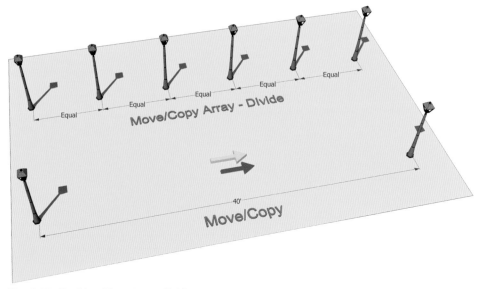

Fig. 6-26: The Move/Copy Array – Division

Move/Copy – Rotate The Move/Copy command doubles as a Rotate-on-Axis tool. Select Move/Copy and hover the cursor over the selected component. Little red Xs will appear around the side of the component over which the tool is hovering. Selecting one of the Xs will cause a small rotate protractor to appear, allowing the object to be rotated on an axis (Fig. 6-27). Learn how to quickly locate the crosshairs on various sides and play with how the Move/Copy Rotate functions.

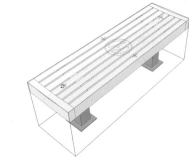

Fig. 6-27: The Move/Copy crosshairs and rotation

Rotate Tool The Rotate tool (View ➤ Toolbars ➤ Modification menu) allows you to select two points of rotation for a selected component: the center axis and the angle of rotation. The Rotate tool can array objects using the same commands as Move/Copy Linear and Division Array (Fig. 6-28).

Scale Tool The Scale tool (View ➤ Toolbars ➤ Modification menu) allows a component to be enlarged, reduced, or distorted in size and shape (Fig. 6-29).

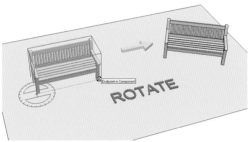

Fig. 6-28: The Rotate tool

Example: Select a component and activate the Scale tool. A series of green square handles will appear around the component. Grab a handle and move it in and out to adjust the size and dimension of the component (Fig. 6-29).

Components can be scaled to retain proportion by using only one of the four corner handles. You can scale them to a specific value by entering the value after a green handle has been selected. You can also use Scale to create an exact mirror image of a component by selecting one of the handles and entering the value **−1**.

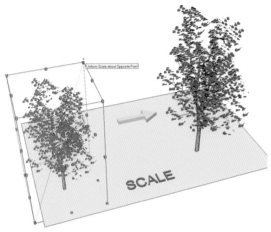

Fig. 6-29: The Scale tool

You should practice scaling components using the various handles and seeing how they affect the size, shape, and proportions of a component. Also, the Scale tool can be used on flat surfaces.

PathCopy This is a custom extension (see Chapter 5) available for free on the Extension Warehouse (search for **PathCopy** in Window ➢ Extension Warehouse). It allows components and groups to be copied along arcs and other nonlinear lines. Follow the instructions in Chapter 5 to install the extension.

From the Extensions menu, select PathCopy. There will be two options: Copy to Path Nodes and Copy to Spacing. For now, select Copy to Spacing. Enter a value in the Measurement window and press Enter. Next, select an arc and then the component. The component will be copied along the arc at the specified interval (Fig. 6-30).

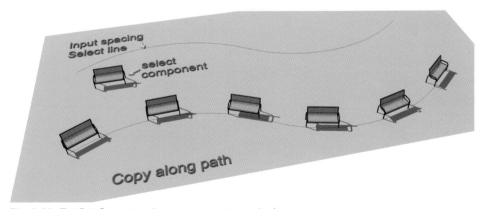

Fig. 6-30: The PathCopy extension can array components along arcs.

Adding Components to the Flatwork Base

Using components downloaded from 3D Warehouse, add some detail to the Flatwork Base. Make sure to import each object type onto a specified and named layer.

Start by adding trees. Go to Window ➤ Components. Select a tree component. Place the tree in the tree lawn area adjacent to the road at one end of the tree lawn.

Next, use the Move/Copy tool to array the tree. Select the tree, select the Move/Copy tool, and Move/Copy the tree along the green axis by Ctrl+clicking. Enter a value of **20′** and press Return. The tree will be copied 20′ along the green axis. Enter the value **4X** and press Enter. Three copies of the tree will be generated along the green axis, each 20′ apart (Fig. 6-31).

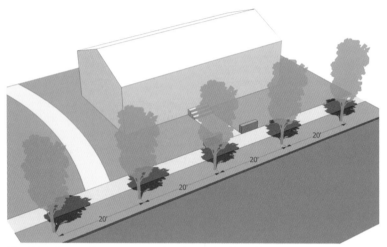

Fig. 6-31: Insert a Tree component into the model. Move/Copy the trees in the tree lawn with a linear array.

If you downloaded PathCopy, use it to place four trees along the trail arc (Fig. 6-32).

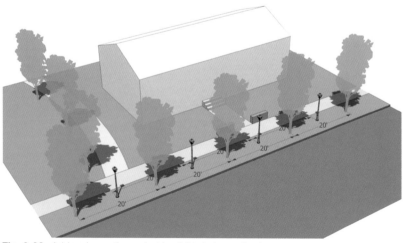

Fig. 6-32: Add and array the pedestrian lights between the trees.

Next, add pedestrian lights between the trees (Fig. 6-32). Place the light between two trees (approximate). Array three more lights into the model between the trees using the Move/Copy command.

Continue to import more detail (such as benches, cars, and people) into the scene. Experiment by using the various tools to adjust size, rotation, and location (Fig. 6-33, Fig. 6-34). Make sure to place all component types onto an appropriate layer.

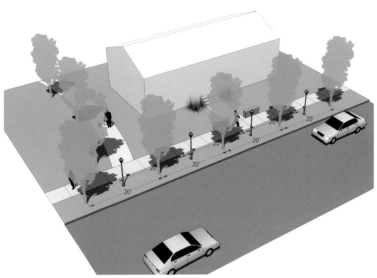

Fig. 6-33: People, cars, and shrubs are added.

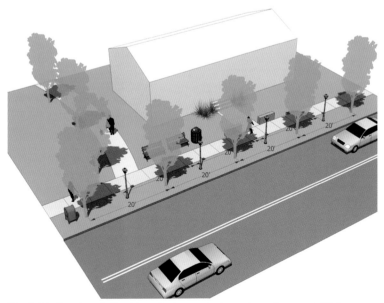

Fig. 6-34: Benches, traffic stripes, trash receptacle, and a mailbox are added.

Adding Component Windows and Doors

The last phase of populating the model is to add detail to the building.

First, free up the modeling space: turn off all of the layers except Layer 0 and the Layer 01 Flatwork Base (Fig. 6-35).

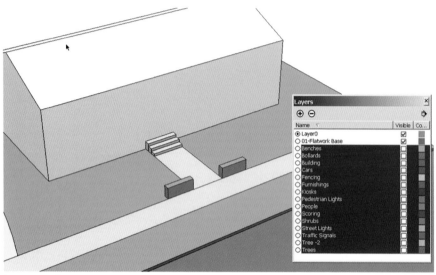

Fig. 6-35: Turn off the component layers to clear the work environment.

If some of the components do not become invisible, select those components, right-click, and activate Entity Info. Place the components on the correct layer. Create appropriate layers as needed. The Flatwork Base group should be the only geometry visible.

SketchUp components have the ability to "cut holes" in surfaces. This ability is very useful when you create windows with transparent materials or colors that allow the objects or spaces on the other side to be visible. Chapter 9 discusses how to create components that cut through a surface, a technique that is most useful in architectural modeling.

Enter the group instance and zoom in on the building. Add detail to the building surface using Window and Door components. (You can download Window and Door components from 3D Warehouse.) Select a Window component for the building. Place the window onto one of the building's vertical surfaces (Fig. 6-36). The component will stick to the surface and cut a hole, making the interior space of the building visible. If the component window were deleted, the surface of the building would heal.

Using the various Window and Door components available, add them to the building surface (Fig. 6-36, Fig. 6-37). Add a door component aligned with the steps and entrance.

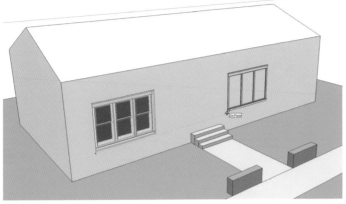

Fig. 6-36: Use Move/Copy to place the Window components on the building face.

Fig. 6-37: While fixed to a face, Building components can be scaled and adjusted just like regular components.

Adjusting the Building Components

Components placed on buildings can be scaled, copied, moved, arrayed, rotated, and edited the same as other components.

Select the Door component and adjust its size using the Scale tool (Fig. 6-37). Adjust the door to match the length of the steps. You can see the completed building in Fig. 6-38.

Fig. 6-38: The completed building with component detail

Reviewing the Completed Model

Turn on all the layers and review the model (Fig. 6-39). If you followed along with the book, you created a basic and simple model, populated with details that define the character of an outdoor space. The model was created without any reference material.

Fig. 6-39: An eye-level view of the completed model

The Flatwork Base was created by:

1. Drafting and subdividing surfaces on a 2D face
2. Adding color to the defined surfaces
3. Giving volume with Push/Pull

Objects were included by:

4. Using components to represent objects
5. Arranging component objects on the Flatwork Base

The model was organized by:

6. Making the Flatwork Base a group
7. Placing the Flatwork Base group on its own layer
8. Importing component objects directly onto their own layers

These are the steps that define the SketchUp Process Modeling method. The same sequence is used to help construct models from a variety of sources: hand drawings, Computer Aided Design files (AutoCAD), and when working with Digital Elevation Models. Understanding these basic principles is essential for working through the remainder of this book.

An Advanced Example

These example images illustrate a model created by following the outlined process (Fig. 6-40 through Fig. 6-43). The model was created in under 30 minutes and incorporates rich detail, perspective, and many types of features found in the built environment. Using the processes described in this chapter, try to re-create the design. Do not sweat being accurate, but attempt to re-create the outline base, shapes, and volumes as best possible.

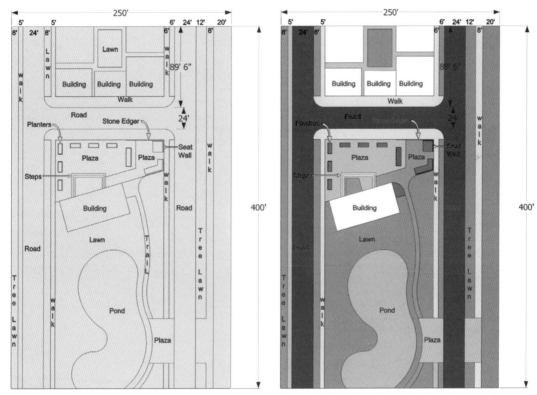

Fig. 6-40: Flatwork Base drafted from scratch   **Fig. 6-41:** Color is added to the drafted Flatwork Base.

You can download three models that represent the three stages of the included examples (Fig. 6-40, Fig. 6-42, and Fig. 6-43):

- ▶ Advanced Example – Flatwork Base
- ▶ Advanced Example – Color
- ▶ Advanced Example – Completed Site Plan

You can check your progress against these models. The Completed Site Plan model includes site object components.

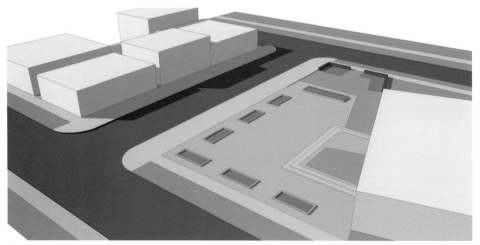

Fig. 6-42: Volume is added to surfaces—planters, stairs, road, walks, buildings, and walls.

Fig. 6-43: Component details are added to the Flatwork Base. Components were downloaded from Google 3D Warehouse Bonus Pack for SketchUp 7 and from **www.formfonts.com**.

Modeling Your Own Designs

Before moving on with this book, try to create an original model from your own imagination using the SketchUp Process Modeling method. Use any available reference materials, such as site plans or Google Earth images. Start small and build up to larger model areas, and then apply more detail in the landscape and buildings.

Explore the various tools outlined in this chapter. Discover how Ruby Scripts can be used with SketchUp to aid in modeling.

Always be mindful of layers and use them. Start to collect your own pre-made component library.

CHAPTER 7

Detailed Site Plan Modeling

Now that you've been introduced to SketchUp Process Modeling, it's time to explore some additional process methods. In this chapter, you'll expand on the techniques you've already learned—drafting a Flatwork Base, adding color, and applying volume—and apply them while working from a scanned image.

Using Site Plans

Site plans are drawn and scaled drawings that represent two-dimensional layouts of a built environment (Fig. 7-1). They range from hand-drawn sketches on tracing paper to elaborate pencil, marker, Photoshop, or AutoCAD plans.

This chapter focuses on constructing a Flatwork Base from a scanned hand-drawn plan of a courtyard and surrounding buildings. To complete this exercise, download the Conceptual Site Plan Image model from 3D Warehouse. The model is part of the SPM Part 2 collection (**SPM Part 2** is the search term). Use the downloadable tutorial model when indicated.

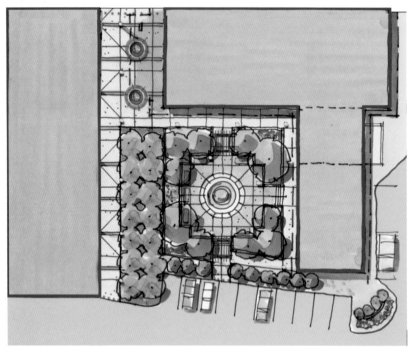

Fig. 7-1: A hand-drawn site plan scanned into SketchUp for use with the chapter tutorial

Importing Site Plans

SketchUp lets you import several standard image formats: JPEG images (.jpg), tagged images (.tif), bitmap images (.bmp), and Portable Network Graphic images (.png). When you use a site plan, make sure it was scanned or saved in a compatible image format.

To import an image, go to File ➢ Import and select the file extension that supports the plan image. Several options will appear to the right of the file import screen. Select the Use as Image option. Click Open and the image will appear in SketchUp. You'll have to place and size the image for SketchUp.

Place the plan image at the 0 insertion point of the drawing axes, much the same as you did with the initial rectangle for the Flatwork Base in Chapter 6 (Fig. 7-2). Once the insertion point is selected, you'll need to size the plan. Simply click and drag the image and left-click to select the final size. The plan image won't be scaled, but you'll learn how to do that later in the chapter.

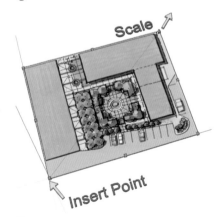

Fig. 7-2: Inserting and scaling a plan

If you select the plan image, you'll see that SketchUp has converted it into a group.

Imported-Image Resolution

Unlike Photoshop, SketchUp is not an image viewer. Imported plan images will seem to lose their clarity, or they may appear pixelated when viewed. When they are imported and scaled, images are stretched to real-world proportions and lose image quality. However, these images are still quite usable as drafting references. Because of their decreased image resolution, SketchUp site plans are meant to be viewed from a comfortable distance.

Processing image files can tax computer performance. To help keep your system from bogging down, use JPEG images if possible. They use a compressed format that doesn't eat up as much computer space.

Placing the Plan Image on a Layer

Place the plan image on its own layer. Create a new layer (Window ➤ Layer ➤ Add Layer button) called 02-IMAGE.

Select the Plan Image group, open the Entity Info menu, and place the imported plan image on the new layer. Once the transfer is complete, make Layer 0 the active layer again. This prepares the modeling environment for drafting.

Scaling the Image

A built environment is comprised of surfaces and objects that usually have standard dimensions. Because plan images describe objects and surfaces of the built environment, you can reference many of their dimensions with standard lengths or widths. Follow these steps to scale a plan image (Fig. 7-2).

1. Use the Tape Measure tool (View ➤ Toolbars ➤ Construction ➤ Tape Measure) to measure an area that correlates to real-world dimensions that you know.

    The following widths and lengths are fairly typical ones that you can use to help determine scale:

    Roads: Average 12′ for single lane, 24′ to 34′ for most two-lane roads

    Steps: 1″ tread width

    Benches: 6′ or 8′ in length

    Cars: 9′ width or 18′ length

    Walks: 5′ to 10′ in width

2. Immediately after measuring an area with the Tape Measure tool, enter (in the Measurement window) the real-world value of the area you measured. Press Return. SketchUp will ask if the model should be resized. Select Yes. The plan image will be resized.

3. Use the Tape Measure tool to check the dimensions on the image to make sure they are the correct length or width. Resize the image as needed, repeating steps 1 through 3.

Preparing the Drafting Trace

You can use the downloaded Conceptual Site Plan Image mentioned earlier for the rest of this chapter. This exercise's image is already scaled to the correct size. The image group is on its own layer, and the group itself is locked.

As described in Chapter 6, the Flatwork Base will be sculpted on a rectangular face. Because the plan image will be traced onto the rectangular face, the surface needs to be transparent. To prepare the drafting face, follow these steps:

1. Create the drawing surface.

    a. With Layer 0 as the active layer, draw a rectangular face over the entire image.

    b. Snap the first point of the face at 0 insertion; make sure to cover and overlap the entire image surface (Fig. 7-3).

2. Make the face transparent.

    a. From the Paint Bucket tool, select Color 001 from the Colors palette (select Colors from the drop-down menu).

    b. Apply Color 001 to the face.

    Fig. 7-3: Draft a rectangle face over the plan image.

    c. Select Edit in the Materials menu.

    d. Under Edit, find Opacity. (In some systems it may be hidden. Expand the menu by dragging the corners to locate Opacity at the bottom.) Set the Opacity value to 50 percent.

The image plan underneath is now visible through the face, and the face is ready for drafting (Fig. 7-4).

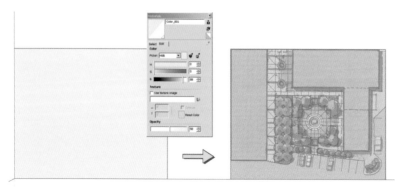

Fig. 7-4: Paint the drafting face and make it transparent.

Drafting Tips

When you are drawing lines, arcs, and faces, you can create clean geometry that is easy to manipulate and edit by following these tips:

Don't sweat accuracy. Trying to be accurate when you're tracing lines from a fuzzy plan image is difficult at best. Trace the lines as accurately as possible, but don't sweat it.

Draw on the axes. Try to draft orthogonally and on the axes. Utilize linear inferences and snap to endpoints and midpoints. Most if not all image plans, including the provided site plan, have lines that are not orthogonal. If possible, snap nonorthogonal lines to orthogonal lines.

Don't overlap lines. Overlapping lines will cause problems with faces and the ability to generate volumes and edit geometry. When you're drawing rectangles, snap edges to edges and ensure that no overlaps exist (Fig. 7-5).

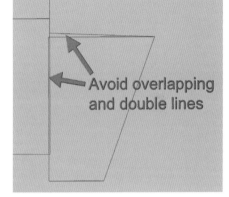

Avoid double lines. This occurs when two lines compete to be the same edge. When you're drawing nonorthogonal geometry, check for double lines (Fig. 7-5).

Align the edges. The built environment in many cases is defined by surfaces and edges that are parallel, perpendicular, and aligned. Line up drafting edges using adjacent linework as guides. This is easily accomplished by using the Tape Measure tool (View ➤ Toolbars ➤ Construction ➤ Tape Measure)

Fig. 7-5: Avoid overlapping and double lines.

to create construction guides. *Construction guides* are dashed edges that serve as reference edges and do not affect geometry (Fig. 7-6).

Use the Tape Measure tool (View ➤ Toolbars ➤ Construction) to add construction lines. Play around with the Tape Measure to learn how it works. It will be very useful for the chapter tutorial.

Use rectangles. Trying to subdivide faces with the Line tool does not always work. Instead, use the Rectangle tool to define areas. Then subdivide the edges and faces of the rectangle to fit the desired outline. This will ensure that the face geometry is subdivided.

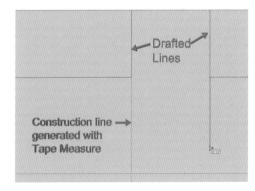

Fig. 7-6: The Tape Measure tool can be used to create construction guides.

Identify all the surfaces before drafting. This will help you determine the drafting order. Also, surfaces provide reference points in which edges and faces can be connected (Fig. 7-7). Some typical hard surfaces include concrete, colored concrete, pavers, asphalt, stone, walls, curbs, and building footprints. Some typical landscape surfaces include lawns, crusher fines (gravel), and planting beds.

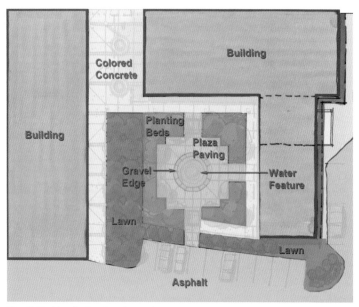

Fig. 7-7: Identify the site plan surfaces.

A bug in SketchUp versions 6 and below sometimes prevents faces from being subdivided after the lines are drawn to define an individual face. Working around the bug is easy, but figuring out how to do it will take some detective work. Make sure that all the faces are divided into their own areas. If they are not, try the following:

- Make sure all the edges are snapped to other edges.
- Make sure none of the lines overlap. This commonly occurs when the Offset tool is used. Delete and redraw the lines as needed to remove all the overlaps.
- Delete an edge that composes the face that should be subdivided and redraw it. Go around the edges, and delete and redraw lines until the face is subdivided.

Drafting Order

These steps, which will be described in more detail, provide general guidelines for drafting and for effectively using the inference system. First, draft the outline of the plan image. Gradually subdivide the surface into smaller, more detailed faces. Use all of the drafted geometry to snap and align the other edges and faces as more detail is added. The smallest surfaces (for example, steps and walls) should be the last geometry that you draft.

Drawing the Site Perimeter and Building Footprints

Perimeter edges and building footprints provide references for snapping and aligning other drafted geometry. First, draw the building footprints using the Rectangle tool. Snap the footprints to the outer edges of the rectangular drawing surface. Next, draw the outer edges of the site plan; in the example plan, this is the curb line between the plaza and the parking area. Notice that some of the perimeter edges can be snapped to a building footprint (Fig. 7-8).

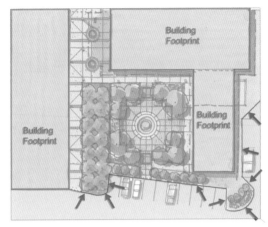

Fig. 7-8: Draft the building footprints and site perimeter.

Drafting the Identified Surfaces

Steps 1 through 7 are fairly complex. Read through the steps prior to attempting the tutorial. Draft the previously identified surfaces. Use the perimeter and building edges as references and snap points when applicable (Fig. 7-8).

Align the edges. The interior of the plaza, defined by the edges of the planter areas, is composed of several edges at right angles. Follow these steps to draw lines that are aligned, parallel, or perpendicular. Use the image as reference to locate all edges.

1. Draw a rectangle to define the main surface of the plaza (Rectangle 1) (Fig. 7-9). Further define the plaza edges using smaller rectangles. Draw a small rectangle (Rectangle 2) above the first rectangle (Fig. 7-10).

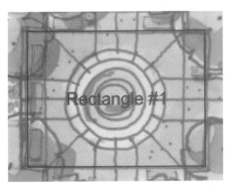

Fig. 7-9: Define the inner plaza with a rectangle.

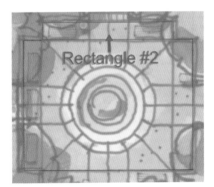

Fig. 7-10: Drawing the inner plaza

2. Use the Tape Measure tool to draw construction guides from the right and left edge of Rectangle 2 to the bottom edge of Rectangle 1. At the intersection of the construction guides and Rectangle 1, draw Rectangle 3 to finish defining the interior plaza space (Fig. 7-11).

3. Draft Rectangle 4. Place Rectangle 4 over most of the tree lawn area (pink trees). Align the right edge of the rectangle with the corner endpoint of the perimeter edge (Fig. 7-12).

4. Draw Rectangle 5 over the indicated linework of the plan image. Align the top edge of the rectangle with the top edge of Rectangle 4 (Fig. 7-12).

5. Draw Rectangle 6; make sure to align the rectangle with the right and left edges of Rectangle 5. Use construction lines to guarantee the alignment. The bottom edge of Rectangle 6 should end at the left corner of the planter indicated on the plan image (Fig. 7-12).

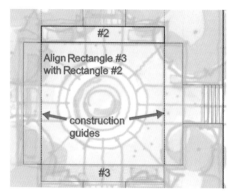

Fig. 7-11: Align the edges of Rectangle 3 with Rectangle 2.

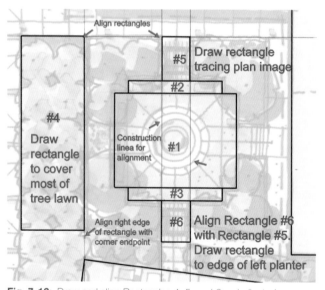

Fig. 7-12: Draw and align Rectangles 4, 5, and 6 as indicated.

6. To create Rectangle 7, draw an edge from the midpoint of the left edge of the plaza to the right. Four feet above this line, on the outside edge of Rectangle 1, draw a 10′-6″ × 8′ rectangle to define the entry (Fig. 7-13).

7. Draw the edges to complete each area as indicated in the diagrams. Make sure that the edges are drawn on axes (green and red) where applicable, and that the faces are subdivided. If faces do not subdivide, zoom in to the endpoints of the drawn line and make sure they are connected to the correct edges they were drawn to (Fig. 7-14 through Fig. 7-16).

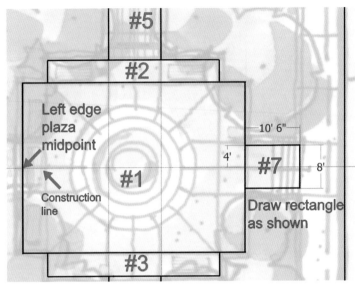

Fig. 7-13: When you draw Rectangle 7, align it with the left edge midpoint of the plaza.

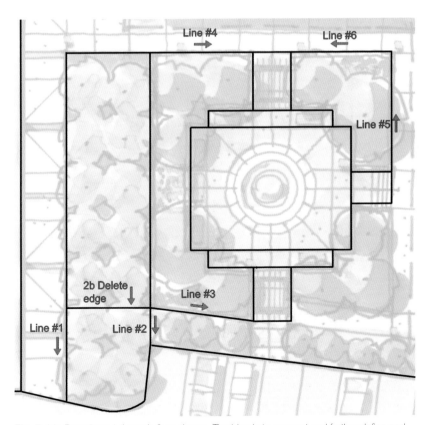

Fig. 7-14: Draw lines 1 through 6 as shown. The idea is to connect and further define and subdivide areas of the plaza.

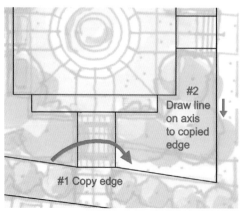

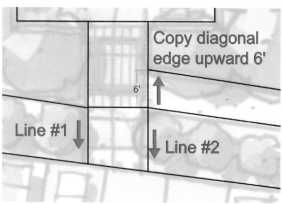

Fig. 7-15: Copy the diagonal edge (line 3 from Fig. 7-16) over to the right.

Fig. 7-16: Add two lines from the bottom edge of the rectangle to the perimeter.

Adding the Small Edge Details

To draft the small details (steps, curbs, and walls), follow these steps.

1. Create the steps.

    a. Move/Copy the edges at the plaza's bottom (Rectangle 6) and east (Rectangle 7) entries to create steps (Fig. 7-17).

    b. At the south entry, offset the edge 2′ to create a landing. Offset the landing edge to create three 1′-wide steps.

    c. At the east entry, from the right edge, offset three edges, each 1′ apart, to create three steps (Fig. 7-18).

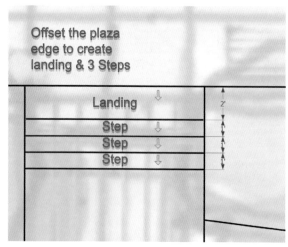

Fig. 7-17: Move/Copy the steps and landing at the bottom entry (bottom of Rectangle 6).

2. Create the entry sign wall and planting area.

   a. At the bottom right of the plan, trace a single arc to define one edge of the wall (Fig. 7-19).

   b. Offset the arc to create the wall thickness and to define the planter edges as shown in the plan.

   c. Further subdivide the wall and planting bed with arcs and lines (Fig. 7-20, Fig. 7-21).

3. Create the water feature located at the center of the plaza.

   a. Draw a diagonal line from one corner of the plaza to the opposite end.

   b. Use the Circle tool (View ➤ Toolbars ➤ Drawing ➤ Circle) to draw a round surface on the midpoint of the diagonal line, matching the central circle on the plan (Fig. 7-22).

   c. Delete the diagonal line. Offset the first circle to match the concentric round edges, as shown in the image (Fig. 7-23).

4. Create the curbs. The edges between roads and walks and lawns are typically defined by a 6″ curb. Adding curbs to models provides a visual cue to viewers; it conveys a subtle realism (Fig. 7-24).

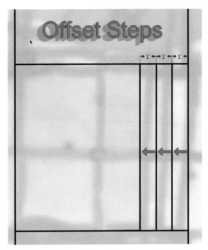

Fig. 7-18: Move/Copy the steps at the right entry (right edge of Rectangle 7).

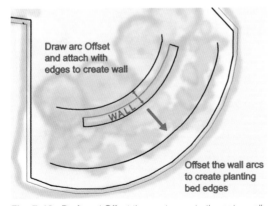

Draw arc Offset and attach with edges to create wall

WALL

Offset the wall arcs to create planting bed edges

Fig. 7-19: Draft and Offset the arc to create the entry wall sign and planting area.

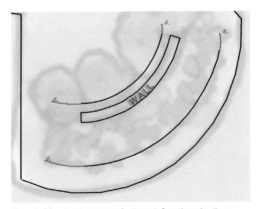

WALL

Fig. 7-20: Apply arcs to further define the planting area.

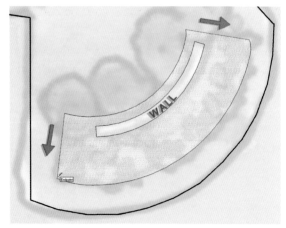

Fig. 7-21: Use edges to finish the planting area form and create the subdivided faces.

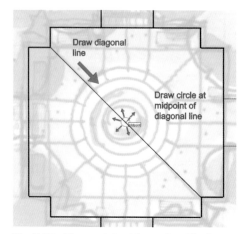

Fig. 7-22: Place a circle at the center of the inner plaza.

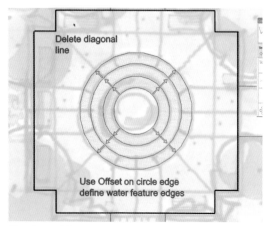

Fig. 7-23: Offset the center circle to create the fountain edges.

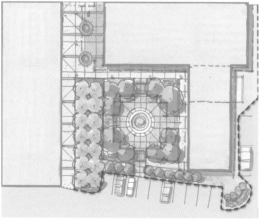

Fig. 7-24: Area of plan that will have a curb

a. Select the face of the surface where curbs can be located. Offset the face inward 6″. This will offset all the edges that compose the surface (Fig. 7-25).

b. Draw perpendicular lines between the edge of the road and the offset line at locations where the curb would end; curbs should be located only adjacent to the road (Fig. 7-26). Repeat this step for areas

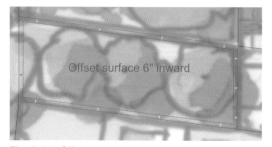

Fig. 7-25: Offset the face to create edges used for a curb.

that can accommodate a curb (Fig. 7-27). Ensure that the surface faces you defined for curbs are subdivided from the adjacent faces.

5. Create the walls and planters using the same technique you used to create the curbs. Identify areas with walls, use the Offset tool to provide thickness, and (if needed) close off the ends by adding edges with the Line tool (Fig. 7-28, Fig. 7-29).

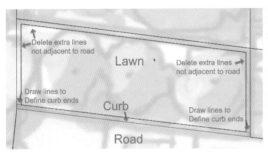

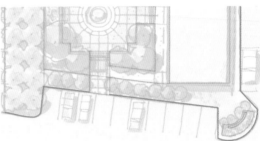

Fig. 7-26: Define ends of curb locations. Delete extra lines created from using the Offset tool.

Fig. 7-27: A curb is added to the site perimeter.

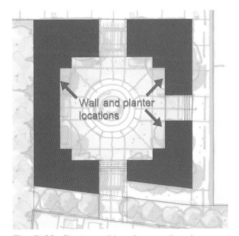

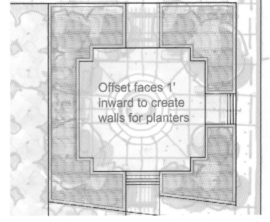

Fig. 7-28: Planter wall locations on the plan image

Fig. 7-29: Offset the planter area faces to create edges for the wall.

Review the plan before you move on to the next step. If you missed anything or something needs to be adjusted, draft the necessary lines. Select faces that define locations to make sure they have been subdivided.

Creating the Flatwork Base Group

You'll need the plan image to help identify and place components. However, adding colors or textures will obscure the plan image underneath. Therefore, before you add colors or textures to the faces, copy the Flatwork Base and place it next to the current base (Fig. 7-30).

1. Using a selection box, select the drafted edges and geometry that compose the Flatwork Base.

2. Right-click and select Make Group.

3. Create a new layer called 01 - Flatwork.

4. Select the Flatwork Base group, right-click and select Entity Info, and place the group onto the 01 - Flatwork layer.

5. Use Move/Copy and place a copy of the group near the original.

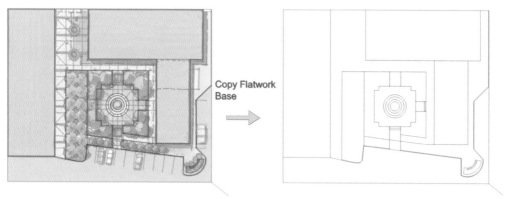

Copy Flatwork Base

Fig. 7-30: Copy and paste the Flatwork Base next to the original.

Adding Color and Texture

By striking a balance between solid colors and textures, you can make your model more visually appealing and expressive. Use colors and textures that best define the material that represents the surface. As a general rule, apply more solid colors than textures. This will help delineate between the surfaces (Fig. 7-31).

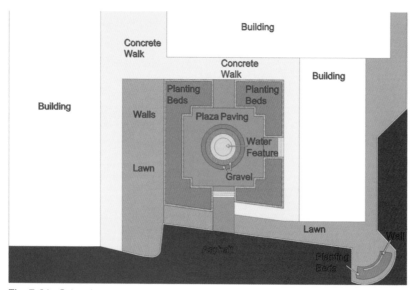

Fig. 7-31: Colored areas on a site plan

You can adjust Hue, Saturation, and Contrast under the Materials Edit tab. Make the colors lighter or darker or change the hues as needed. Table 7-1 lists the colors used on the Flatwork Base faces.

Surface	Material Menu	Texture / Color
Asphalt	Asphalt and Concrete	Asphalt_New
Building	Color	Color_000
Concrete Walk	Vegetation	Vegetation_Bark_Marble - Texture removed
Gravel – Inner Ring	Groundcover	Groundcover_Sand_Smooth
Gravel – Outer Ring	Groundcover	Groundcover_Brick_Crushed -Texture removed
Lawn	Vegetation	Vegetation_Grass1 -Texture removed
Planting Bed	Vegetation	Vegetation-Blur7- Texture removed
Plaza Paving	Asphalt and Concrete	Concrete_Stamped_Ashler -Texture removed
Wall	Stone	Stone_Sandstone_Ashlar_Light
Water Feature	Marker	Light Blue

Table 7-1: Colors Used on the Flatwork Base Faces

Textures are images you use to paint a face. Textures can be *scaled to size* (made larger or smaller). To scale a texture, select the texture in the material's window and click the Edit tab. Adjust the values in the Use Texture Image dialog box.

Removing the texture image converts the texture into a solid color. In the Edit tab, uncheck Use Texture Image.

To keep the focus on the site plan, paint the building faces white.

Adding Volume

When you add volume to a Flatwork Base, just as when you draft, you should do so in a definitive order.

Lower the road surfaces first. For most bases, they are the lowest points in the model and establish the baseline of volume depth and height.

Next, determine the highest elevated surface in the model. An easy rule of thumb is to locate the stairs first. Because the steps in the model ascend upward, the surface to which they transition is the tallest surface. This will help determine the height of other surfaces and volumes.

Road and Curb

Push/Pull the road 6″ down. Remember to delete the excess edges (and faces) created by Push/Pull on the perimeter of the road face (Fig. 7-32).

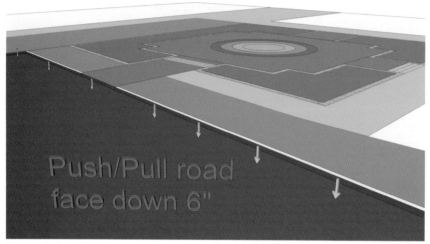

Fig. 7-32: Push/Pull the road 6″ down.

In some situations, you'll need to reapply the color to the face of a created volume to correctly match its intent. For example, the vertical face of the curb is generated when the road is pulled downward. This causes the color of the curb to match the road. Using the Paint Bucket, match the color of the vertical curb to the horizontal surface above it (the curb and walk color) (Fig. 7-33).

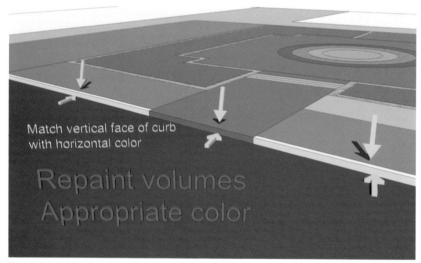

Fig. 7-33: Add colors to vertical faces along the road.

Steps and Plaza

Locate both sets of steps. Each step should have a 6″ riser. Push/Pull the steps to create an ascending stair to the plaza. The *landing* or the face between the last step and the plaza should be level with the last step. Push/Pull the plaza faces (including the water-feature faces) to match the height of the landing (Fig. 7-34).

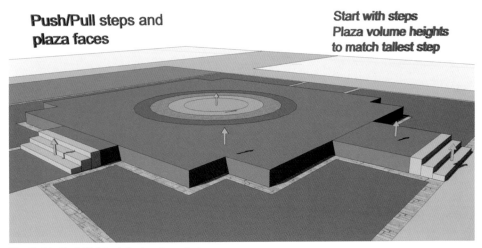

Fig. 7-34: Push/Pull the tallest surfaces first.

Planter Walls

Elevate the adjacent planter walls to the same height as the plaza. Push/Pull will "stop" and match the height of any adjacent surfaces. Apply Push/Pull until the desired height is achieved. Additional height will be added to the walls after the next step (Fig. 7-35).

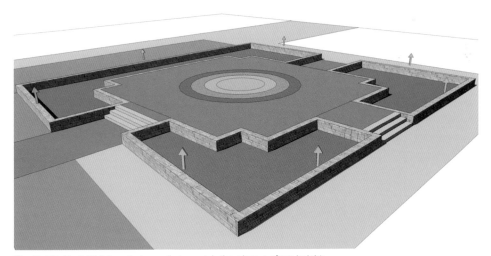

Fig. 7-35: Push/Pull the planter walls to match the plaza surface height.

Ramp

A cursory pan around the plaza will reveal that the north entry to the plaza is blocked by the vertical surface generated in the previous steps. The plan does not indicate any steps. Draw a ramp to accommodate the entry.

There are many ways to add ramps. You'll learn other methods in Part 3, "Terrain Modeling," when you study the Sandbox tools. For this ramp, use the Line tool and draw edges from the top point of the plaza (where the plaza edge and the wall intersect), along the face of the wall to the endpoint of the entry. Do this on both sides (Fig. 7-36).

SketchUp should generate a face between the two drawn edges. However, in some cases, the edges may not be aligned, so SketchUp will not be able to generate a surface. If that occurs, draw a diagonal line from the bottom edge of the entry to the opposite top edge. This will create a surface/ramp into the plaza. Apply the appropriate color to the surface (Fig. 7-37).

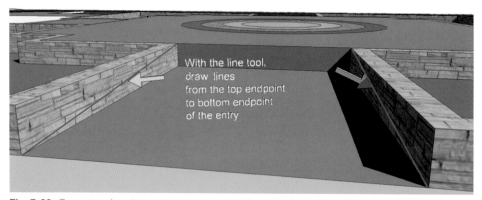

Fig. 7-36: To create a face that serves as a ramp into the plaza, draw diagonal lines from the top of the entry to the bottom.

Fig. 7-37: Add color to the ramp's face.

Planter Wall Adjustments

Adding volume to the planter walls helped create references to the edges and faces to create the ramps. Now, adjust the planter walls above the elevated face of the plaza. Push/Pull the planter walls upward another 1′. This partially encloses the plaza.

Push/Pull the planting bed surface slightly below the top surface of the planter walls (Fig. 7-38). The three elevated surfaces (the plaza, planter walls, and planting bed) help create scale and visual interest.

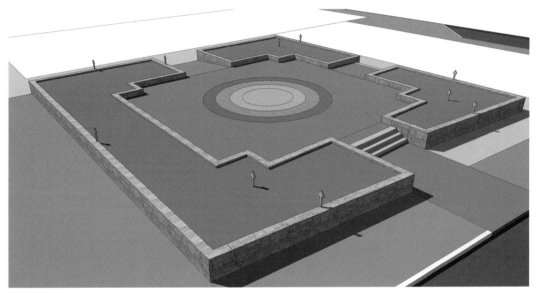

Fig. 7-38: Push/Pull the planter beds just below the top of planter wall.

Entry Sign Wall

Push/Pull the entry sign wall to 3′ height/volume (Fig. 7-39).

Buildings as Components

Before you add volume to the building area, make each building surface into a component and then place each component onto a Building layer.

1. Select the face and one edge that comprise a building surface. Right-click and then select Make

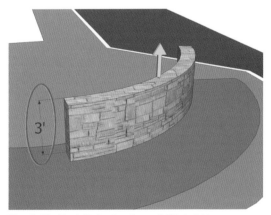

Fig. 7-39: Push/Pull entry sign wall 3′ in height.

Component from the context menu. Make sure to check the Replace Selection with Component box (Fig. 7-40, Fig. 7-41).

2. Do this for each building.

3. In the Component dialog box, input a name for each building: **Building 1**, **Building 2**, and **Building 3.** Create a layer called Building, and use Entity Info to place the buildings on the layer.

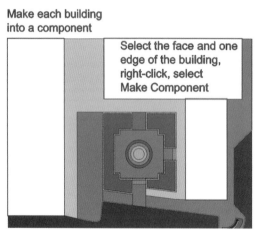

Fig. 7-40: Turn each building surface into an individual component.

Fig. 7-41: Name each Building component in the Component Creation menu. Place the Building components on the Building layer.

This step accomplishes two things:

▶ It separates the building geometry from the Flatwork Base, which allows the buildings to be placed on their own layer.

▶ By placing buildings on their own layers, they can be toggled off so they do not interfere when you model.

▶ It will be easier to add details such as windows and doors to the buildings. This is reviewed in Chapter 9.

Building Volumes

The height of a building is determined by the number of floors and the floor-to-floor heights. *Floor-to-floor height* refers to the distance between one floor and the next floor. Typical floor-to-floor heights range from 10′ to 14′, with exceptions that range from 18′ to 22′ for a loft or vaulted ceilings (Fig. 7-42).

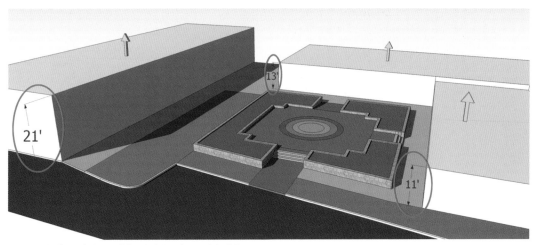

Fig. 7-42: Specify the building heights for each building.

To add volume to the buildings, edit the Building components. Make them 11′ and 13′ in height, respectively. Select the third building and Push/Pull the volume to 21′ high. Once the volumes are added, turn off the Building layer. The buildings are now hidden from view.

Adding Detail to Volumes

Now that the basic volumes have been Push/Pulled, it's time to include additional details that help provide more articulation to the model.

Detailing the Sign

The corner wall is designed to serve as a sign in the plaza; therefore, it can use some additional detail.

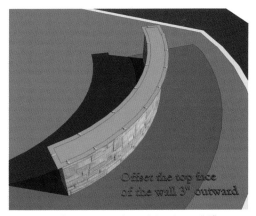

Fig. 7-43: Offset the top face of the sign wall 3″ outward.

1. Add a simple wall cap.

   a. With the Offset tool, select the top face of the wall. Offset the face outward 3″. The edges of the face will offset 3″ and create a face overlapping the original edges (Fig. 7-43).

   b. Push/Pull the new surface 3″ in height. Push/Pull the inner face 3″ to match the first face.

   c. Delete the excess lines of the inner face and add color to the faces (Fig. 7-44).

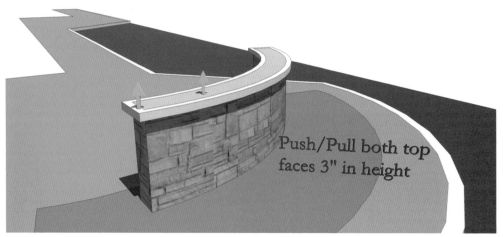

Fig. 7-44: Push/Pull the top faces of sign wall 3″ in height.

2. Add 3D text to the surface of the curved sign wall. 3D Text (View ➤ Toolbars ➤ Construction ➤ 3D Text) will generate typed text with edges, faces, and volume. The menu allows you to input the font type, alignment, extrusion (volume), and size of the text. Select OK to generate text as a component that can be placed on surfaces.

   a. Select View ➤ Hidden Geometry. Vertical dashed lines will appear on the curved surface of the wall. These lines show that the curved wall is not a true curve but is composed of a series of flat faces that create the illusion of a curved wall.

   You can apply 3D text to each wall face so that it can also be used as a sign.

   b. Place a single letter on each face (Fig. 7-45).

   c. Open the 3D Text menu and specify the following settings:

   Font: Garamond

   Size: 1′

   Extruded: 2″

   d. One letter at a time, type **Google**. Place each letter on the faceted surfaces that define the vertical walls of the planter.

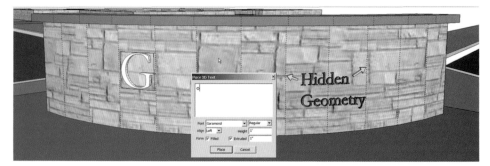

Fig. 7-45: To create a sign, add 3D text to the wall face.

Once all the letters are placed, turn off Hidden Geometry (View ➤ Hidden Geometry). Add color to each letter (Fig. 7-46).

Fig. 7-46: Add color to the 3D text.

Detailing the Planters

The Scale tool can help you model existing geometry to create irregular shapes. In this example, you'll use it to create sloped walls.

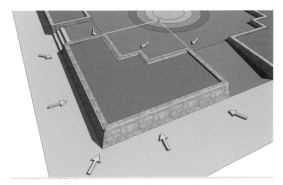

Fig. 7-47: Scale the top face of wall inward to create a sloped surface.

1. Select only the top face of one of the smaller planter walls.

   a. Activate the Scale tool. Because the face is flat (2D), only eight green scale handles will appear. Ctrl+Alt and select a corner green handle and push it inward. This will accomplish two things (Fig. 7-47):

      ▶ The face will be uniformly scaled inward on all sides.

      ▶ The vertical wall faces will fold inward with the scaled top surface, creating a sloped wall (Fig. 7-48).

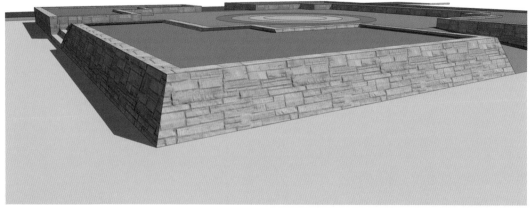

Fig. 7-48: The sloped vertical faces of the planter wall

2. Go to the next small planter wall. Select the top face and repeat step 1. This time, select a corner green handle and push it outward (Fig. 7-49). The walls' vertical faces will fold outward with the scaled top surface (Fig. 7-50).

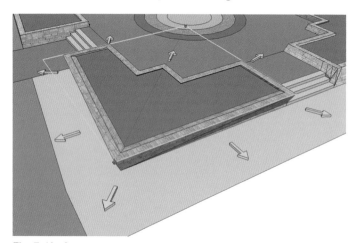

Fig. 7-49: Scale the top face of the wall outward to create a levered wall.

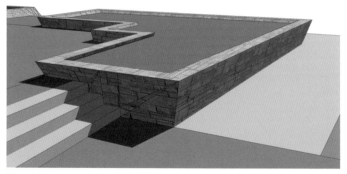

Fig. 7-50: The levered vertical faces of the wall

Part 2: SketchUp Process Modeling

Although this method adds detail, it does create some problems with the geometry around the walls. Locations where the wall faces are attached or are sticking to other geometry, such as the steps, will contain irregular geometry (Fig. 7-51). This is unavoidable; fortunately, irregular geometry can be masked. While holding the Shift key, use the Eraser tool and select the irregular edges. This will hide the lines.

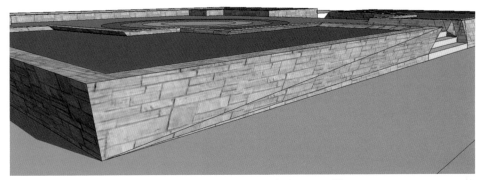

Fig. 7-51: Hide any irregular geometry created when you scale the top wall faces.

When you finally generate images or animations of models with any such irregular geometry, avoid focusing on those areas. Instead, focus your images where the sloped walls appear clean and calculated.

Now that the various elements and surfaces have been added and detailed, the Flatwork Base is finished (Fig. 7-52). Make sure to save the model for use in later chapters and tutorials. The next step for the site plan model is to populate and arrange pre-made and custom components.

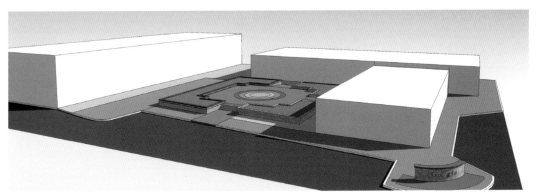

Fig. 7-52: The completed and detailed Flatwork Base and volumes

CHAPTER 8

Custom Site Furnishings

Components are versatile. They can stand alone. They can be flipped or mirrored. They can be unique and separated from the parent component. They can be used to build other components. You can construct your own components to populate a Flatwork Base with custom site furnishings. The tutorials in this chapter reinforce the drafting techniques you have already been utilizing to quickly and cleanly generate custom site furnishings.

Each exercise introduces a new tool or method, builds on the previous component, and requires you to apply the skills you learned in earlier chapters. You will use the completed components to help populate the Flatwork Base from the previous chapter.

The Modeling Process

The process used to create custom site furnishings is almost identical to the general steps used in SketchUp Process Modeling. To make custom components, follow these steps:

1. Draft the proportions and detail in a 2D plan.
2. Delete the extra edges and faces.
3. Convert the remaining edges and faces into a component.
4. Rotate the component to stand on the vertical axis.
5. Add volume and detail.
6. Add color.

When you are modeling a site-furnishing component, you apply the color last. This is different from the order you used to model a Flatwork Base. Color is most effectively added to faces after the component volumes are complete.

Components within Components

Components and groups can be modeled, created, or placed in other components or groups. There is no limit to the number of subcomponents a main component can have (Fig. 8-1, Fig. 8-2).

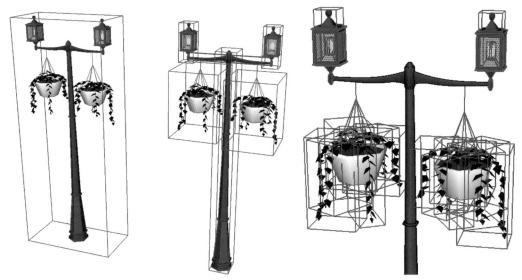

Fig. 8-1: The main light component (left) is constructed from many subcomponents (right).

Fig. 8-2: Subcomponents are composed of other subcomponents.

Mirroring Components

The Scale tool can make a mirror image (reverse) of any selected geometry. This ability is quite handy when you're working with components. This versatile tool lets you create new inverted shapes without creating any new geometry (Fig. 8-3, Fig. 8-4).

To mirror an object, select the component and then activate the Scale tool. Select one of the green corner handles that appear. Push the handle inward on the component. Enter **-1** in the Value Control Box (Measurement window) and press Enter. The component will mirror itself in the opposite direction.

The direction and type of mirroring accomplished is determined by which handle was used to create the mirror.

Entering **-1** into the Measurement window tells SketchUp to scale the object 100 percent in the opposite direction (inward), keeping the object at the same scale (size and proportion). Entering a different value, either positive or negative, will scale the component to a different proportion. For example, if you enter **.75**, the component will be reduced in size by 25 percent. If you enter **1.25**, the component will be enlarged by 25 percent. The same is true if the values entered were negative, the difference being that the component would be mirrored or flipped on itself.

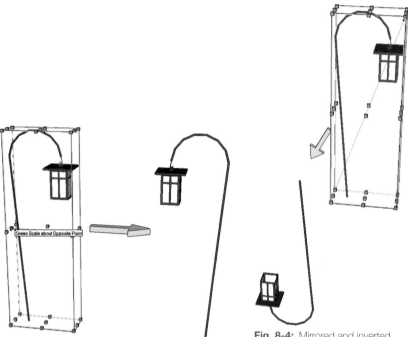

Fig. 8-3: Mirrored and reversed component

Fig. 8-4: Mirrored and inverted component

Making Unique Components

To activate the Make Unique option, select a component or group of components and right-click. Selecting Make Unique will convert any of the selected components into their own new component types, separate from the original (Fig. 8-5).

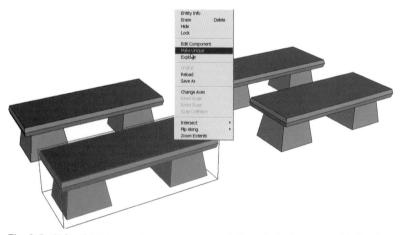

Fig. 8-5: All four benches are the same component. The selected component is "made unique."

These new components can be edited without affecting the original component type (Fig. 8-6). Make Unique is not available if there is only one copy of a component in a model. SketchUp automatically renames components after Make Unique is used. It adds a version number such as (1) to the end of the original component name.

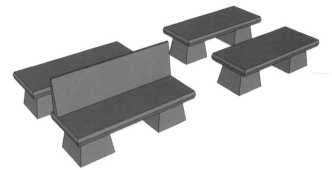

Fig. 8-6: The Made Unique component is edited, but it does not affect other components. It is now its own component.

The Follow Me Tool

The Follow Me tool is a versatile tool that allows you to create complex geometric forms with relative ease. It is used extensively in the chapter tutorials.

Example 1:

1. Create a cube 10′ × 10′ × 10′ (Fig. 8-7). At the bottom right corner of the cube, draft an edge 50′ in length with the Line tool. Draw the edge so it aligns with either the green or red inference axis (Fig. 8-8).

2. At the end of the edge, draft two arcs. Try to make the arcs tangent to the edge and to each other. Place the arcs so that they form a smoother, continuous path (Fig. 8-8).

3. Make sure that the edge and two arcs are "flat" and not at all vertical.

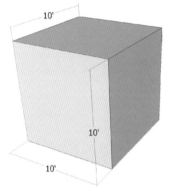

Fig. 8-7: Draft a 10′ × 10′ × 10′ cube.

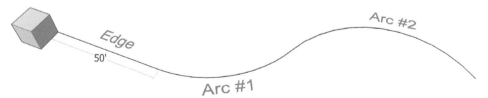

Fig. 8-8: Starting at the cube, draft a 50′-long edge and two arcs as indicated.

4. Select the edge and the two arcs. With all three selected, activate Follow Me (View ➤ Toolbars ➤ Modification ➤ Follow Me) and then select the face on the cube that is perpendicular to the edge and arcs (Fig. 8-9).

The face of the cube will Push/Pull along the selected edges (Fig. 8-10).

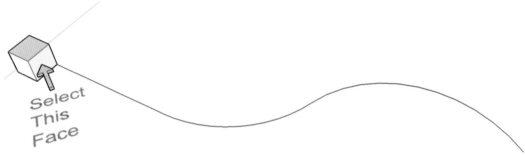

Fig. 8-9: Select the edge and two arcs. Activate Follow Me and select the indicated face on the cube.

Fig. 8-10: Follow Me will Push/Pull the cube face following the path of the selected edges.

Example 2: This example includes steps that are common to most of the tutorials in this chapter.

1. Using the Circle tool, draft a 20′-diameter circle face on the ground. Select the face and edges of the circle, right-click, and convert the geometry into a component (call it Sphere) (Fig. 8-11).

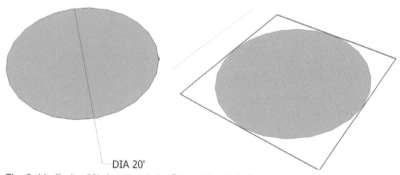

DIA 20'

Fig. 8-11: Draft a 20′-diameter circle. Convert the circle face into a component.

2. Use the Move/Copy tool to rotate the circle to the vertical position. While you are hovering the cursor over the component with the Move/Copy tool, notice the little red crosshairs that appear.

3. Hover/Snap the Move/Copy tool to one of the crosshairs. At the center of the component, a rotation circle will appear. Selecting the crosshair will allow Move/Copy to rotate the component. You can do this for both the horizontal and vertical side of the component.

4. In this case, the vertical side of the component is paper thin because it does not have any volume. Hover the Move/Copy tool over the thin-edge sides of the component and snap to the crosshairs that appear (Fig. 8-12). This should allow you to rotate the component vertically. This is a useful skill to practice, and you'll need to be able to do it to successfully complete the tutorials.

5. Rotate the circle component so that is standing directly vertical (Fig. 8-13).

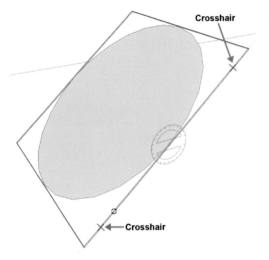

Crosshair

Crosshair

Fig. 8-12: Use the Move/Copy tool to rotate the component to stand vertically. Use the small red crosshairs on the side of the component to complete the rotation. (The crosshair size is exaggerated in this diagram.)

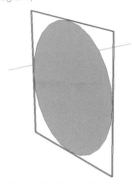

Fig. 8-13: Rotate the component to stand vertically.

6. Enter the component instance of the circle. At the bottommost edge of the circle, draft another 20'-diameter circle. Make sure the circle is horizontal (Fig. 8-14). Learning to align with the Circle tool can be tricky, but have the patience to orient the new circle to the horizontal plane.

7. With the bottom circle in place, while still in the component instance, select the edge of the horizontal circle, activate the Follow Me tool, and select the face of the vertical circle (Fig. 8-15).

8. The vertical circle's face will "follow" the selected edge of the horizontal circle and create a sphere (Fig. 8-16).

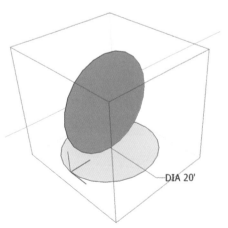

DIA 20'

Fig. 8-14: Enter the Circle component instance and draft another horizontal circle at the base of the vertical circle.

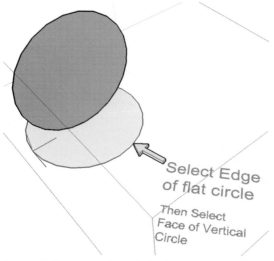

Select Edge
of flat circle

Then Select
Face of Vertical
Circle

Fig. 8-15: Select the edge of the horizontal surface, activate Follow Me, and select the face of the vertical surface.

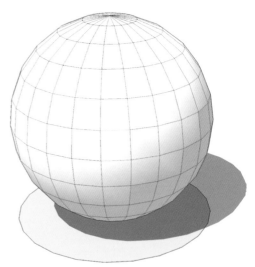

Fig. 8-16: The Follow Me tool will cause the face of the vertical circle to follow the edge of the horizontal circle edges, generating a sphere.

Although it is very versatile, Follow Me can be a troublesome tool. It can have difficulty extruding more complex forms and can work inconsistently. Profile Builder is a powerful alternative extension that is reviewed at the end of this chapter.

Model Organization

Save each custom component in its own separate SketchUp file. This accomplishes two things:

▶ It provides an obstruction-free modeling environment. This is important given the small size and details of custom components.

▶ A component saved in its own file can be imported into any site model.

The filename should describe the component for easy identification when importing.

Tutorials

Complete each of the component tutorials in the order presented. The components from each tutorial will be used in Chapter 10 to populate the Flatwork Base from Chapter 7.

As you work through the following tutorials, remember these important tips:

▶ Do all of your drafting and modeling on Layer 0.

▶ Work in a separate file.

▶ Remember to save the SketchUp file frequently.

▶ Name all of the components.

▶ Make sure you are working within the component instances when they are called for or are needed.

- ▶ Use Move/Copy to practice rotating flat geometry to the vertical position.
- ▶ Be patient when working with the Follow Me tool. If it does not seem to work correctly the first time, go back and repeat the steps.

The Bollard

In this first tutorial, you will draft an outline of a bollard and then use Follow Me to generate the three-dimensional form.

Download model: Bollard

1. Draft the bollard on a 2D rectangle face.
2. Draft the bollard ribs as arcs with a 1/4" bulge. Move/Copy and array the first arc to create the other four (**5x**).

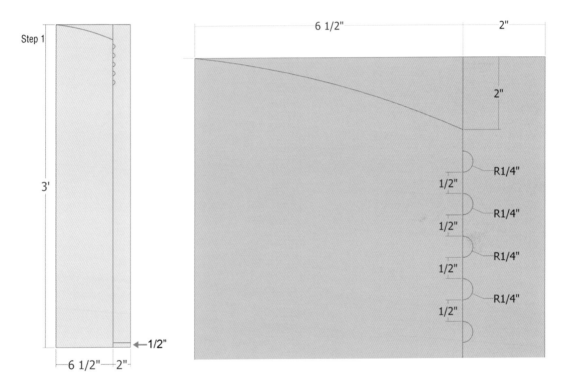

3. Delete excess faces and edges. You should have a 2D outline of the bollard. Select and make the face and line geometry into a component.
4. Rotate the component so that it stands vertically. Draw a circle in the component instance. The circle must be perpendicular to the component (horizontal). Snap the circle midpoint to the left endpoint of the bollard face.

   Snap the circle edge to the right-edge endpoint of the bollard face. Make sure that the circle is drawn within the component instance.

5. The circle added in the previous step is the reference edge for Follow Me. You will have to reselect the circle edge each time to perform Follow Me on the bollard faces. Use the Follow Me tool on the faces in this order:

   a. Center face

   b. 1/4" bulges

   c. Base

Step 5A

Center face

Base

1/4" bulges

Steps 3–4

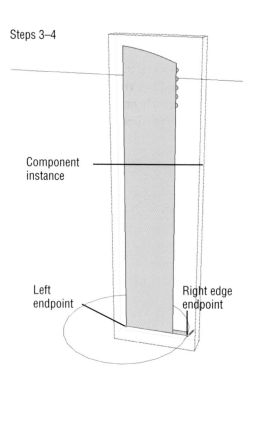

Component instance

Left endpoint

Right edge endpoint

6. Add the color. Make the base black and the bulk of the bollard red.

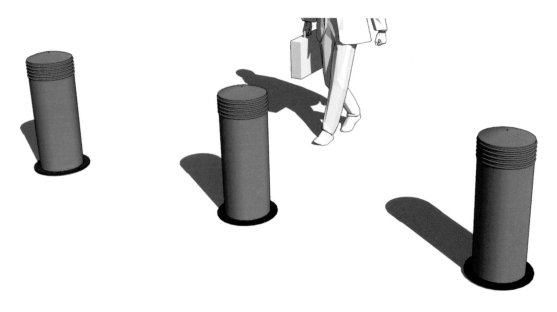

The Pedestrian Light

This tutorial expands on the previous bollard model. It teaches you how to model a pedestrian light and paint color and materials to specific parts of a faceted form.

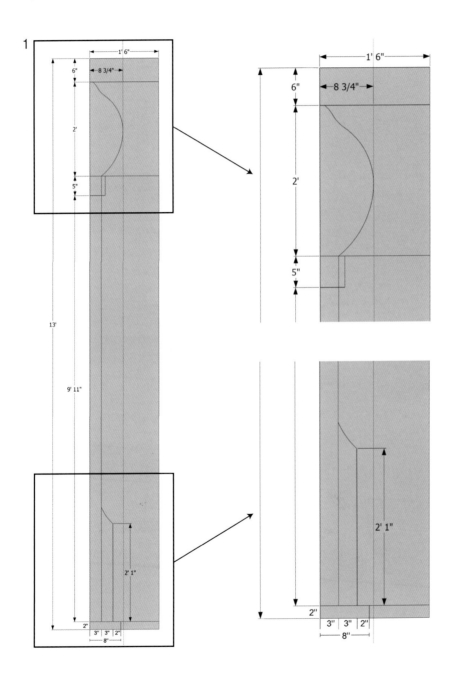

Download model: Pedestrian Light

1. Draft the face. Dimension as indicated in the diagrams.
2. Outline and make the component. Rotate it to vertical.
3. In the component instance, draw a circle at the base.
4. Use the Follow Me tool on the faces. Do the outside fin last.

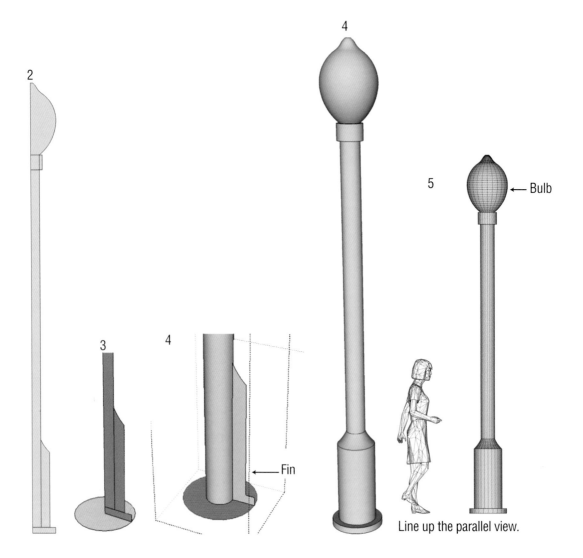

Line up the parallel view.

5. Add color to specific faces using Hidden Geometry. Turn on View ➤ Hidden Geometry. Under Camera, select Parallel Projection. From View ➤ Toolbars ➤ Views, select any of the four front, right-back, left views. This will line up the view axis to look directly at the light. Pan into the bulb. Using the Select tool, place a selection box around the

central bulk of the bulb. Leave the faces at the top and bottom of the bulb unselected. Apply a transparent color (Transparent_Glass_Bold) to the selected faces.

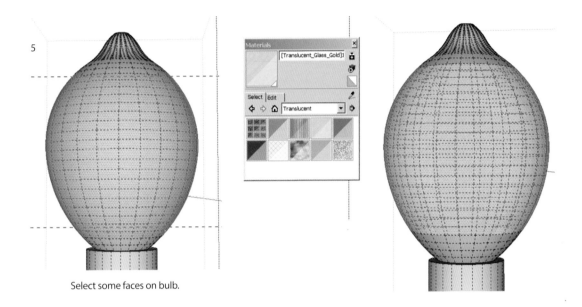

5

Select some faces on bulb.

6. Repeat step 5 to add color to the top and bottom of bulb. Add Color_005. Turn off Hidden Geometry when you are done with this step. Under Camera, select Perspective.

7. Add color to the rest of the lightfaces as shown.

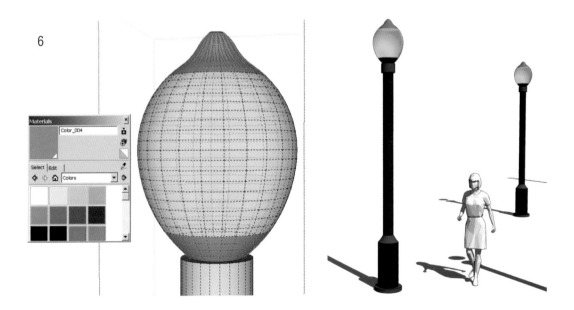

6

The Modern Bench

The Modern Bench tutorial will demonstrate how Push/Pull can be used to create subtracted volume.

Download model: Modern Bench

1. Draw the volume.

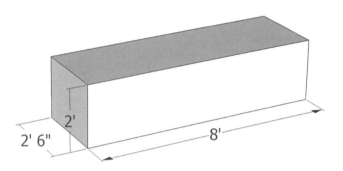

2. Draft the faces on the front surface as indicated in the diagram. The colors are for reference only, to delineate the faces.

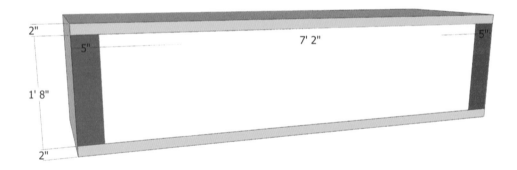

3. Push/Pull the center face inward. Snap the face to an edge on the opposite side of the volume. This will cause the center face to disappear.

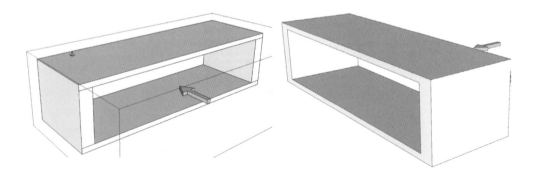

4. Use the Line tool and draw edges to define the top seating surface of the bench. Make sure to go around the volume.

5. Add color.

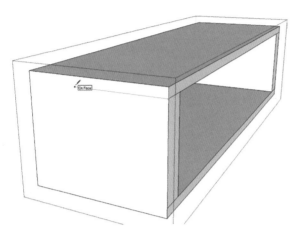

The Park Bench

In this example, you will learn to mirror and make components unique while also utilizing components within components.

Download model: Park Bench

1. Draft the edges on the face.

2. Convert the geometry into a component. Call it Frame. Add volume as indicated. Note: if Push/Pull causes the other side of the volume to lose its faces, heal the faces (in the component instance) by going from endpoint to endpoint with the Line tool along the "hollow" edges. This simple component will be used to make the Bench Frame.

3. Copy the Frame component. Perform a Mirror/Scale of the copied component: select the component and activate Scale. Select one of the corner handles and enter **−1** in the Measurement window.

4. Move/Copy and snap the ends of the two Frame components as shown in

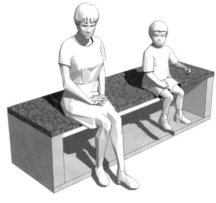

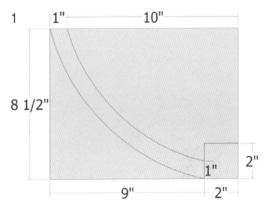

the diagram. Select both connected components. Use Move/Copy and make a copy of both Frame components.

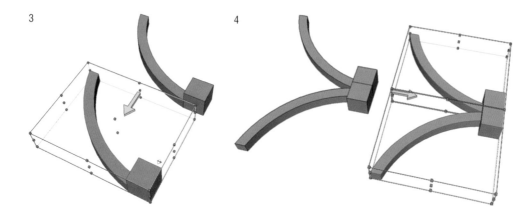

5. Select the copied Frame components. Activate Scale and mirror the copies. Snap the mirror-copies to the ends of the previous components as shown.

6. Select the top-right Frame component. Right-click and select Make Unique.

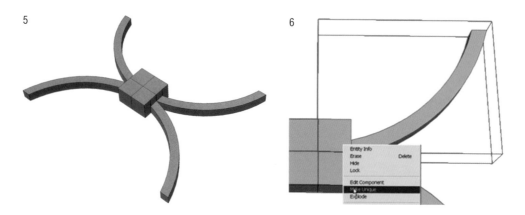

7. Enter the component instance of the Frame that was made unique. Draw an edge 1'-6" out from the top edge of the component. Make sure the edge is drawn perpendicular (magenta color edge when being drawn).

8. Select the line, activate Follow Me, and select the face adjacent to the drawn edge. This will create the future backrest for the bench.

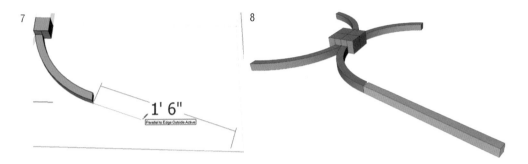

9. Select all four components and make them a single component called Bench Support. Use Move/Copy and rotate the component so that it is vertical.

10. Within the component instance of Bench Support, draw a 1/2″ radius circle at the intersection of the four components. This will create a circle face.

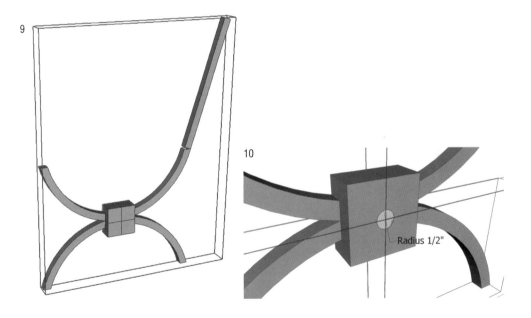

11. Push/Pull the circle face 2′-6″ outward. Exit the component instance.

12. Copy and mirror the Bench Support. Attach the two components at the ends of the Push/Pulled circle face. Select both components and make them into a single component called Bench Frame. Draw an edge from the top front end corner to front end corner of the Bench Frame.

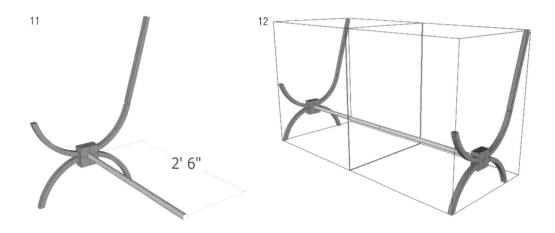

13. In front of and parallel to the Bench Frame component, draw a 6′ × 4″ × 2″ volume. Make the volume a component named Wood Slat. Select the midpoint of the Wood Slat component on the side furthest away from the Bench Frame. Move/Copy and snap it to the midpoint of the edge drawn at the top-front of the previous step.

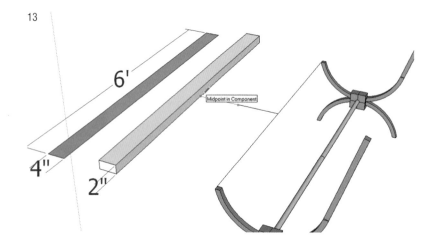

14. Use Move/Copy to copy the Wood Slat component to the opposite end of the Bench Frame. Next, array the component: type **4/** to create three evenly spaced copies of the Wood Slat.

15. Copy a Wood Slat component upward along the bench back. Place the component a little below the top of edge of the frame.

16. Use Move/Copy to rotate the Wood Slat component to sit parallel along the bench back.

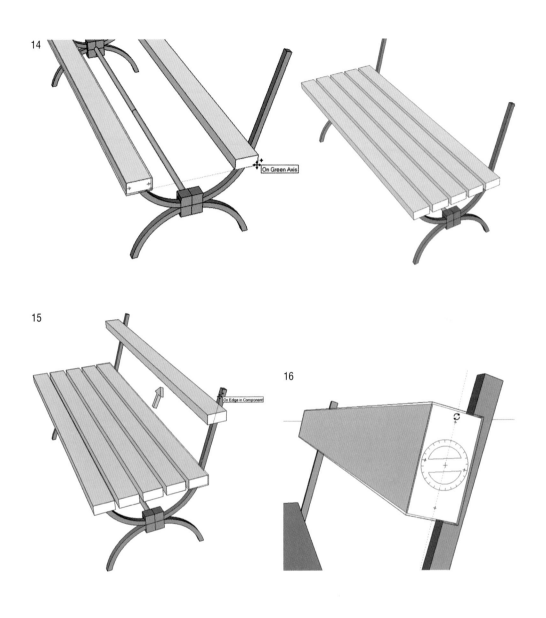

14

On Green Axis

15

On Edge in Component

16

17. Copy the top Wood Slat downward.

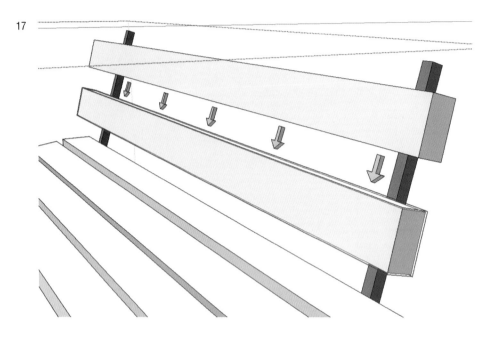

18. Add color. Select all the components that compose the bench. Right-click and select Make Component. Call it Park Bench.

The Decorative Planter Bench

The Decorative Planter Bench in this tutorial will be composed of several individual components. You will learn to use the first constructed component as a reference to build the rest of the objects that compose the planter.

Download model: Decorative Planter Bench

1. Draft the edges on the face. Make it a component called Pot and rotate the component vertical.

2. In the component instance, add a circle at the bottom and use the Follow Me tool to generate the Pot volume.

3. Select the top face of the Pot and Offset it inward 3″. Push/Pull the center-top face downward 1″ to create a slight lip.

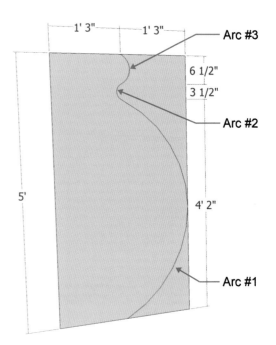

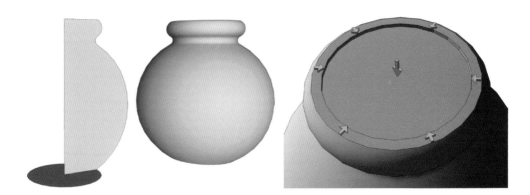

4. Add a green color to the lowered face at top. Add color to the rest of the Pot.

5. Exit the component instance and pan to the bottom of the Pot. Draw a line across the center axes of the planter bottom. From the drafted line midpoint, snap a circle outward 4′ in radius. This will create a circular face around the base of the Pot component outside the component instance.

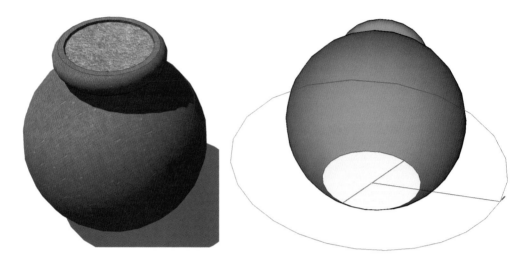

6. Offset the face of the circle inward in this order: 4″, 1″, 4″, 1″, 4″. Delete the faces in-between the 4″ faces created by the 1″ offset and delete the inner (center) face.

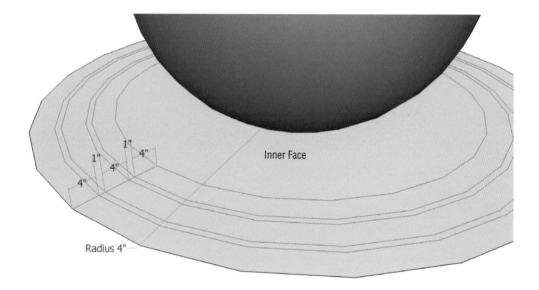

7. Push/Pull each 4″ face 2″ in height. Make each volume into a component called Slat 1 through 3. Select all three Slat components and make them into a component called Bench Seat.

8. Select the Bench Seat component and move it up along the vertical axis 1′-6″.

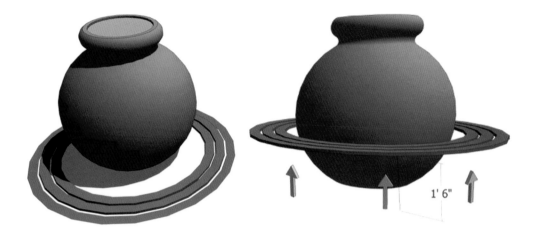

9. Near the Pot, create a square face 2'-6" by 2'-6". Draft the outline for the bench rail on the face as indicated. Push/Pull the surface to a 1" thickness. Make it a component called Bench Rail. Add color. Rotate the component to vertical.

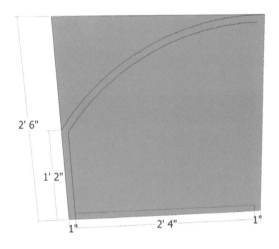

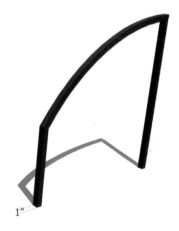

10. Move the view to the bottom of the Pot. Draw a line from the endpoint of the edge at the bottom of the Pot drawn in step 5. Make sure the line extends along the same axis as the existing edge outward beyond the Bench Seat. Select a bottom endpoint of the Rail component. Move and snap the rail to the drawn line. With the Rotate tool, rotate the rail to be parallel to the line. Move the Rail component along the drawn line so that the rail straddles the Bench Seat.

11. Rotate/Copy the rail along the midpoint of the bottom face. Select the rail and activate the Rotate tool. Select the center of the bottom of the Pot (midpoint of the drawn edge across the bottom) for the first rotation point. Select the outside (furthest) bottom edge of the rail. This is the second rotation point. Hold the Ctrl key (to create a copy of the rail) and rotate the rail 45 degrees. Enter the value **45** in the Measurement window.

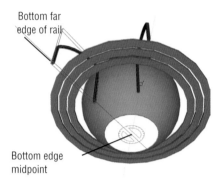

Bottom far edge of rail

Bottom edge midpoint

12. Immediately after the first Rotate/Copy, enter **7x** to create six duplicates, each rotated 45 degrees.

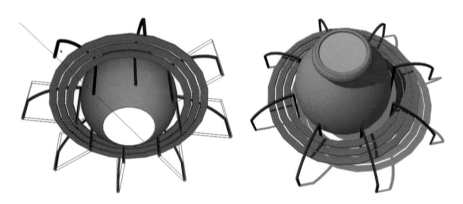

13. Import a 3D tree. Place it at the center of the planter. Scale the tree to the appropriate size, as shown in the diagram. Select all the components and make a single component called Decorative Planter Bench.

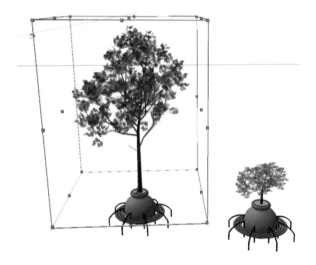

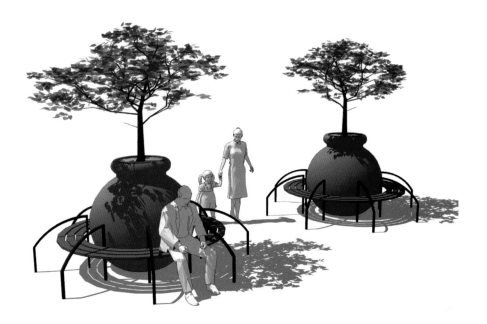

The Decorative Rail

This tutorial will teach you how to draft and compose small edges and faces to create a tiny detailed model. The instructions for this tutorial are held to a minimum. Use some of the processes from the previous tutorials to complete the steps.

Download model: Decorative Rail

1. Draft the edges on a 12″ × 8″ face.

2. Convert each lattice segment into a component called Lattice 1, Lattice 2, and Lattice 3. Select and copy the three components simultaneously.

3. Use the Scale 1 tool and Mirror the copied lattice components. With the Move/Copy tool, snap them to the endpoints of the originals.

4. Push/Pull all the faces 1/2″. Select all of the geometry and convert it into a component. Call it Edger. Rotate the component to vertical.

5. When you are using Move/Copy to create the array of Edgers, overlap the ends of each component.

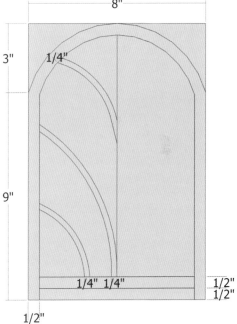

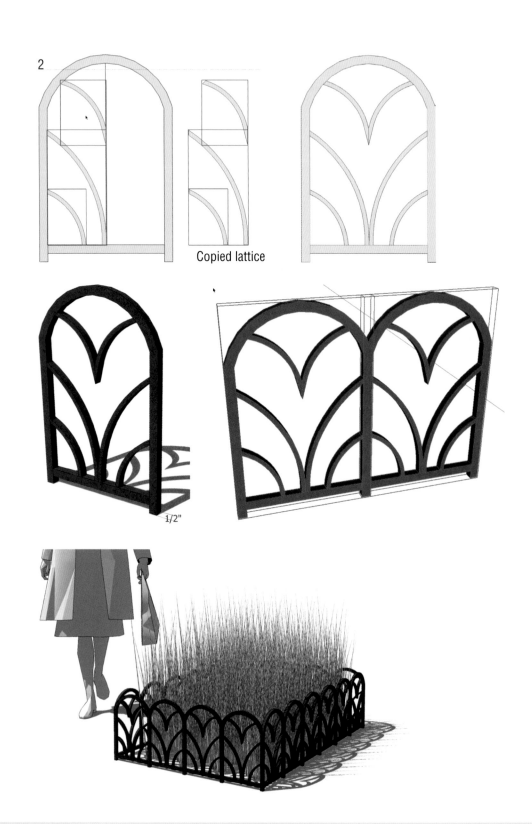

Copied lattice

1/2"

The Handrail

This tutorial shows one method to create accurate (ADA-compliant) handrails for steps. As with the previous tutorial, instructions are kept to a minimum.

Download model: Handrail

1. Draft the edges and faces of a standard set of steps.

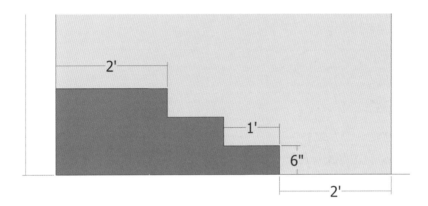

2. Draft the line work as indicated by the diagram. The outline forms the perimeter of the handrail.

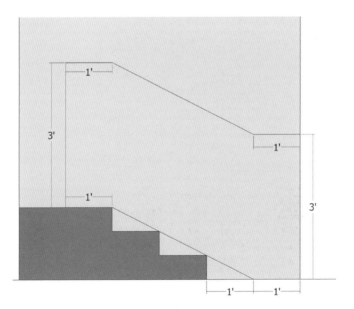

3. Offset the face generated by the outline in step 2 inward 2″. Delete the bottom edge of the offset. Delete the diagonal line across the top of the steps. Draw edges downward and upward at the location indicated by the red circles. Make sure the face of the rail is subdivided.

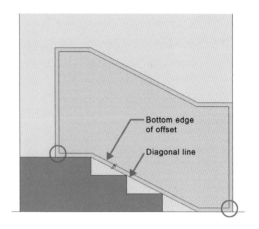

Bottom edge of offset

Diagonal line

4. Delete the faces and edges outside and around the handrail and step faces.

5. Select the faces that compose the vertical bars of the rail. Make each a component called Vertical Rail. Move each component inward 5-1/2″.

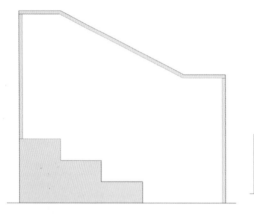

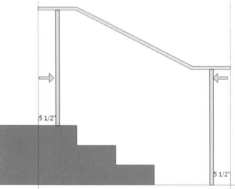

6. Push/Pull the top rail 4″. Push/Pull the vertical bars 2″. Center the vertical bars on the top rail. Select all the geometry of the rail and convert into a component called Handrail. Rotate the component to vertical.

Profile Builder

Profile Builder is a powerful extension that can outperform FollowMe. It allows you to build complex forms and organic shapes quickly and easily. It can be found on the Extension Warehouse (Fig. 8-17). There are free and Pro versions of Profile Builder. The free version allows you to extrude pre-made forms (Fig. 8-18, Fig. 8-19, and Fig. 8-20). The Pro version enables you to extrude a custom form that you draft.

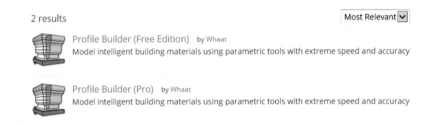

Fig. 8-17: Profile Builder (both the free and Pro versions) can be found in the Extension Warehouse.

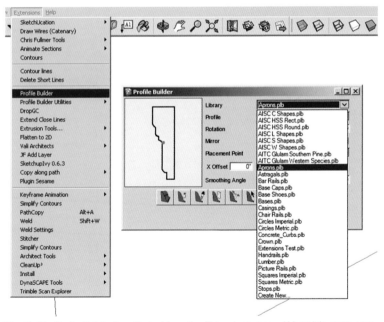

Fig. 8-18: Profile Builder is activated from the Extensions menu. When it is open, you can select pre-made shapes to extrude along a selected path. (The preloaded Apron profile is selected in the image.)

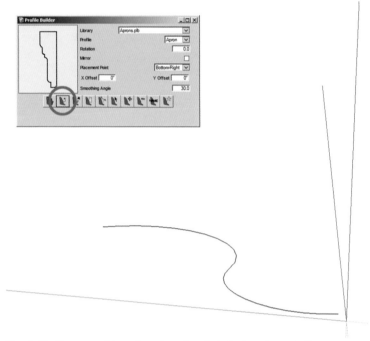

Fig. 8-19: The arcs will have the selected profile built along the path. The red circle indicates the Build Along Path (Follow Me) option, which is the main tool you will use when working with Profile Builder.

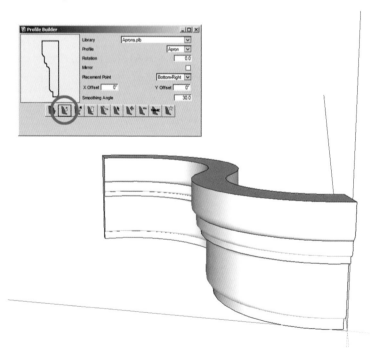

Fig. 8-20: The form is generated along the path.

The Pro version of Profile Builder enables greater customization, allowing you to build complex forms. For example, Fig. 8-21 shows a 2D face of a road profile. Using the Pro version, the road profile will be extruded along the two connected arcs (Fig. 8-22). With the surface selected and clicking the Create a New Profile button (Fig. 8-23), the road profile is added to Profile Builder and can be applied using Build Along Path (Follow Me).

Fig. 8-21: The 2D surface road profile. The upper portion shows the road concept. The lower portion will be selected and used to create the profile.

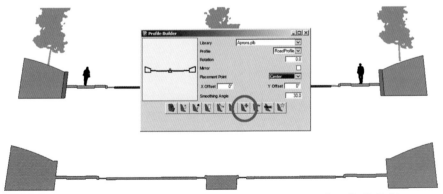

Fig. 8-22: Use the Create New Profile button (circled) to add the road profile to Profile Builder.

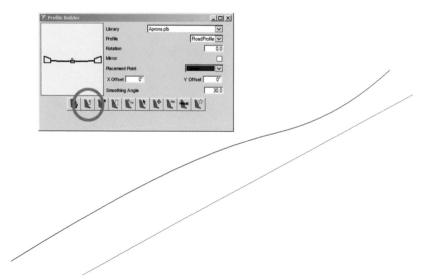

Fig. 8-23: Use Build Along Path (Follow Me) to extrude the road profile along the selected arcs.

The resulting 2D profile is constructed along the path, creating a 3D road profile (Fig. 8-24). Adding color and completing the road with terrain and vegetation took minutes to complete (Fig. 8-25). Profile Builder can be purchased by following the link in the Extension Warehouse for the Pro version website.

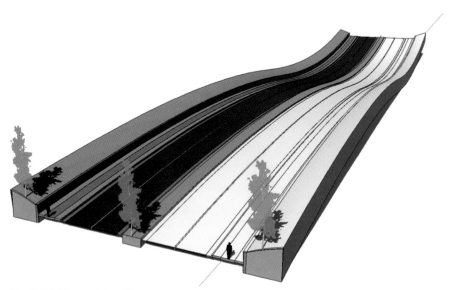

Fig. 8-24: The result is a 3D road and walk. You can add color to the surfaces for better representation.

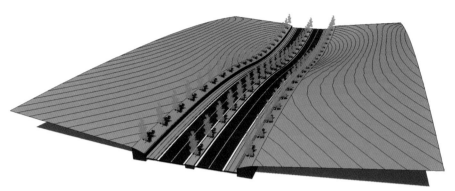

Fig. 8-25: The completed road profile with terrain made using the Soap Skin Bubble extension. 3D trees are added using PathCopy.

Custom Architecture

The processes described in this chapter provide an introductory framework for the construction of architectural models. More advanced methodologies will be explained in Chapter 11. In Chapter 7, you learned how to draw 3D *building volumes,* or the basic shapes and outlines of buildings. The tutorials in this chapter use the building volumes you generated in Chapter 7 to model *building masses* (articulated building forms and volumes) and create custom Window, Door, and Balcony components. You will use the completed architecture to populate the Flatwork Base site plan from Chapter 7.

Sculpting the Building

Modeling buildings in SketchUp is like making a sculpture out of stone: First, you define the overall form, and then you chisel the minute details. In modeling terms, this means you model the building mass out of the building volume and then create and populate the building mass with components.

Building the Mass

When modeling buildings, your first task is to mold the building volume into a building mass. The *building mass* is a series of Push/Pulled faces that define levels, edges, and areas. There are many ways to manipulate a volume to create mass. The easiest method for articulating building mass is to use existing building geometry to generate more detail.

Start with the roof. Subdivide the vertical faces of the building volume (Fig. 9-1) by selecting the flat "roof" face of a building volume and copying the face down, using the vertical building edges as references. The subdivided faces can be Push/Pulled to create building arcades, overhangs, and other details (Fig. 9-2).

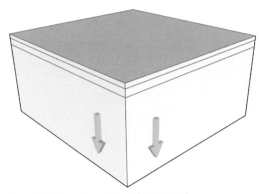

Fig. 9-1: Move/Copy the roof downward.

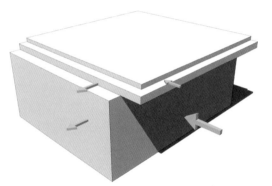

Fig. 9-2: Push/Pulling volumes of subdivided faces

You can further articulate the building mass by using the Line tool to subdivide faces (Fig. 9-3). Subdivided faces can be Push/Pulled to create a specific look and feel for the building (Fig. 9-4).

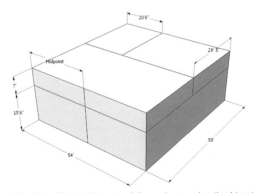

Fig. 9-3: Subdividing a building volume using the Line tool

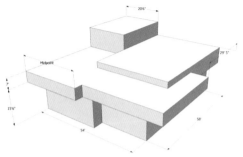

Fig. 9-4: Push/Pulled faces subdivided by the Line tool

Making Window and Door Components

Window and Door components provide scales and detail, and further define a building's aesthetics. These specialized components are created from building mass geometry to cut holes through the surfaces on which they are placed. When window faces are transparent, geometry on the other side becomes visible.

To create a Window component, follow these steps:

1. Create a 10′ × 10′ × 10′ cube (Fig. 9-5).

2. On one of the vertical faces, draw a rectangle 8′ wide × 6′ high (Fig. 9-5).

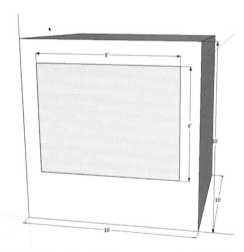

Fig. 9-5: Creating a Window component on the 10′ × 10′ × 10′ cube

3. Delete the subdivided center face.

4. Select the remaining edges of the deleted face.

5. While hovering the cursor over one of the edges, right-click and select Make Component (Fig. 9-6).

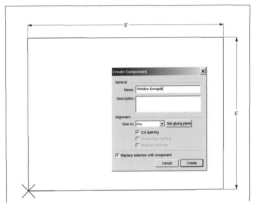

Fig. 9-6: Select the edges of the deleted face, right-click, and select Make Component.

6. In the Component menu, the Glue To drop-down box should be set to Any and the Cut Opening box should be checked. Once it is checked, enter a name for the component (**Window Example**) and select OK. This will create the base for the Window component (Fig. 9-6).

7. Edit the newly created component. In the component instance, use the Line tool to heal the missing face (Fig. 9-7).

8. Offset the new face 2″ inward. Push/Pull the center face in 2″ (Fig. 9-8).

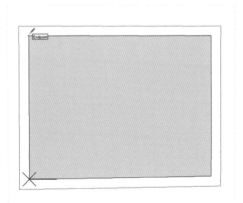

Fig. 9-7: Heal the face in the Window component instance.

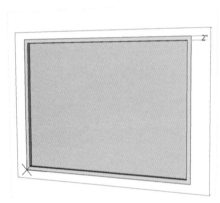

Fig. 9-8: Offset the component face 2″. Push/Pull the face 2″ inward.

9. From the Materials ➤ Translucent menu, select Translucent_Glass_Blue. Paint the color onto the center face.

10. Exit the component instance.

11. Copy (Edit ➤ Copy) and Paste (Edit ➤ Paste) the window and place it around the cube. Notice how it cuts a hole in the surface, allowing the other placed windows to be visible (Fig. 9-9).

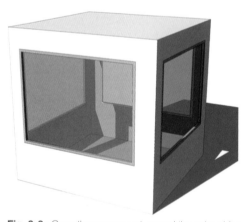

Fig. 9-9: Copy the component around the cube sides.

12. Delete one of the placed components. Notice that the face of the cube reseals after the window is deleted (Fig. 9-10).

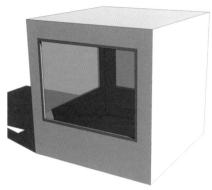

Fig. 9-10: Deleting the Window component causes the cube face to reseal.

The created component can be scaled in place. In many cases, windows need to be scaled to better fit their locations. This can be tricky.

It is best to use the middle-corner scale handles to scale the Window component. When a Window or Door component is placed on a face, these middle handles can be hard to find.

Zoom into the corners or edges of the component to help locate the scale handles (Fig. 9-11). Turning on View ➤ Face Style ➤ Xray can help in selecting the middle Scale tool. Once selected, turn off the Xray style. Practice trying to scale the window on the cube surface (Fig. 9-12).

Fig. 9-11: Zoom into the corner of the component to select the middle scale handle.

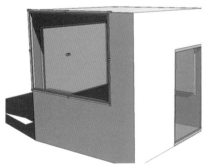

Fig. 9-12: The scaled Window component on the cube face

Problem Solving the Window Components

In step 6, Glue To must be set to Any (the default) and Cut Opening must be checked. If they aren't, the window will not be created correctly; it will not cut the openings in the faces where it is placed. To fix this problem, check the following:

▶ Make sure the window geometry was not drawn outside the Building component instance.

▶ Make sure the rectangle drawn in step 2 is not connected to or touching any other building geometry except the face to which it is affixed. SketchUp has a bug that can prevent Window components from being created if any edges touch other building geometry. It is not a consistent bug, but it is worth noting.

Copying and Inserting

As indicated, the simplest way to duplicate a Building component is to copy (Ctrl+C) and then paste (Ctrl+V) the component onto a face (Fig. 9-13, Fig. 9-14)—or you can use the Move/Copy tool. However, in some instances, components can behave improperly; they may not align or may cut an opening into a face. If this occurs, simply reinsert the component from the Component browser.

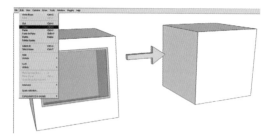

Fig. 9-13: To copy a component, select it and then select Edit ➤ Copy or Ctrl+C.

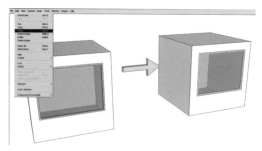

Fig. 9-14: Use Edit ➤ Paste or Ctrl+V to paste the copied component.

The Component browser is located under Window ➤ Components. To display all components in the model, select the button that looks like a little house (called In Model). Any component created in the model will be visible under this tab (Fig. 9-15). Selecting the component in the browser will insert a copy of the component into the model.

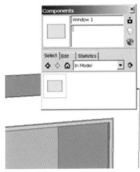

Fig. 9-15: The Component browser shows all the components in a model.

Copying and Pasting Between Instances

The following architectural tutorials use the same Window and Door components on multiple buildings. To repeatedly use components, you can copy them between component instances. Simply select and copy a component while in a building instance. When you enter the next Building component instance, you can paste the copied Window or Door component onto the face. As always, make sure you are working in the correct building instance.

Or, while in a Building component instance, you can use the Component browser to insert the constructed Window or Door component onto a building face.

Making Unique

In many instances, buildings are composed of repetitive elements that share similar functions and design qualities. Elements such as windows, doors, and columns can be composed of the same material, share a particular style, or be of related proportions. These repetitions can be useful when you are modeling a building in SketchUp. Constructing a single component and replicating it along the face of a building mass is a quick way to detail a building.

A useful shortcut to creating multiple types of windows, doors, or other components is to use the original component and edit or adjust it. Selecting a Window or Door component and making it unique (right-click on the component and select Make Unique) will create a new and separate version of that component (Fig. 9-16). This new component can then be edited and adjusted without affecting the original component (Fig. 9-17, Fig. 9-18). This method can be faster than creating a new component from scratch.

Fig. 9-16: The original component is made unique and then adjusted.

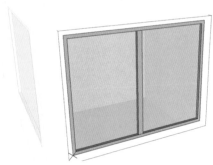

Fig. 9-17: The new component can be adjusted to create a new style without having to create a new component.

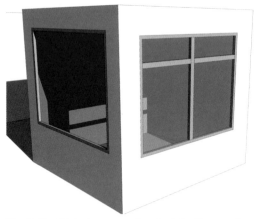

Fig. 9-18: Original component on the left with new adjusted component on the right

Tutorials

The following tutorial applies the concepts discussed throughout this chapter. First, you'll set the workspace by saving the Building components into their own file. Then you'll model the building mass and create custom Window, Door, and Balcony components.

While you are working through the tutorial, be sure to keep the following tips in mind:

- ► Window components need to be created on the building face itself.
- ► Be cognizant of the component settings when you make the Window components.
- ► Work within each Building component instance when you add mass or place components.
- ► Do not move the building locations.
- ► While you are trying to scale windows and doors on the building faces, be patient.

Setting the Workspace

The Building component volumes and the site plan geometry from Chapter 7 are saved in the same file. However, it is easier to work with buildings in their own separate file. Follow these steps to "set the workspace" and make a separate file for the Buildings component. You can apply these steps to separate any component out of a model for easier modeling.

1. Open the completed site plan model from Chapter 7. Select all three buildings (each should be a component). With all three buildings selected, right-click and select Make Component. Name the new component **Buildings**.

2. Right-click the Buildings component created in step 1. From the context menu, choose Save As. SketchUp will prompt you for a location to save the Buildings component as a separate SketchUp (.skp) file. Save the file in the same folder as the site plan model. The Buildings component is now its own SketchUp model file. Make sure to save the Flatwork Base file to include the creation of the Buildings component.

3. Open the saved Buildings component file. Note that the buildings in the saved file are no longer part of the large Buildings component created in step 1; each structure is again an individual component.

4. Once all the details are added to the Buildings components in the model, the file will be saved and reloaded into the site plan model. Do not change the physical locations of the buildings. Changing the physical locations will cause the buildings to shift positions once they are reloaded in the site plan.

Adding Mass to Buildings 1 and 2

This tutorial adds mass and detail to Buildings 1 and 2 (Fig. 9-19). You will add massing detail to the roof and the vertical faces of the building. Please note that you should add the details primarily to the sides of both buildings that are facing the site plan plaza.

Download Model: Conceptual Site Plan – Building Masses

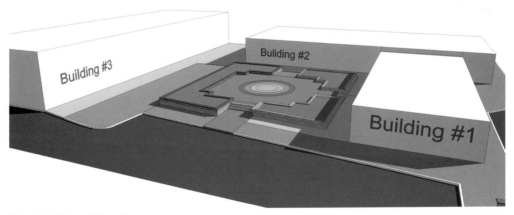

Fig. 9-19: The building reference

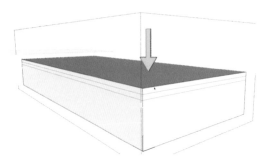

1. Starting with the roof of Building 1, select the top face. With the Move/Copy tool, make two copies downward of the roof face along the building's vertical axis at 1′ intervals. Use the vertical edge of the building as a reference point.

2. On the adjacent building, copy the roof face downward. Snap the copies to the roof edge copies made in step 1. The copied face and edges will subdivide the vertical faces of the building.

3. Push/Pull the vertical bottom faces of both buildings inward 4′ to create a building arcade as indicated.

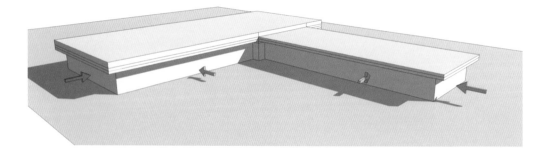

4. Offset the top face of each building 2′ inward. Push/Pull the Offset center face 1′ down. This creates the subtle impression of a roof with a lip.

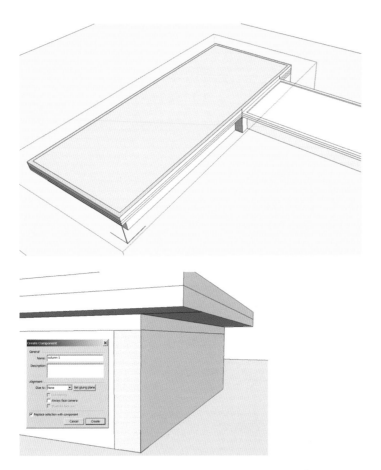

5. On the corner face of Building 1, draw an 18″-wide rectangle from the bottom of the overhang to the building bottom edge. Select the face and edge of the subdivided face. Make it a component called Column 1. Enter the component instance and Push/Pull the face outward 8″ to create an extruded column.

6. Move/Copy the component along the building face 70′. Array-divide (**5/**) immediately after the initial Move/Copy.

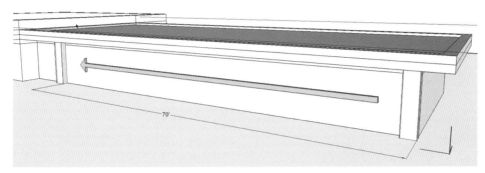

Columns arrayed along the face of the building

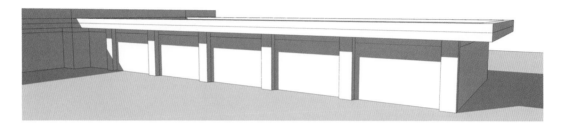

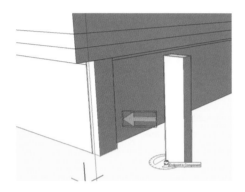

7. Copy the column of Building 1 onto Building 2. The Column component will need to be copied from the Building 1 instance into the Building 2 instance. Rotate the component so that it is parallel to the Building 2 face. Array-divide the component (**4/**) along the Building 2 face.

8. Return to Building 1 and Push/Pull the second vertical face down from the roof, inward 6″ on all sides. Repeat this step for Building 2.

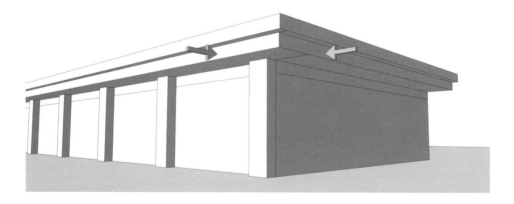

Adding Mass to Building 3

This tutorial adds mass to Building 3. Building 3 will have some additional detail added in comparison to the previous buildings. As with previous buildings, the detail should be added to the side of the building facing the plaza.

1. Copy the roof downward 1' and 9'-6" along the vertical axes. The second copied edge indicates the split between the first and second floors. Draw an edge dissecting the length of the roof from midpoint to midpoint.

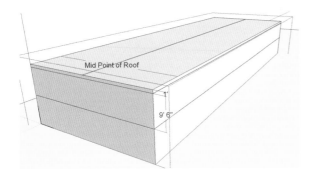

2. Push/Pull the two lower building faces 1' inward. Push/Pull the lower front face of the building 5' inward. Raise the roof edge drafted in step one 8' in height to create a sloped roof.

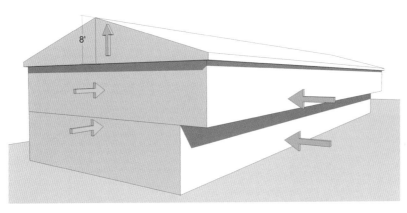

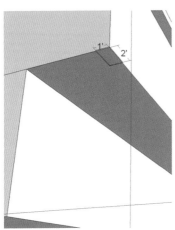

3. On the corner ledge of the building arcade, draw a 1′ × 2′ rectangle. Convert it into a component called Column 2. Push/Pull it downward toward the ground to add volume.

4. Copy the column to the opposite edge endpoint of the building length. Array-divide the columns (**9/**).

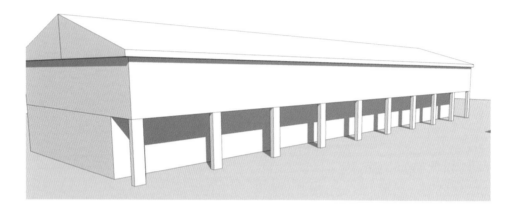

Window Components

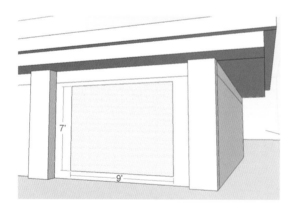

Now that you've added mass to the buildings, you can add the Window components. You will learn to create window variations from a single component.

1. Draw a 7′ × 9′ face on Building 1, between the columns. Delete the subdivided face. Make sure to be working in the Building 1 instance.

2. Select the four edges, right-click over one of the edges, and select Make Component. Make sure that Glue To is set to Any and that the Cut Opening box is checked. Name the component **Window 1**.

3. In the component instance, heal the face with the Line tool.

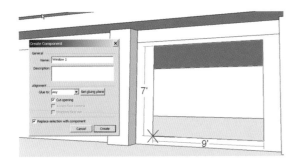

4. On the face, draw and offset the face with the dimensions shown in the graphic.

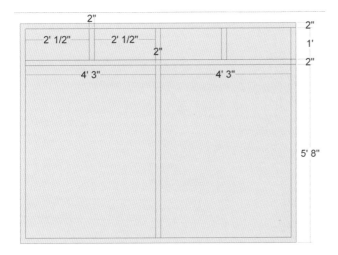

5. Push/Pull the large faces inward 3″. Add color (Translucent_Glass_Corrugated) to the large faces. Paint the window *mullions* (window supports) using Color_008.

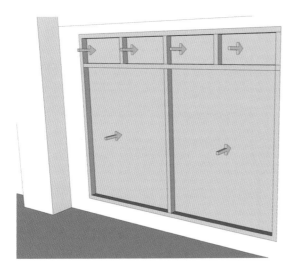

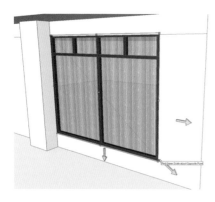

6. Exit the Window 1 instance. Move the window to the top-left corner, intersecting the overhang and the column edge.

7. Scale the component to fit between the two columns.

8. Select the window and copy it over by using the column endpoint as a reference. The copied window will cut the face on which it is placed.

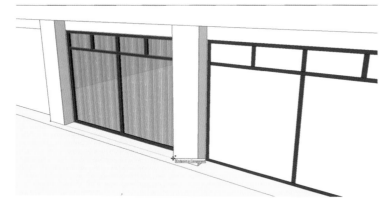

9. Array the windows four times (**5x**) immediately after copying the component in step 8. The windows should be copied between the columns.

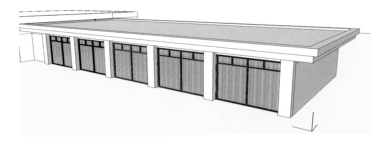

10. Copy the window from Building 1 into the component instance of Building 2. Select the copied component and then select Make Unique.

11. Scale the Window component width in half (Scale Factor of .5). Copy the scaled window next to the original. There should be two Window components between the columns.

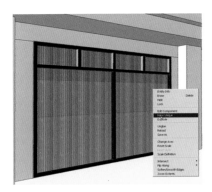

12. In the Window component instance, at the base of the window, draw a rectangle with the indicated dimensions. Convert the drawn rectangle into a component. Name it **Awning**.

13. In the Awning component instance, Push/Pull the rectangle face 3″ in height.

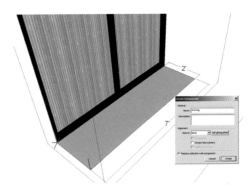

14. Exit the Awning component instance, and move the component upward on the window as indicated.

15. Edit the Awning component. Select the two front edges. Move the edges down along the vertical axis. The faces will fold downward, creating an angled awning.

16. Edit the Building and Window component colors.

    a. Color the larger faces: Translucent_Glass_Gold.

    b. Color the top four windows: Translucent_Glass_Green_Dark.

The windows have been added to Building 1 and Building 2.

Door Components

This tutorial adds the Door components. As with window variations, the Door component will be created using the already created Window components.

1. Select the middle Window component of Building 1. Make the component unique.

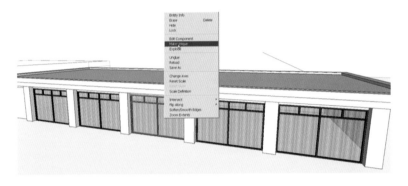

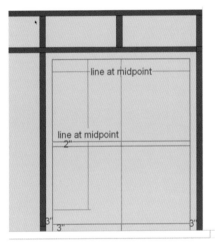

2. In the unique component instance, draft the lines as indicated in the diagram.
   a. Offset the two large window faces 3″.
   b. Draw a line down the center of each face along the midpoint.
   c. Draft a line across the face. Offset the horizontal line 2″.

3. Paint the faces of the subdivided faces.

4. Repeat the previous steps and add door geometry to the indicated window on Building 2.

Balcony Component

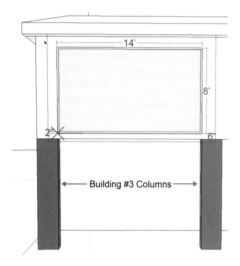

This tutorial adds the Balcony component, which will be added to Building 3.

1. On the second-floor face of Building 3, between the first columns, draft a component for a balcony.
   a. Draft a 14′ × 8′ face, 6″ from the bottom edge of the second level.
   b. Delete the face, select the edges, and make the edges in a component called Balcony.
   c. Within the component, heal the face.
   d. Offset the face 2″.
2. Push/Pull the center face 4′ inward.

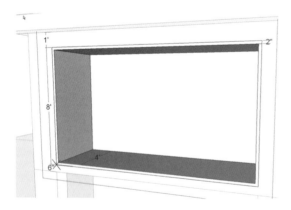

3. On the Push/Pull face from step 2, draft additional linework to define the balcony doors and windows. Offset the face 2″. Draw in the window mullions (2″ width), as shown in the diagram. Push/Pull the larger faces inward 3″.

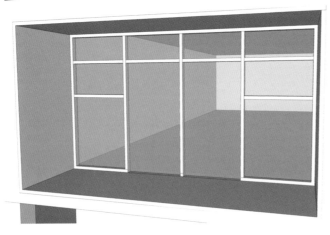

4. Add Translucent_Glass_Blue color to the window faces. Paint the mullions using Color_001.

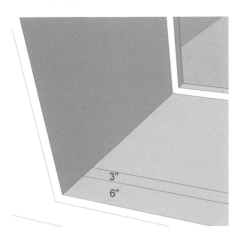

5. Offset the bottom edge of the balcony 6″ inward. Offset it again 3″. Make sure the face is subdivided.

6. Push/Pull the 3"-wide face 3' in height to create the balcony rail.

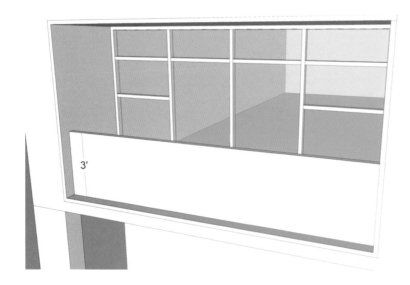

7. Copy/Array the Balcony component between the building columns.

8. Copy and Make Unique the Window and Door components from Building 2. Place them along the faces of the first floor of Building 3.

   Adjust the color of the copied Window and Door components' glass to match the balcony color (Translucent_Glass_Blue).

9. Save the file.

CHAPTER 10

Arranging and Presenting the Model

Now that the Flatwork Base, custom site furnishings, and building architecture have been completed, you have one final step to complete your model. You still need to piece together all the geometry and components to create presentable images. As you read about the concepts presented in this chapter, you will update the Flatwork Base site plan model from Chapter 7.

In this chapter, you'll be introduced to the following concepts:

▶ Arranging vegetation and site-furnishing components

▶ Placing components in a logical order

▶ Creating and exporting scenes

✱ To complete the exercises in this chapter, you will need three types of 3D tree components. Review the end of Chapter 3 for detailed instructions on obtaining components.

Arrangement Methods

As you work more with SketchUp, you'll find that you frequently need to relocate objects from one location to another. For example, you may need to relocate components from one SketchUp file to another or from a 2D plan image to a 3D Flatwork Base. Understanding how and why components such as vegetation and site furnishings are relocated is valuable when you are working with SketchUp. This chapter discusses two different methods of arrangement: the Accuracy method and the Speed method.

The Flatwork Base site plan that you generated in Chapter 7 provides an opportunity to consider different methods for arranging site components. In this tutorial, you will place vegetation components using the Accuracy method, and you'll add site furnishings using the Speed method.

The Accuracy Method

The 2D plan image provides accurate locations for all vegetation and site furnishings. After the components are imported and placed on the 2D plan image, they can be relocated to an identical location on the Flatwork Base.

Using the plan image endpoints and the Flatwork Base endpoints, you can relocate selected components with the Move/Copy tool (Fig. 10-1).

Plan Image **Flatwork Base**

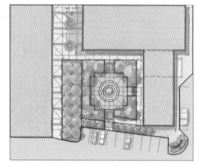 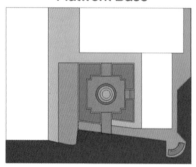

Fig. 10-1: The plan image and Flatwork Base

If the Flatwork Base includes elevated volumes (such as the plaza, steps, and curbs), any relocated components will appear below the faces and surfaces of the base. You will need to move each component upward on the vertical axis to sit on top of the Flatwork Base surfaces.

The Speed Method

You can approximate the location of objects on the Flatwork Base using the plan image as a visual reference. This method of arrangement is faster (it does not require the components to be moved up), but it is less accurate.

Logical Order and Adjustments

Placing components in a specific order can help streamline component layout, maintain layer organization, and optimize computer performance. By placing these component objects in the following order, you will easily be able to add more details.

1. Buildings
2. 3D vegetation
3. Site components

Buildings

Reload the Building components that were saved out of the original model (Fig. 10-2). This simple step gives life to a site plan and provides context when you import the vegetation and site furnishings.

In the Flatwork Base model, select the unarticulated Building components. Right-click and select Reload. Browse to the folder location of the articulated Building components from Chapter 9. Select the correct file and click Open. The buildings will be updated to reflect the changes and components that were completed from the Chapter 9 tutorials.

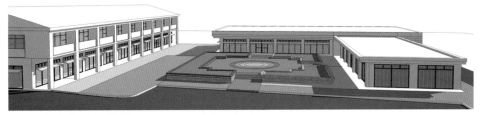

Fig. 10-2: Reload the Building components in the site plan.

The adjusted buildings have left gaps in the Flatwork Base. The gaps were caused when the building arcades were added to the massings.

Turn off the Building layer. With the Rectangle tool, enter the Flatwork Base instance and add faces to fill in the building locations (Fig. 10-3). Paint the faces to match the adjacent concrete of the Flatwork Base.

3D Vegetation

Three-dimensional trees are highly desirable components; they add realism, scale, and aesthetics. They are composed of many edges and faces—and they can hinder computer performance. The following tips can help you manage these components by maintaining organization and performance, while adding rich detail.

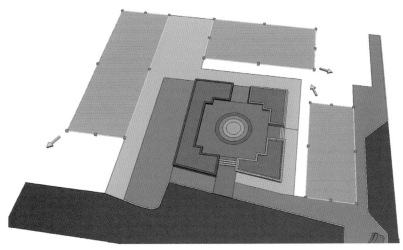

Fig. 10-3: Fix the surface geometry at the building locations.

Add and adjust three varieties of 3D trees using the Accuracy method (Fig. 10-4 through Fig. 10-12).

1. Different types of vegetation should be placed on separate layers. For example, the site plan model indicates three different tree types. Include three layers to accommodate each tree variety. Suggested layer names are Trees 01, Trees 02, and Trees 03.

2. If you have a lot of a particular vegetation component, divide the component onto multiple layers. Separate vegetation by location or groupings if needed. As an added exercise, instead of creating three Tree layers, create six. Break up each grouping of trees into two sets.

3. Imported 3D vegetation of a uniform type looks artificial and repetitive; it lacks natural and organic qualities (Fig. 10-4). This unnatural appearance can be easily fixed with a custom extension called CLF Scale and Rotate Multiple. CLF Scale and Rotate Multiple randomizes the rotation axes and the height of selected components to create a more natural and organic habit (Fig. 10-5, Fig. 10-6). It can be found and installed from the Extension Warehouse for free. (See Chapter 5 for additional information.) Go to Extension ➢ Chris Fulmer Tools ➢ Scale and Rotate Multiple ➢ Scale and Rotate Randomly. This will bring up a menu allowing you to adjust the scale factors.

Fig. 10-4: Import and arrange 3D trees onto the plan image.

Fig. 10-5: Apply CLF Scale and Rotate Multiple to the 3D trees.

Fig. 10-6: Adjust the scale of some trees.

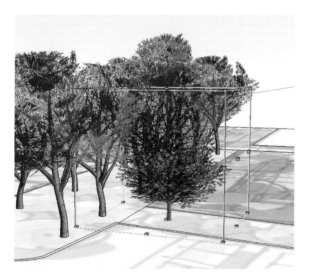

Fig. 10-7: Import and adjust a second vegetation type.

Fig. 10-8: Apply CLF Scale and Rotate Multiple.

Fig. 10-9: Add a third 3D vegetation type. Remember to use layers.

Fig. 10-10: Apply CLF Scale and Rotate Multiple and then adjust.

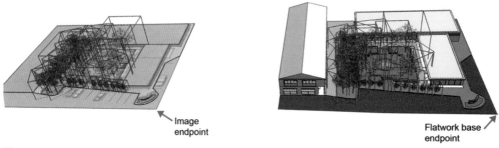

Image endpoint

Flatwork base endpoint

Fig. 10-11: Using the bottom-right endpoints on the base as references, move trees from the plan image to the Flatwork Base.

Part 2: SketchUp Process Modeling

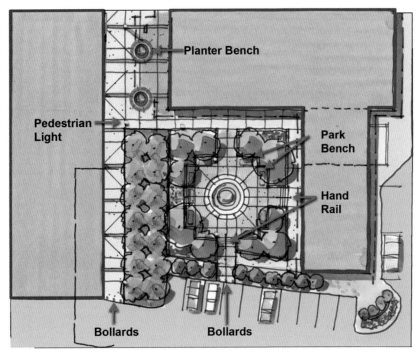

Fig. 10-12: The plan image and site elements location

4. Select all of the vegetation once it is placed and adjusted. Move it using the Accuracy method (Fig. 10-11). Select the Tree components located on the 2D plan image and move them to the Flatwork Base. Reference the same corner endpoints of the 2D image and the Flatwork Base to move the components.

5. To help with computer performance, turn the Vegetation layers off as they are completed. This will allow you to continue working in the model without SketchUp slowing down due to the high face count of the 3D vegetation. For example, once a tree variety is included in the model, make it invisible before you add more tree types. Turn the Vegetation layers on only when:

   ▶ The model is being evaluated for design and aesthetics.

   ▶ You are exporting views of the model to image or animations.

Furnishing the Components

Site furnishings don't need to be arranged in any particular order. This is true whether you are arranging the ones generated in Chapter 8 or similar pre-made components (Fig. 10-13). As a general rule, though, you should make sure each component type is on its own layer. Before you import your components, create a layer for each furnishing type and make it active.

Fig. 10-13: Import and insert custom-made site components from Chapter 8. Insert the bollards, pedestrian lights, park bench, planter bench, and hand rail.

Even when custom components are available, including pre-made components can augment model details (Fig. 10-13, Fig. 10-14). For this exercise, first import, arrange, and scale the custom components created in Chapter 8 using the Speed method. Next, add pre-made components (Fig. 10-14, Fig. 10-15).

Fig. 10-14: Include pre-made components to complement the custom site furnishings. Include additional components such as tables and chairs, trash cans, cars, people, and water jets.

Fig. 10-15: Pre-made water jets included in the central fountain

FormFonts offers the most versatile library of well-constructed, pre-made site components (architectural elements as well). These components can be downloaded quickly to establish a substantial and reusable component library. To subscribe, go to www.formfonts.com.

Creating and Exporting Scenes

Once the Flatwork Base is populated with buildings, vegetation, and site furnishings, use the following tools to set the camera position, adjust the field of view, and turn on Sky and Shadows. As you read this section, try to re-create the scenes shown in steps 1 through 7.

Selecting Your Scenes

Pan around the model to find the view you want. When you find it, save the scene by opening to Window ➤ Default Tray ➤ Scenes and selecting the Add Scene button (plus sign) (Fig. 10-16) to add a scene. Find and create all of your scenes before you export any images.

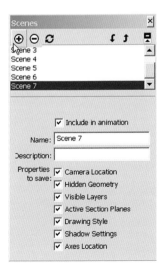

Fig. 10-16: Creating scenes with the Scenes menu

The Scene Menu

When the Add Scene button is selected, SketchUp will save the relative position of the camera. A Scene tab will be created below the menu lines. Panning away from the scene and then selecting the generated Scene tab will return the camera to the saved scene.

The Scene menu allows you to fine-tune a saved scene (Fig. 10-16). Many different options can be adjusted when saving a scene. By default, all the options are selected, which means that whatever values or positions were present when the scene was added will be reloaded when the scene is made active again. Review the options under the Scene menu and experiment with how they can be adjusted.

The Position Camera Tool

When the Position Camera tool (View ➤ Toolbars ➤ Walk Through ➤ Position) is active, you can select a location in the model by snapping to an edge or face. Once selected, the view will shift to place the camera at the precise location chosen as a first-person point of view, 5′ above the ground—the view will be as if you were standing in that location.

The Look Around Tool

You can adjust the view even more using the Look Around tool (View ➤ Toolbars ➤ Walk Through ➤ Look Around). Once the tool is active, you can pan the camera in any direction while maintaining its present location.

The Zoom Tool

Selecting the Zoom tool (View ➤ Toolbars ➤ Camera ➤ Zoom) allows users to adjust the width and breadth (field of view or depth of field) of the camera view by simply typing values into the Measurement window and pressing Enter. This feature works similarly to a real camera lens; selecting Zoom and entering **35mm** into the Measurement window will adjust the camera view similar to a 35-millimeter camera lens.

Plan Views and Elevations

SketchUp lets you view elevations (side views) and plans (top-down views) of a model. Go to the Camera menu and select Parallel Projection. This will adjust the camera to a nonperspective view. Next, select View ➤ Toolbars ➤ Views. The Views menu provides isometric, plan, and side views of the model. With Parallel Projection active, in tandem with Views, SketchUp will produce a plan view (Top) and elevations (Front, Right, Back, Left).

People and Cars

People and cars are the last objects you add to a model. By using pre-made people and car components, you can enliven a model and show building context, scale, and how spaces are used.

An efficient way to place cars and people is on a scene-by-scene basis—especially for eye-level views. Determine what scenes are desired and add people and cars as needed.

Trees and Scenes

When you are trying to determine a scene by navigating around a model, try turning on the Tree layers. If this causes serious performance issues, you can always turn off the Tree layers. Find the view location you like, and turn on the trees so you can assess the view. If you find a scene you like, first turn on the Tree layers, then add the scene. This will ensure that the Tree layers are turned on when that specific Scene tab is chosen.

Only turn on the Tree layers that will be visible in the scene. Trees that are not in the view screen for a particular scene should remain invisible, if possible. This will help generate faster exports. Do this by placing tree types on multiple layers, as indicated earlier.

Adding Sky

SketchUp can simulate the color of the sky. Adding a sky background provides depth and realism to an eye-level scene. To turn on the sky, go to Window ➤ Default Tray ➤ Styles ➤ Edit Tab ➤ Background Settings ➤ check the Sky box.

To adjust the color of the sky, double-click the color swatch next to the Sky box.

Exporting Scenes and Shadows

Shadows should be turned on only when you are exporting an image. The detailed 3D trees coupled with Shadows will make navigation impossible even on the best computer systems.

When your scenes are ready to be exported, select the desired Scene tab, wait for SketchUp to navigate to the scene, and then turn on Shadows. Export the scene.

Exporting scenes with Shadows turned on can take from 5 to 15 minutes, depending on the computer. Using 3D trees with Shadows turned on can increase render times by a factor of 10. When such scenes are being exported, computer resources are used to the maximum. It may be possible to use other applications, but it will be difficult to re-enter SketchUp. Wait for the render to be completed. SketchUp will seem to be *frozen* (not responding); however, this is usually not the case. SketchUp's ability to provide shaded real-time rendered scenes is unique and does take time. The exported scenes are worth the wait.

Once the export is completed, turn off Shadows before you select the next Scene tab.

Troubleshooting Shadows

If an object is casting a shadow on the vantage point of an eye-level view, the scene shadows will be distorted. There are two solutions to this problem:

▶ You can adjust the location or shadow settings of the scene.

▶ You can determine which object is casting the shadow on the camera's vantage point. Select that object (typically, this will be a Building or Tree component behind or directly adjacent to the scene position) and right-click to open Entity Info. Under Entity Info, uncheck the Cast Shadow box. The object will not cast shadows when they are turned on, so it will not distort the camera (Fig. 10-17).

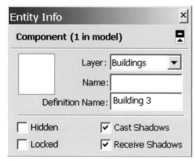

Fig. 10-17: The Entity Info menu with the Cast Shadows option

In this tutorial, you will learn to duplicate the scenes in Fig. 10-18 through Fig. 10-24 and troubleshoot problems with shadows.

Download file: Conceptual Site Plan – Completed

1. Turn on the Tree layers once the view is set (Fig. 10-18). Set the Field Of View to 55mm. Add the scene. Turn the Shadows on. Once Shadows are on, do not pan around or move in the model.

Fig. 10-18: Navigate to and try to re-create this scene.

2. Under File ➤ Export, save the scene as a JPEG. (The level of detail in the model will cause the image export from SketchUp to take between 2 and 10 minutes. This is the cost of adding such detail. However, the images will be expressive and rich.) Practice exporting more images.

3. Once the image is exported, turn off Shadows.

4. Adjust the model view to be looking down and focusing on the plaza (Fig. 10-19).

Fig. 10-19: Birds-eye view of the plaza

5. Add the scene from the Scene menu.

6. Turn Shadows on and export the image, as in step 2.

7. Turn Shadows off once the export is completed.

8. Under Camera, turn on Parallel Projection.

9. Select Top from the View menu. This will create a true plan view of the model (Fig. 10-20).

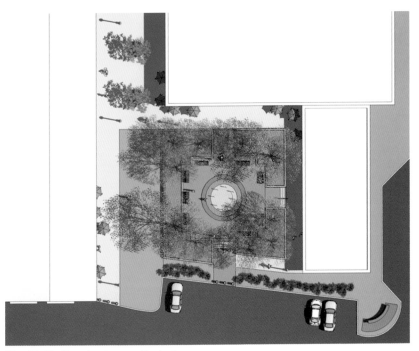

Fig. 10-20: Plan view image with shadows

10. Turn off the trees in the larger tree lawn.

11. Turn on Shadows.

12. Export the image.

13. Turn Shadows off once the export is complete. Under Camera, select Perspective.

14. Under the Camera menu, select Position Camera.

15. Snap to a location at the front of the plaza allowing the stairs to be visible in the foreground (Fig. 10-21).

16. Add the scene.

17. Turn on Shadows and export the scene. Turn Shadows off once completed.

18. This next scene is a trickier to set up (Fig. 10-22).

Fig. 10-21: View of the plaza from the front steps near the road

Fig. 10-22: View of plaza from inside second floor of building. The trees are turned off for a clear shot of the plaza.

19. Navigate to Building #3.

20. Using Position Camera, try to position the view to view the plaza from behind the glass window of one of the balconies. Choose a balcony location on the building that shows a view down to the center of the plaza. Turn off any Tree layers that might obstruct the view. The trick is to navigate from the chosen position, backward behind the glass.

21. Add the scene.

22. Turn on Shadows. If the shadows are distorting the view, turn off the shadows, pan away from the position, and select Building #3 (you will have to enter the building's component instance to accomplish this). With the building selected, right-click and open Entity Info. Uncheck the box for Cast Shadow. Select the Scene Tab button. Now turn on Shadows and export the scene.

23. Turn Shadows off once the scene is exported.

Try to re-create and export the scenes for the last two images (Fig. 10-23, Fig. 10-24). Use the steps outlined for previous exports to add the scene, turn on the shadows, and export an image.

Fig. 10-23: View of the bench planters from under the building arcade

Fig. 10-24: View of the walk between the plaza and buildings adjacent to the plaza ramp

Architectural Tutorial

This chapter tests your drafting and modeling skills. To successfully complete the tutorial model, you will need to apply the lessons and procedures you learned in earlier chapters. The exercise focuses on the construction of a complex building from scratch. You will draft an intricate floor plate, generate an involved building massing, and apply a set of custom Window and Door components to finalize the structure. In addition, you will learn how to work with arcs and circle edges and how to graft components onto curved surfaces.

The tutorial uses the Jefferson County Courthouse building, located in Lakewood, Colorado, as its inspiration. You will create a conceptual and reasonable facsimile model of the building. The challenging nature of the building design makes it a great exercise.

This tutorial utilizes SketchUp Process Modeling. Once again, the process is as follows:

1. Draft a 2D base plan/outline of the building footprint.
2. Push/Pull the volumes.
3. Add color.
4. Construct the custom Window and Door components.
5. Arrange the components on the building.

Working with Arcs and Circles

Arc and circle geometry is not constructed from true curves or circles. Rather, arcs and circles are composed of a series of linear edges, or *facets*, to depict curvature and roundness.

SketchUp lets you adjust the number of edges composing arcs and circles. When first activating an Arc or Circle tool (simply click it), the Measurement window will display Sides. The default number of sides for an arc is 12, and the default for circles is 24. This means that any drawn arc or circle—no matter the length, orientation, or size—will be composed of 12 or 24 facets (Fig. 11-1) unless you change the default.

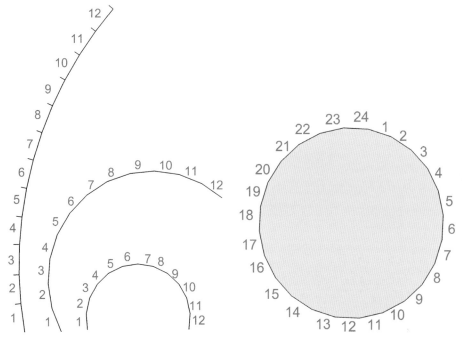

Fig. 11-1: Edges composing the arcs and circles

The default value can be adjusted to increase or decrease the number of sides. More sides make smoother and rounder curves. However, more facets can make it more difficult to include components. This is explained in detail in the "Components and Faceted Surfaces" section.

For the Courthouse tutorial, just make sure that arcs and circles are set to their default values of 12 and 24 sides. The tutorial model cannot be constructed properly if you use other values.

Hidden Geometry

Extruded 3D faces originating from arcs or circle edges are constructed of faceted faces. The number of faceted faces is equal to the number of sides that compose the arc or circle.

To set the dashed edges that compose the curvature to be visible (Fig. 11-2), turn on Hidden Geometry (View ➤ Hidden Geometry). This will allow each individual face to be selected and adjusted (Fig. 11-3).

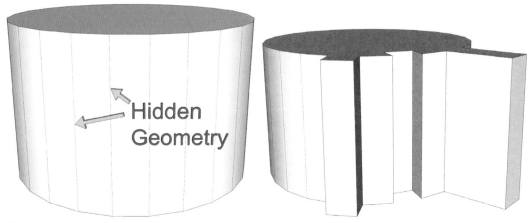

Fig. 11-2: Hidden geometry composing the cylinder

Fig. 11-3: By making the hidden geometry visible, you can Push/Pull the individual faces on the cylinder.

Components and Faceted Surfaces

Components, such as windows and doors, can be affixed to the individual faces of a curvature. When the hidden geometry is visible, placing a component onto the surface is no different than placing a component on any other face (Fig. 11-4).

Faceted faces can interfere with a component. For example, the Window component in Fig. 11-5 is arranged between two faces, with the hidden edge in the middle. This will cause the component to be hidden or disrupted by the adjacent face. Components can be placed only on a single flat face, and they can't overlap an adjacent faceted face.

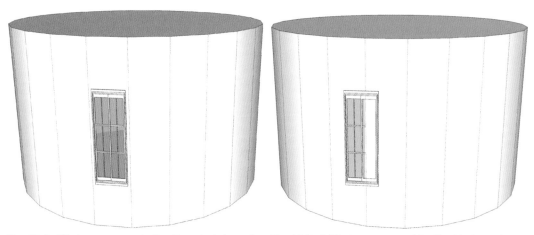

Fig. 11-4: Window component affixed to a single face of a cylinder

Fig. 11-5: A Window component is affixed between two edges, causing it to be obscured.

Components that are constructed to be glued to surfaces (as discussed in Chapter 9) can be copied and applied to other faceted faces. A selected component, either copied by reference or simply moved, will affix and align to the destination face. When you are applying a component to a faceted face, let SketchUp align the component to the face before you place it (Fig. 11-6).

Fig. 11-6: A Window component being copied from one cylinder face to another using endpoints of edges for reference (1). Copied component correctly affixed to destination face (2). Once placed, the window will cut a hole in cylinder face (3).

Faceted objects can contain so many surfaces that placing the components can be difficult. Fig. 11-7 shows two similar building massings with a curved wall. The massing with 12 facets does not allow the placement of the Door components; they simply do not fit on the narrow face. Conversely, the structure with five facets easily includes the Door component. When you are modeling, make sure you use only the number of sides necessary.

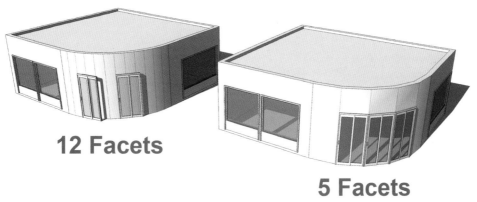

12 Facets

5 Facets

Fig. 11-7: The number of edges used to create arcs and circles can affect component placement.

To add more volume detail, you can also Push/Pull any faces that have components affixed to them. If a face is Push/Pulled, the glued component will move with the adjusted volume (Fig. 11-8).

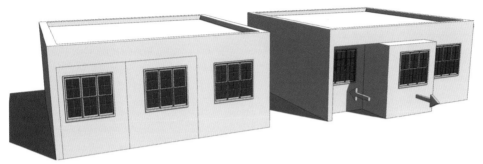

Fig. 11-8: Components will move and adjust when a face is Push/Pulled.

The Courthouse Tutorial

The Courthouse tutorial will take more time to complete than the previous exercises. To complete it, you will have to pay attention to the small details: drafting and laying out the base plan, making sure the massing volume is correct, and correctly placing the custom components.

Download Model: Jefferson County Courthouse

As you work through this exercise, remember and apply these tips:

▶ Work with Hidden Geometry toggled to visible (View ➤ Hidden Geometry).

▶ Double-check the dimensions and locations before you move on to the next steps.

▶ When drafting the base plan, make sure that the edges and lines that connect parallel (offset) arcs are drawn perpendicular.

▶ When you are drafting edges and arcs, pay close attention to the starting points, endpoints, and bulge locations.

▶ Ensure that drafted arcs and circles have the correct number of facets. For this tutorial, arcs should have 12 sides and circles should have 24.

▶ Pay close attention to instructions indicating whether you should offset a *face* or an *edge*.

▶ Draft on Layer 0.

▶ Make sure the building massing heights are created as indicated. The massing must be accurate so that the components can be placed properly.

Only four custom components will be created and used to populate the massing. For this exercise, only the front area of the building needs to be populated with Window and Door components.

▶ Arrange the components as indicated by the instructions. Dimensions reference both hidden and regular edges. In some cases, you will need to draw, create, or offset edges to place the components.

- ► You will need to learn to copy and arrange components on adjacent faceted surfaces. This can be tricky, and it takes time to master.
- ► Remember not to overlap components with dashed (hidden) edges.

Drafting the Floor Plate

Begin modeling the Jefferson County Courthouse by first drafting the floor plate, as described in these steps:

1. Study the floor-plate base diagram and familiarize yourself with it. Draft a rectangle face. Draw an edge from the top-left corner to the bottom-right corner of the rectangle face. Add a circle (radius 50′) to the midpoint of the diagonal edge.

2. Create the arc at the left side of the floor plate. Delete the diagonal edge outside of the circle.

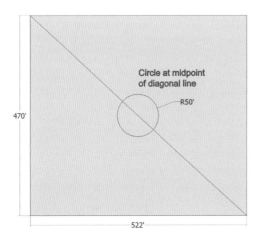

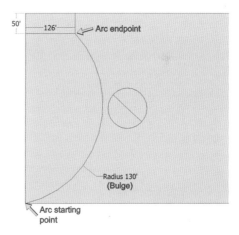

3. Offset the initial arc outward 100′.

4. Draw an edge along the green axes. Connect both endpoints to the offset arc from step 3. Draft a second arc (right side of plate) and offset it 100′.

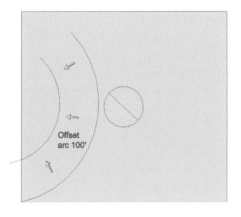

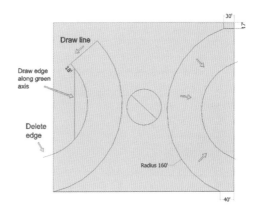

5. Draw perpendicular edges from the endpoints of the offset arc to the first arc. Draft an edge starting 27′ inside the offset arc, down along the green axis.

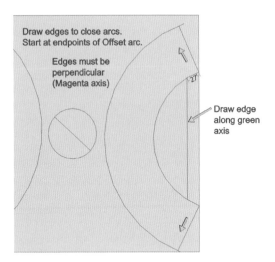

6. Draft the edges along the red axis, starting from the endpoints of the diagonal edge of the circle out toward the adjacent arcs. Use construction geometry if needed. Make sure the edges subdivide the face between the circle and arcs.

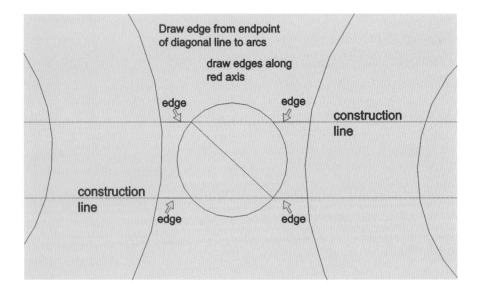

7. Draft the edges from the indicated locations. The edges will be connected from facet-edge endpoint to facet-edge endpoint. Draft a total of six edges: four on the left and two on the right of the floor plate.

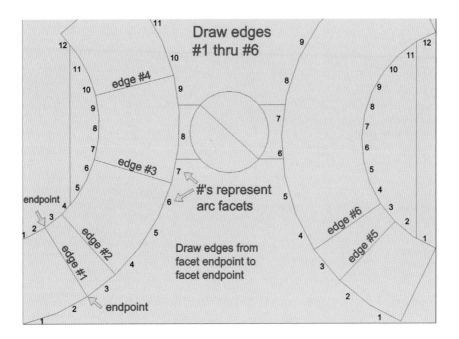

8. Offset the inner arcs 26′ and 27′ on both sides to create a double line 1′ apart.

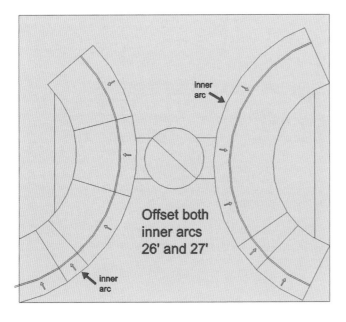

9. Delete the faces outside of the outlined surfaces. The floor plate should resemble the image.

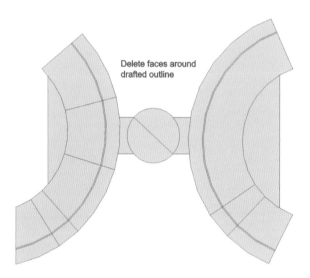

Delete faces around drafted outline

Adding Volume

Now that you've drafted the floor plate, continue modeling the Courthouse by adding volume. To do that, Push/Pull the faces on the left side of the floor plate, as indicated in steps 10 through 14.

10. Push/Pull the base to a height of 27'-6". Add a parapet. A *parapet* is the wall-like barrier at the edge of a roof or structure. The parapet height is 7'-6". The parapet surfaces are defined by the offset arcs in step 8.

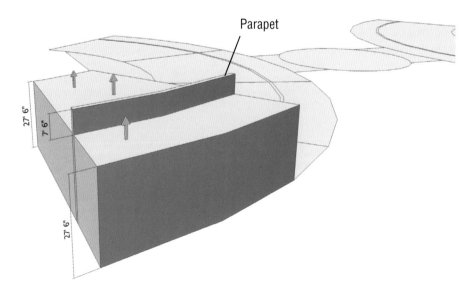

Parapet

11. Push/Pull the adjacent set of faces to total 42'-6". Push/Pull the parapet an additional 7'-6".

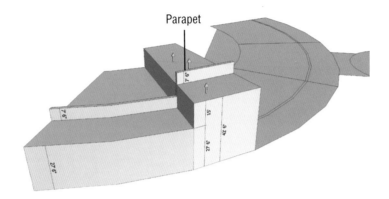

Parapet

12. Push/Pull the next set of faces to a total 67'-6". Push/Pull the parapet an additional 7'-6".

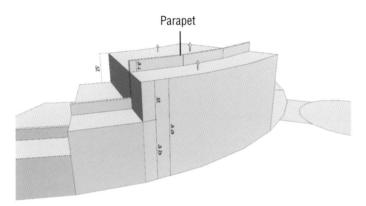

Parapet

13. Push/Pull the next set of faces to a total 77'-6". Push/Pull the parapet an additional 7'-6".

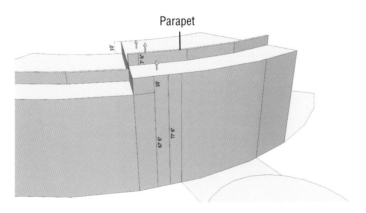

Parapet

14. Push/Pull the last set of faces on the left side of the base to a total 75′. Push/Pull the parapet an additional 7′-6″.

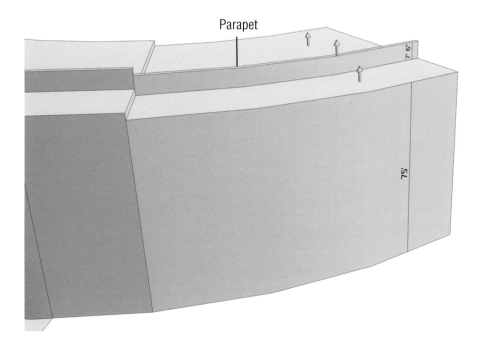

Now it's time to Push/Pull the faces on the right side of the floor plate, as indicated in steps 15 through 17.

15. Push/Pull the first set of faces to the base height of 27′-6″. Push/Pull the parapet an additional 7′-6″.

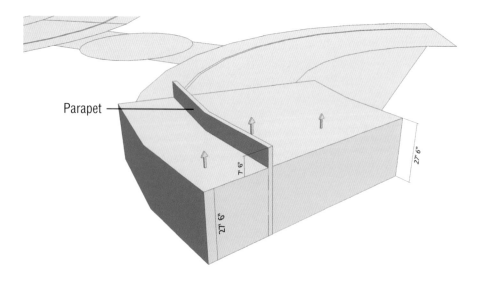

16. Push/Pull the adjacent set of faces to total 42'-6". Push/Pull the parapet an additional 7'-6".

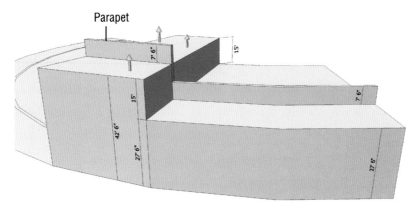

17. Push/Pull the last set of faces to total 77'-6". Push/Pull the parapet an additional 7'-6".

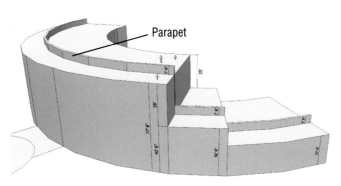

18. Push/Pull the semicircles located on the outside of the left-hand floor plate to 15' in height.

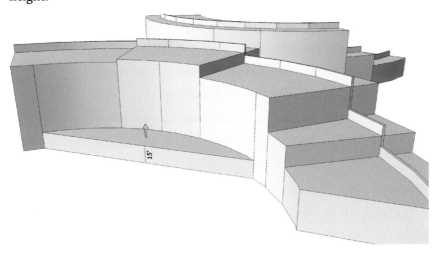

19. Push/Pull the semicircles located on the outside of the right-hand floor plate to 15′ in height.

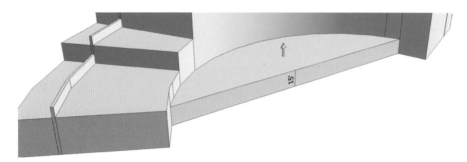

20. Push/Pull the center circle to 82′-6″ in height. Push/Pull the adjacent faces on either side of the center circle to 75′ in height.

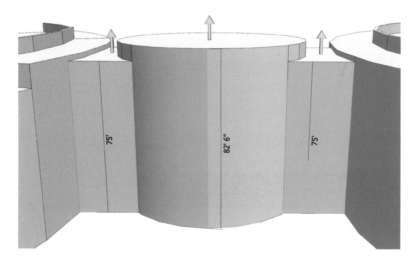

21. Offset the top face of the central circle as indicated.

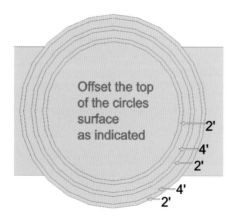

Offset the top of the circles surface as indicated

2′
4′
2′
4′
2′

22. Push/Pull the four inner faces that you offset in the previous step to 7'-6" in height. The last two inner faces should be 7'-6" higher than the adjacent faces. Do not Push/Pull the outer two faces.

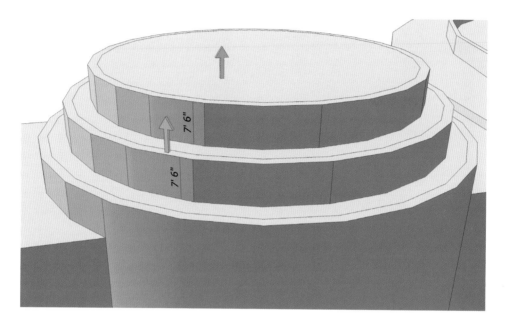

23. Insert the Courthouse Glass Dome component. This component can be found at 3D Warehouse under the SPM 2 search term. Place the component onto the top of the central circle. Scale and adjust the Glass Dome component to fit the top portion of the inner circular surface, as shown.

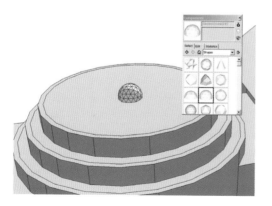 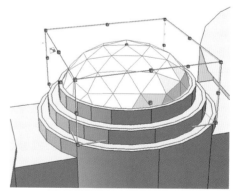

24. The hidden geometry must be visible for this step to work. Copy the six edges composing the front area of the central building mass downward along the blue axis, 68'-6". Make sure the copied edges subdivide the faces below. Push/Pull the two faces that are second to last from the outside, 4' outward.

25. Push/Pull the side inner faces of the faces extruded in the previous step toward the center of the mass, 5′.

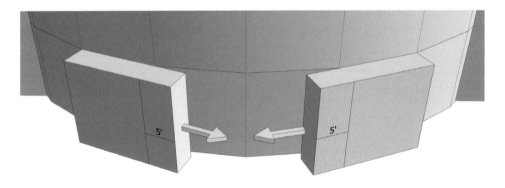

26. Draw two edges to connect the two extruded faces. Draw the edges from the top and bottom outside endpoints. Done correctly, this will heal faces on the top and front.

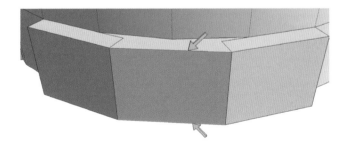

27. Add color to the massing. Paint the entire massing beige (Materials ➤ Marker ➤ Beige). Do not alter or apply color to the Courthouse Glass Dome component.

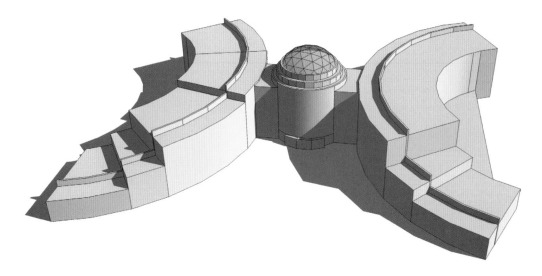

Adding the Custom Components

Now it's time to add the windows and doors.

✱ When you convert the geometry representing the windows and doors into a component, make sure you use the appropriate method and steps as outlined in Chapter 9 (pages 156–161).

28. On the building massing face, draft the Window 1 component outline as indicated.
29. Push/Pull the window surfaces inward 2″. Add a transparent color.

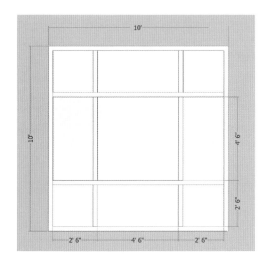

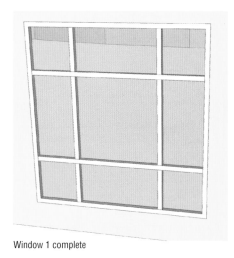

Window 1 complete

30. On the building massing face, draft Window 2. Draft the basic outline and offset the face inward 1′. Make sure to draft a 2″ mullion for the window.

31. On the Push/Pulled face, draft the window frame as indicated. Push/Pull the window surfaces inward 2″. Add color.

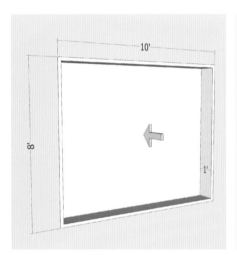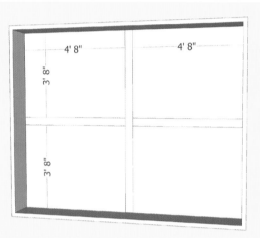

32. Push/Pull the window surfaces 2″ inward. Add color.

33. To make Window 3, copy and paste Window 2. Make the copy unique (right-click and select Make Unique). In the component instance, draw two edges as indicated in the graphic. Make sure they subdivide the faces.

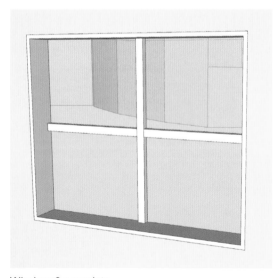

Window 2 complete

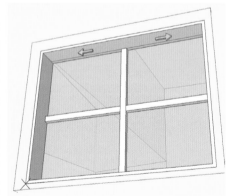

Window 3

34. Select the top two edges of the window frame of Window 3. Move them directly vertical 2′ to create the slanted window panel.

35. To make the door, locate and construct the Door component on the building face as indicated. Draft it on the face created in step 26.

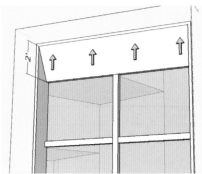

Window 3

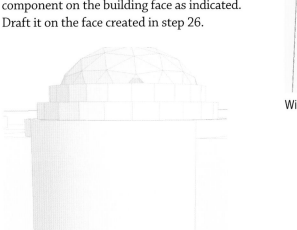

36. Draft the Main Entry Door component in three stages. Use the dimensions provided in the graphics for the general and detailed component outline. First, draft the general outline for the door.

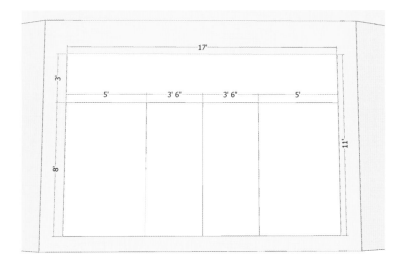

37. Add mullions and further divisions to the Main Entry Door component started in the previous step.

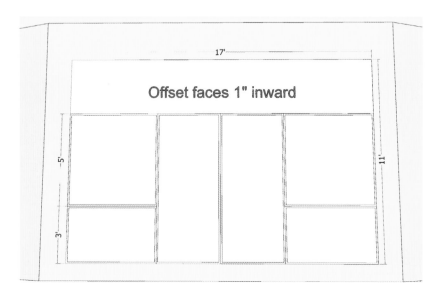

38. Add edges on the two center faces of the Main Entry Door component. This will define the door handles on the component.

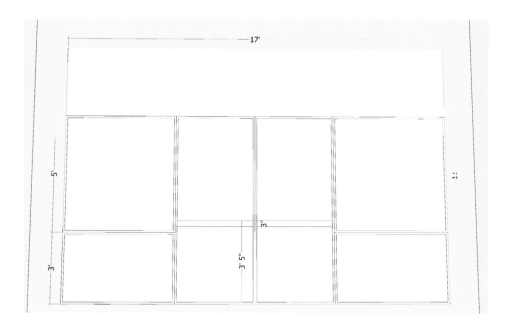

39. To further define the Main Entry Door component, add and adjust volumes: Push/Pull the window faces inward 3″. Apply Material ➤ Markers ➤ Yellow to the door frames. Push/Pull the top door face 2′ outward. Apply a transparent color to the window surfaces.

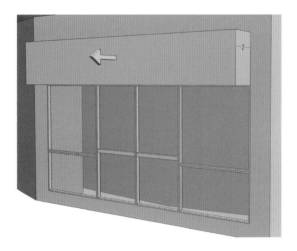

40. Select and move the bottom edge of the top frame inward 1′ to create an angled door-frame panel, as shown in the diagram.

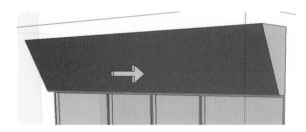

41. Copy and arrange the three Main Entry Door components on the extruded faces of the building mass that were created in steps 24, 25, and 26. Scale the components to fit.

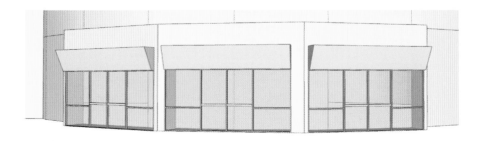

Arranging the Components on the Building

Now that you have made the components, you need to arrange them on the building as indicated in the following steps.

42. Insert Window 1 at the location indicated on the massing.

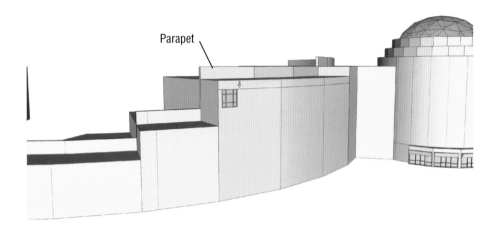

43. Make sure you place the window on the face in the correct location as directed by the dimensions.

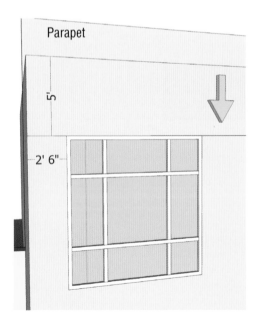

44. Copy and paste the second window 2′-6″ from the adjacent face/dashed hidden geometry edge.

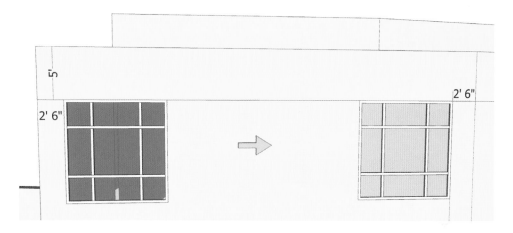

45. Immediately after placing the second window, add the third window equidistant between the other two by entering **2/** in the Measurement window.

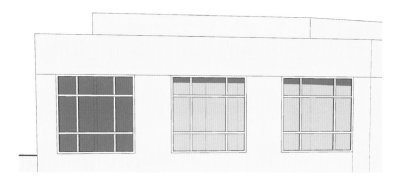

46. Copy and paste all three windows downward 12′-6″ along the blue axis, using the top edge of the windows as a reference.

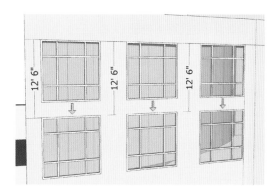

47. Array/Copy the three windows from step 45: enter **4x** into the Measurement window. The faceted face of the building is now composed of 15 Window 1 components. The next steps will utilize the already-placed windows to further populate the adjacent building faces.

48. Select all of the windows that you placed in steps 45 to 47. Using the top-left edge as a reference, copy and paste the entire window set onto the next adjacent face. Reference the left edge of the face for placement. Make sure the copied windows are set correctly onto the face; they should align to and cut holes on the face.

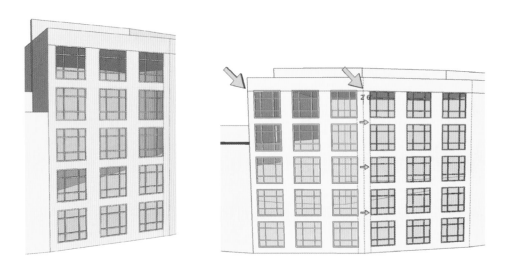

49. Select the two left columns of windows pasted in step 48. Copy and paste them onto the next face (to the right) in the same fashion outlined in step 48.

50. Copy/Add two windows above the pasted windows from step 49. When you place them, make sure to use the correct dimensions as indicated.

51. As indicated, copy the six windows from the same face populated in steps 45–47. Paste the windows onto the adjacent face to the left. Use the edges for reference as indicated by the yellow arrows in the diagram.

52. From the same face (steps 45–47), copy and paste six windows on the faces to the left of the previous surface.

53. Move/Copy the windows from the previous step over to the adjacent face on the left.

This completes the arrangement of windows for this side of the building.

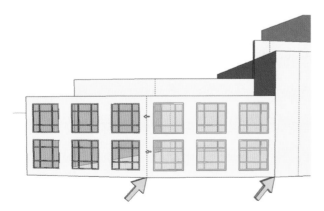

54. Using the same method as in steps 42 to 53, arrange and populate the faces on the other (right) side of the building. The two sides of the building are symmetrical and the composition of windows should be identical.

Once this is complete, populate the center, round mass of the building next.

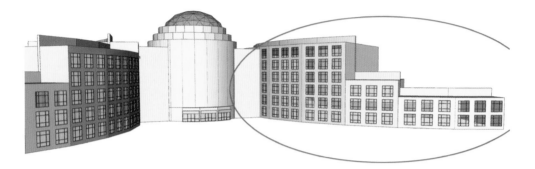

55. Insert Window 3 onto one of the faces of the center mass. The top of the window should be 5′ from the top edge of the outer circle. Make sure hidden geometry is still visible to complete these steps.

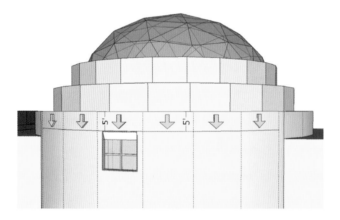

56. Copy and paste five additional windows onto each face, all 5′ below the top edge of the faceted faces.

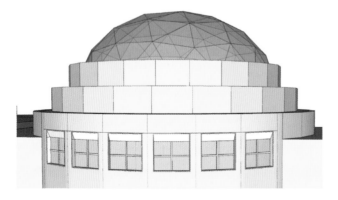

57. Insert Window 2, 2'-6" below Window 3.

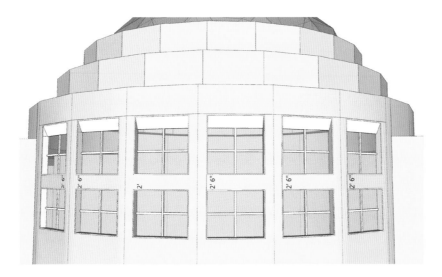

58. Copy/Array Window 2 downward on each face. The top-edge distance from window to window should be 10'-6". Do this for each of the six faces.

Once all the windows and doors have been added, the building center mass should appear as indicated in this image.

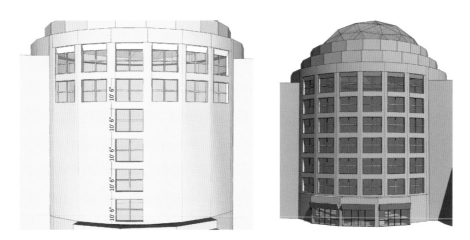

Adding Detail to the Building

Now that the building has doors and windows, you can add the finer details. This set of steps will detail the parapet running at the top of the roofs.

59. Locate the first parapet as shown in the graphic. Detail the parapet as outlined in steps 60 to 62. Repeat these steps to the parapets along the front part of the building.

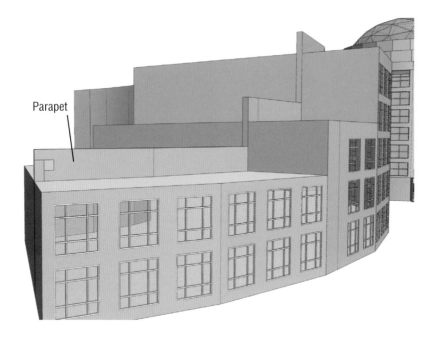

Parapet

60. Starting with the left edge of the parapet face, draw a square as indicated. The square should be 2′-6″ by 2′-6″. It should be located 2′-6″ from the left edge of the parapet and 2′-6″ from the top edge.

61. Use Move/Copy and copy the drafted square to the far end of the face. Place it 2′-6″ from the far, dashed edge. Array/Divide (**4/**) to create three equidistant copies.

62. Using Push/Pull, Push each face in, snapping to the back end of the parapet. The faces should be deleted, leaving a void.

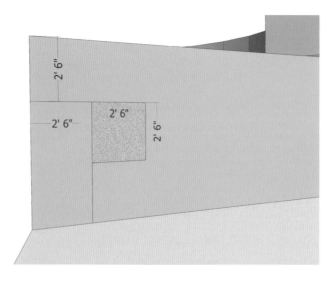

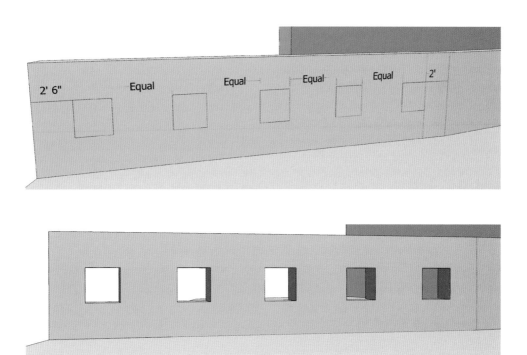

63. Move to the next parapet along the top of the building. Repeat the steps outlined previously to create the 2'-6" by 2'-6" parapet voids. Adjust the number of voids in each face as needed.

64. Repeat the process of creating the parapet voids on the other side of the building. This way the parapet details match on both sides of the building.

65. Focus on the two faces on either side of the round building's central mass. Offset each face 10′ inward. Push/Pull the center face 2′ inward and Add Color: Materials ➤ Markers ➤ Chipboard.

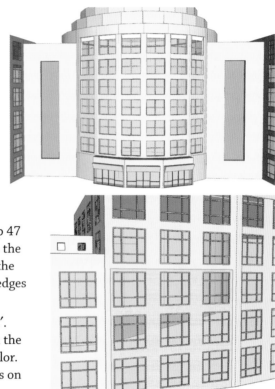

66. Place a rectangle around the bottom nine windows placed on the face in step 47 (the first set of Window 1s). Make sure the rectangle snaps to the bottom edge of the face. Do not overlap or connect to the edges to the left and right of the face.

67. Push/Pull the subdivided face inward 2′. The affixed components will move with the face. Paint the face chipboard to add color. Repeat this step for other face locations on the front end of the building.

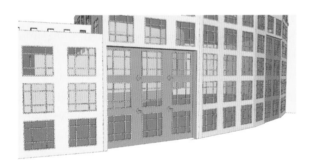

The building model is complete. You can add more detail, such as shadows, to make it look even more realistic.

Terrain Modeling

Introduction to the Terrain Tools

Terrain tools are powerful versatile tools for creating and editing organic geometry. *Organic geometry* refers to edges and faces composed to simulate the appearance of irregular forms and objects. Some examples of organic geometry are the gentle slopes and grades of the land, the curvatures on a building, and the arcing billow of a canopy.

The various terrain tools allow you to generate existing and proposed grades. With these tools, it's possible to quickly and easily transform flat site-plan models to include grades without the need of imported contour edges, spots, or elevations. Similarly, it's possible to model a site plan directly onto existing or proposed digital contour models.

This chapter introduces the Sandbox tools and other terrain extensions. Chapter 13 demonstrates the Sandbox tools' ability to generate grades from flat site models. Chapter 14 shows how to model canopy structures with the From Contour tool. Chapter 15 provides an overview on generating a site-plan model integrated into imported contour lines. Reading Chapter 5 is important so that you'll understand how to find and install the various extensions mentioned in Part 3.

The video tutorials at www.danieltal.com demonstrate how to use all the terrain tools in great detail. Most of the tutorials in Part 3 are available to members of the website. It includes tutorials not found in this book.

Playing in the Sandbox

The primary tools reviewed in Chapter 13 are the Sandbox tools. Native to SketchUp, these tools serve as an excellent set of extensions that allow for the quick and accurate modeling of grades. To activate the Sandbox toolbar, go to View ➢ Toolbars and check the Sandbox Tools box.

The From Contours Tool

From Contours is the premier tool in the Sandbox palette, and it has many uses. It generates a "skin" that stitches together faces between selected edges. The stitched faces automatically form a group.

Although commonly used to create simulated terrain using imported contour data from AutoCAD, it can be used to create almost any geometry, including curb ramps, architectural glass window walls, and tensile structures.

Many of the examples and tutorials in Part 4 focus on ways to utilize the From Contours tool. (See Fig. 12-1 through Fig. 12-4.)

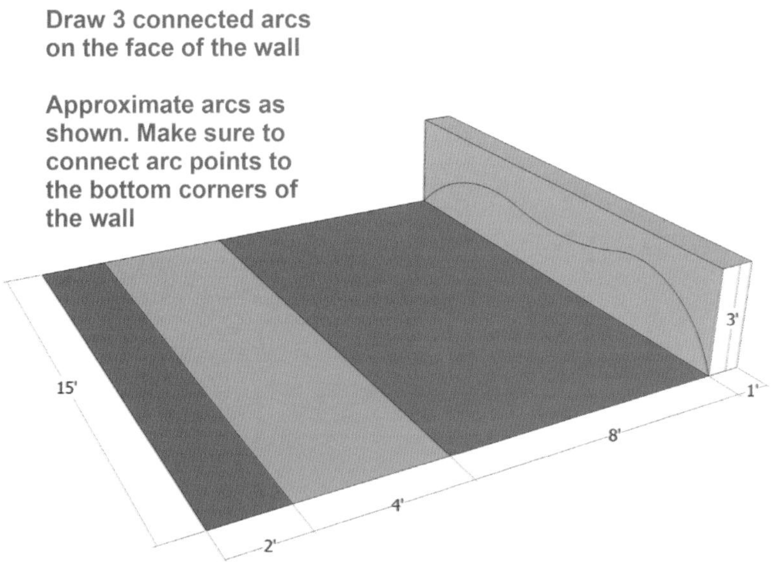

Draw 3 connected arcs on the face of the wall

Approximate arcs as shown. Make sure to connect arc points to the bottom corners of the wall

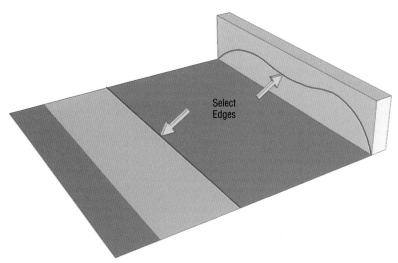

Fig. 12-1: Draft the model as outlined in an image.

Fig. 12-2: Select the edges as shown and run the From Contours tool.

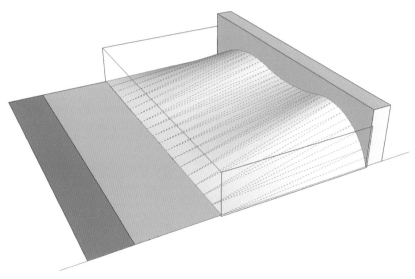

Fig. 12-3: The faces will be stitched between the selected edges.

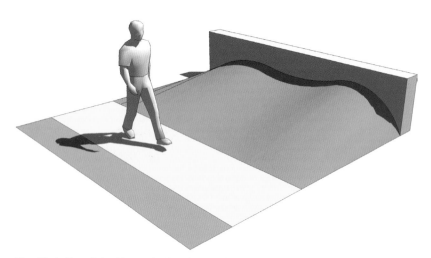

Fig. 12-4: The stitched faces simulate slope and terrain.

The From Scratch Tool

From Scratch creates a series of rectangular faces forming a grid. The size of the rectangles composing the grid can be adjusted by entering a value in the Measurement window. For example, entering **4′** will create a grid composed of 4′ × 4′ squares. Once a value for the grid size is selected, the From Scratch tool requires three selection points: a starting point, a point to define width, and a point providing length. SketchUp will generate the From Scratch grid as a group.

In tandem with the Smoove tool, a From Scratch grid can be sculpted to simulate landforms and elevations (Fig. 12-5).

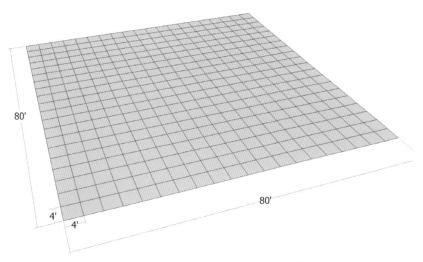

Fig. 12-5: Using the From Scratch tool, draw a grid composed of 4′ × 4′ squares. Make the grid 80′ × 80′.

The Smoove Tool

This tool is intended to be used with From Scratch. When active, it utilizes a circular outline tool to select the edges and faces on a From Scratch grid. The selected geometry can then be pulled up or down to form mounds or depressions. The size of the circular outline can be adjusted to be larger or smaller. (See Fig. 12-6 through Fig. 12-8.) The Smoove tool does take some practice to master.

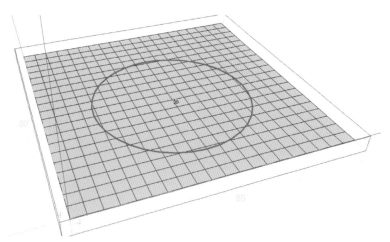

Fig. 12-6: Use the Smoove tool on the From Scratch grid. Adjust the size of the Smoove tool to 35′.

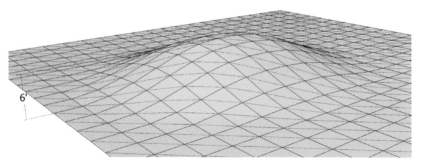

Fig. 12-7: Using the Measurement window, create a mound that is 6′ at its tallest point.

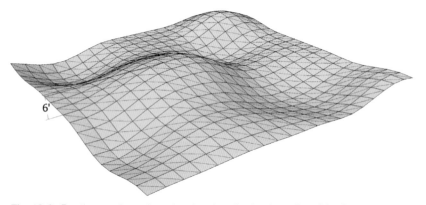

Fig. 12-8: Practice creating various elevations by adjusting the radius of the Smoove tool.

The Drape Tool

The Drape tool projects selected edges onto faces directly underneath. Projected edges should subdivide the affected faces. The Drape tool has many uses, such as defining surface areas and projecting lines onto volumes to create architecture (Fig. 12-9, Fig. 12-10).

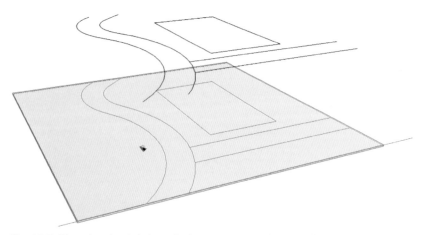

Fig. 12-9: The edges located above the faces are projected onto the face below.

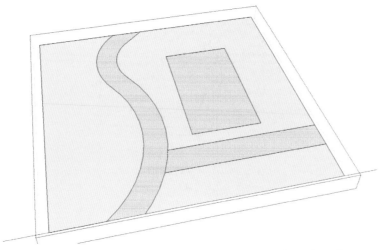

Fig. 12-10: The face below the projected edges now has the edges "draped" onto the face. When possible, draped edges will subdivide a face. This is determined by whether the projected lines form a closed perimeter.

The Add Detail Tool

To add more refined details, the Add Detail tool can further subdivide a From Scratch grid into smaller, subdivided faces (Fig. 12-11).

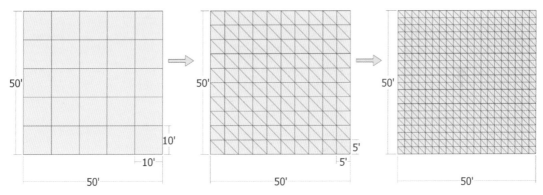

Fig. 12-11: The Add Detail tool applied to grid

The Stamp and Flip Edge Tools

The Stamp tool can help you place objects onto an organic surface. The Stamp tool helps embed the selected item into terrain by adjusting the geometry to enfold the object (Fig. 12-12 through Fig. 12-14).

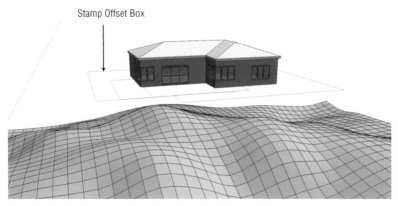

Stamp Offset Box

Fig. 12-12: The Stamp tool is activated on a building model.

The simple Flip Edge tool reverses and adjusts the orientation of edges. When you generate faces using From Contours, some of the edges are aligned in ways that distort geometry. Using Flip Edge on the lines causing the distortion will cause them to flip and "fix" the direction of the face, removing the distortion.

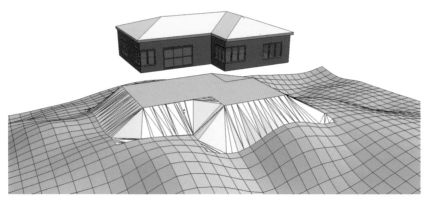

Fig. 12-13: The surfaces below will adjust to help place the building squarely on the model.

Fig. 12-14: An adjusted terrain model with a building

Although the Stamp and Flip Edge tools do have practical uses, the Sandbox tutorials in Part 3 do not utilize them to create grade, architecture, or forms. Even though you won't use them here, feel free to explore them on your own.

Terrain Extensions

As noted, several other terrain extensions are available that can help generate and edit irregular geometry. Most of them are available for free. These scripts are extremely valuable (as are many others not covered in this book).

Tools on Surface

This is a powerful set of tools similar to SketchUp's Drawing commands. They can be used on organic geometry and irregular surfaces to draw lines, arcs, and shapes (Fig. 12-15, Fig. 12-16) in the same fashion as drawing on a flat face. These tools are essential for more complex terrain modeling, as demonstrated in Chapter 15. The Tools on Surface extension is authored by Fredo6; it can be installed only through the SketchUcation Plugin Store.

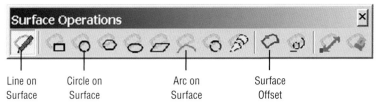

Fig. 12-15: The Tools on Surface toolbar

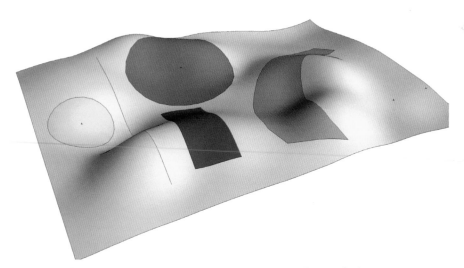

Fig. 12-16: Shapes drafted directly onto an organic surface using Tools on Surface

JointPushPull

This extension is the Push/Pull equivalent for organic geometry. By selecting a group of faceted faces and applying JointPushPull, you can pull the faces up or down to add volume. The script allows you to select multiple, unconnected faces and apply Push/Pull to all the selected faces. (See Fig. 12-17 to Fig. 12-21.) As with Tools on Surface, this script was created by Fredo6 and is available through the SketchUcation Plugin Store.

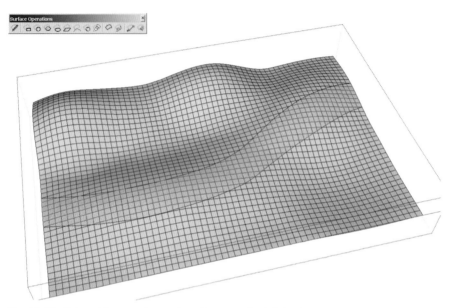

Fig. 12-17: Selected faces on the terrain surface to be Push/Pulled in mass, using the Joint PushPull Ruby

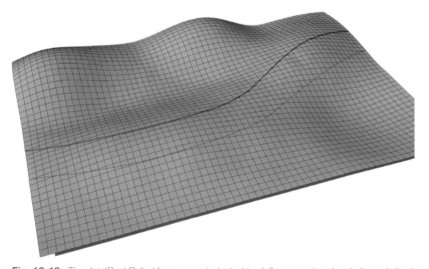

Fig. 12-18: The JointPushPulled faces were indented to define a road and curb through the terrain.

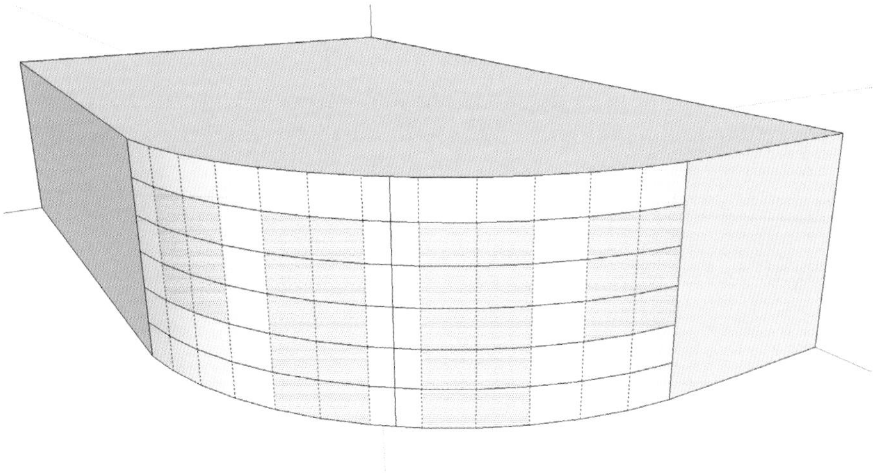

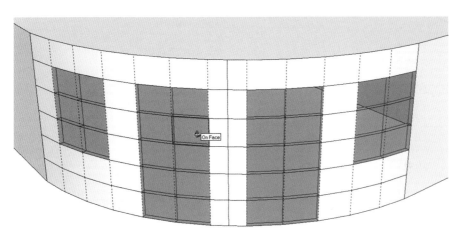

Fig. 12-19: The JointPushPull tool can be used to create features on curved surfaces. Some of the faces on these curved surfaces have been selected.

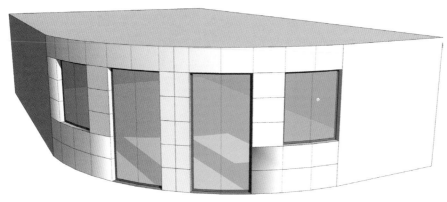

Fig. 12-20: The JointPushPull tool is used on the selected surfaces to indent them.

Fig. 12-21: The pushed faces are offset to form window mullions to create noncomponent windows on a curvature.

Soap Skin Bubble

This extension is similar to From Contour, but it is considerably more powerful. It creates gridded mesh faces between selected edges. The forms created by this extension tend to have greater definition compared to From Contour. The generated faces can be given a value to add bulge and curvature by adding "pressure" to the face, much like a soap bubble (Fig. 12-22, Fig. 12-23). The extension requires some practice so that the selected edges form a connected closed loop, but the results are well worth the time spent mastering it.

The script was authored by Josef Leibinger and can be found on the Extension Warehouse and at http://www.tensile-structures.de/sb_software.html.

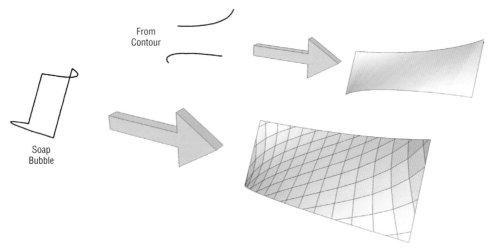

Fig. 12-22: From Contour requires two or more edges. Soap Bubble needs a closed "loop" of edges to stitch the faces.

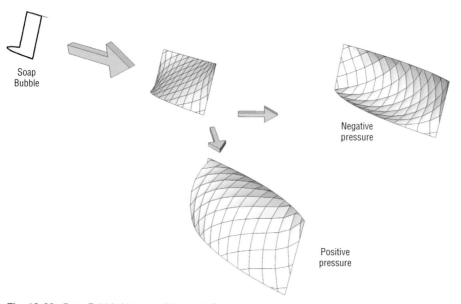

Fig. 12-23: Soap Bubble lets you add more definition to a surface by adjusting the surface's bulges and curvature.

Drop GC

The Drop GC extension drops selected groups or components onto the surface below. You can use this script to help place objects on organic terrain (Fig. 12-24 through Fig. 12-27). It can only be used on components or groups and will not work if there is no surface or object under the selected geometry that is to be dropped. The script was authored by Smustard and can be found on the Extension Warehouse.

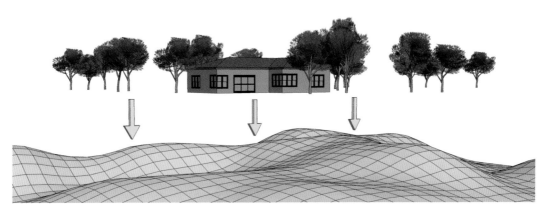

Fig. 12-24: Components floating above the terrain can be dropped directly down with the Drop GC extension.

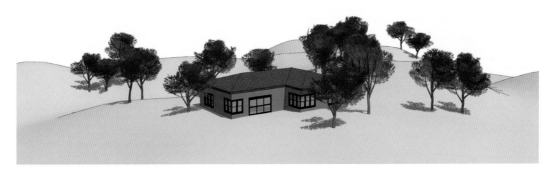

Fig. 12-25: Components land on the terrain at the first face they intersect downward along the vertical axis. The result is that the components "hug" the terrain model. This is easier than trying to place each component on a specific surface location on the terrain.

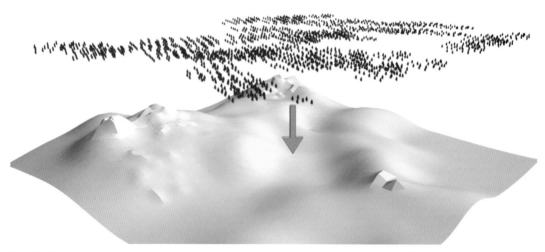

Fig. 12-26: A "forest" of trees is about to be dropped on a large terrain model created using From Scratch and Smoove.

Fig. 12-27: The dropped trees hug the contours of the terrain model.

Artisan

Artisan is a versatile, multipurpose modeling toolset. It can be used to model complex objects such as consumer products or edit grades. Sculpt Brush is the primary tool used to work with terrain. Artisan is a must-have alternative to the Sandbox Smoove tool. Additional terrain tools can also help in selecting, painting, and editing organic surfaces. Artisan can be found on the Extension Warehouse.

Additional Tools and Concepts

The terrain tools are not the only methods for manipulating organic geometry. The following tools and concepts are reviewed in later chapters in conjunction with the Sandbox tools.

Intersect with Model

Intersect with Model creates edges where 3D geometry and volumes overlap. It can be used to help combine objects, subtract volumes, or intersect geometry. It is particularly useful when you are defining surface areas, such as walks and roads, on simulated terrain. Surface area volumes are pulled through a terrain model and then intersected with the terrain model. The surface volume is then deleted, and the outline of the surface is retained on the terrain (Fig. 12-28 through Fig. 12-31).

There are three ways to use Intersect with Model:

- ► It can be used on an entire model with nothing selected (right-click the context menu and choose Intersect ➤ Intersect with Model).

- ► It can be used only on selected geometry (right-click the context menu and choose Intersect ➤ Intersect Selected).

- ► It can be used to add edges to intersecting groups and components (right-click the context menu and choose Intersect ➤ Intersect Context).

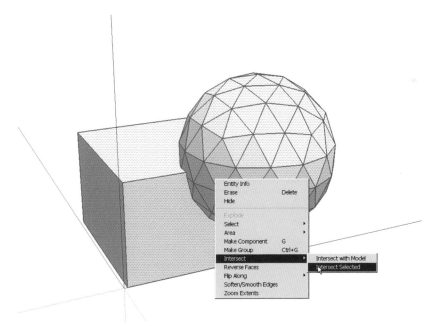

Fig. 12-28: Intersect with Model being performed on a cube and sphere. The sphere will be subtracted from the cube. Notice that neither object is a group or component.

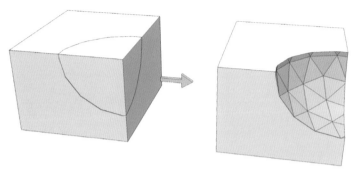

Fig. 12-29: The sphere is deleted from the cube. The face of the sphere remains on the cube where the two objects intersected.

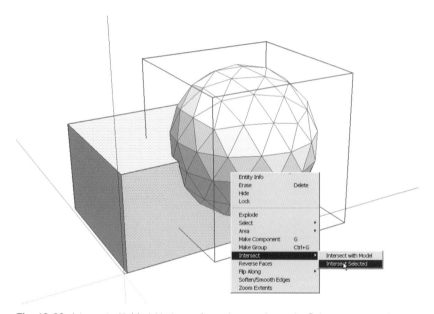

Fig. 12-30: Intersect with Model being performed on a cube and a Sphere component

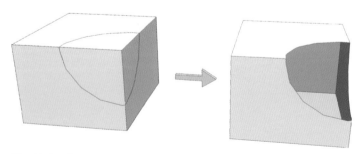

Fig. 12-31: Because the sphere was a component, once it's deleted, the geometry of the sphere does not remain to fill the void in the cube.

Construction Geometry

Construction geometry provides another useful method for generating organic shapes. Construction geometry consists of drawn edges used to create the skeletal forms or *wireframes* of an object. From Contour is applied to the wireframe to generate edges and faces that define the "skin" of the object or form. You will learn how to create edge construction geometry to create slopes, buildings, and complex structures using the Sandbox tools in Chapters 13, 14, and 15 (Fig. 12-32).

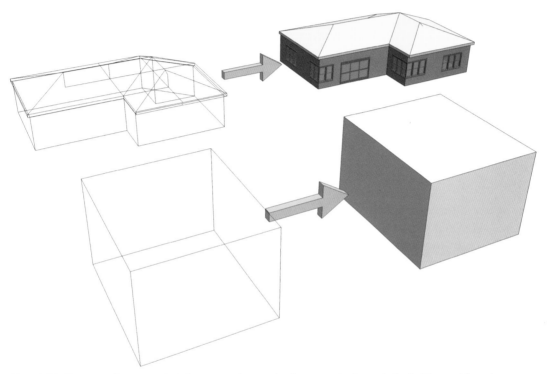

Fig. 12-32: The edges/frames on the left compose the construction geometry to create the building and the cube.

As with other SketchUp tools, the Sandbox tools can be used in many different contexts. The next three chapters include tutorials and examples of how to harness the Sandbox tools and associated Ruby Scripts to create conceptual grading and model architecture, and make complex canopies.

CHAPTER

13

SketchUp Conceptual Grading

SketchUp models should realistically portray architecture, surfaces, and objects. An important part of the built and natural environment is *terrain*: the slopes, grades, and elevations that define peaks and valleys. Using the methods in this chapter, terrain can be realistically represented, adding important definition to a model.

This chapter serves as a primer for Chapter 15; the methods and processes are useful to working with contour models and modeling a site plan on terrain.

Conceptual Grading

Most SketchUp models represent 3D volumes and details on a flat site. They do not typically include terrain or grade. Any vertical relief in a site plan is accomplished with Push/Pulled volumes of elevated areas, typically steps leading to another flat surface.

However, SketchUp can create simulated terrain without a DEM by using the Sandbox tools. With the Sandbox tools, elevations can be sculpted to create identifiable landforms and slopes to achieve a specific look, feel, and scale. The basic approach is no different than adding volume to traditional SketchUp geometry using the Draw and Modification tools. From Contour is the primary tool used to fashion conceptual grading. The versatility of this tool is demonstrated extensively as part of the included tutorials.

Conceptual Grading fits right into SketchUp Process Modeling. Because the simulated grades and terrain are modeled onto the Flatwork Base, they should be added once the base is complete, but prior to the inclusion of site elements. The modeling process would be expanded to flow as follows:

1. Generate a Flatwork Base.
2. Add color.
3. Add volume.
4. Detail the volumes.
5. Add slopes and grades (SketchUp Conceptual Grading).
6. Populate the base with site components and objects.

Modeling and Grading Tips

As you follow along with the tutorials to generate slopes and elevation, keep the following tips in mind.

▶ As discussed earlier, all drafted edges and faces should be drawn on Layer 0.

▶ Geometry generated using From Contour will be created as a group. Place the group geometry onto its own layer called Terrain.

▶ When you are working with groups and components, make sure you are aware of group or component instances within which you are working, especially the Flatwork Base.

▶ You will have to turn on Hidden Geometry (View ➤ Hidden Geometry) when you work with the tools that help generate and edit organic geometry.

▶ In most cases, you will need to draft *construction geometry,* a framework composed of edges to delineate the form and shape of elevation or grade that will be generated.

The Tutorials

The SketchUp Conceptual Grading tutorials focus on creating specific features that are typical of site plans. They are designed to help you learn and understand how to construct some typical objects that can be duplicated and used in other site models. The tutorials build on each other and become more complex as you progress. **You will need to download the specified models to complete the tutorials.**

Pedestrian and Vehicular Ramps You can use the From Contour tool to create pedestrian ramps and vehicular driveways, two important elements of any site plan. Ramps are important for pedestrian crossings and accessibility. By adding these surfaces, you provide realism and context to your site plans.

The tutorial focuses on street curb ramps and driveway entrances.

Simple Slopes Slopes and terrain against buildings and walls are common features in the built environment, and they provide great aesthetic detail in models. By including them in your models, you can create better representations of real-world conditions.

The tutorial demonstrates how to utilize simple lines, arcs, and From Contours to generate slopes; it also shows how to populate the slopes with vegetation.

Swales and Mounds Bioswales and raised elevations serve a variety of purposes. They convey water, screen views, and add aesthetic detail. From Scratch, Drape, and Smoove are ideal for sculpting such terrain.

Pedestrian Ramp

In this tutorial, you will learn to create a simple pedestrian intersection ramp using some simple edges and From Contour.

Download from 3D Warehouse and open model: Pedestrian_Ramp_Tutorial

1. Push/Pull the "corner" surface down to be flush with the adjacent road surface.

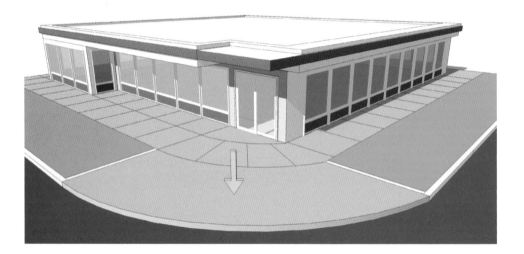

2. Select the curved outer edge (flush with the road) and the top smaller arc-edge adjacent to the buildings and walks. With the edges selected, activate From Contour.

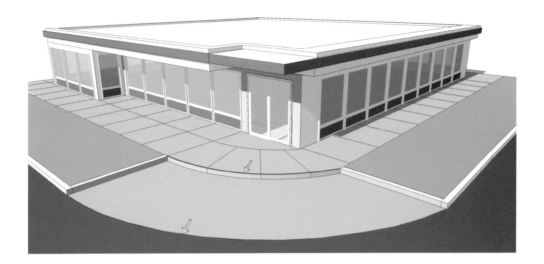

The From Contour tool will stitch the two selected arcs together with a series of faces. The generated faces create a simulated pedestrian curve. In many circumstances, From Contour will generate *artifacts* (extra faces) as indicated by the arrow in the graphic.

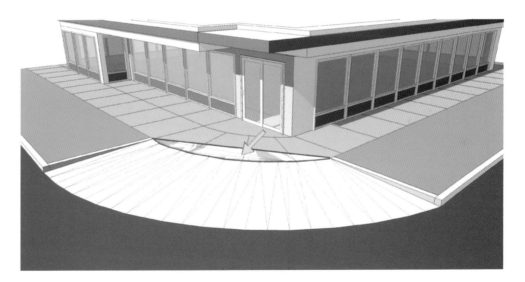

3. By turning the Hidden Geometry to visible (View ➤ Hidden Geometry), you can reveal all the (dashed) edges that compose the stitched ramp. You can easily delete the artifact faces. Enter the group instance of the generated ramp. With the Eraser tool, delete the extra faces and edges.

Make sure to delete enough faces so that there are no overlaps with the adjacent walk. Be as precise as possible, deleting the edges and faces that butt the original arc used to generate the slope.

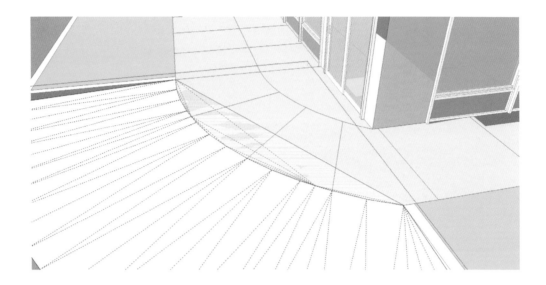

4. Toggle off the hidden geometry and add an appropriate color to the Ramp group.

Driveway Ramp

In this tutorial, you will build a driveway ramp. You will have to draft edges and arcs to help complete the form of the ramp. This is the first instance in which you will use construction geometry that will provide frame for the ramp.

Download from 3D Warehouse and open model: Drive_Ramp

1. Push/Pull the surface indicated by the arrow in the image downward to be flush with the adjacent road surface.

2. With Hidden Geometry set to visible, draw an edge and arc connecting the exposed vertical surfaces. Draw a single edge from the top corner to the midpoint of the first edge of the first face that composes the facet of the curve. Add an arc, starting with the midpoint of the edge to the bottom intersection. Snap the bulge (third arc point) to the edge between Facet 6 and Facet 7.

   Repeat step 2 for the other side of the drive.

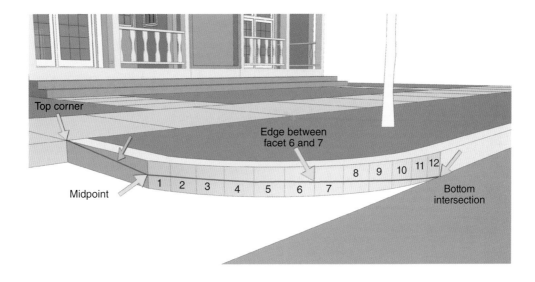

3. Select the drafted edges from step 2. Include the bottom edge adjacent to the road and the top edge adjacent to the walk. Activate the From Contour tool.

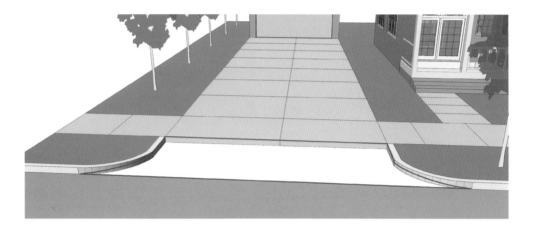

The From Contour tool will stitch all the selected edges with a series of sloping, connected faces simulating a drive ramp.

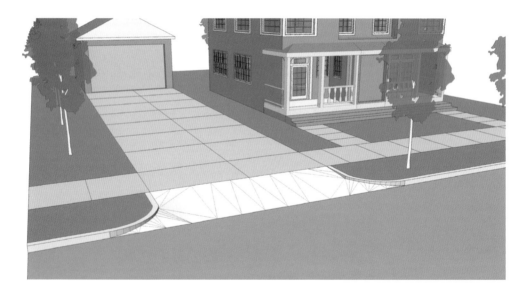

4. Add color to the ramp to match the adjacent walk. Add color to the curb face attached to the slope.

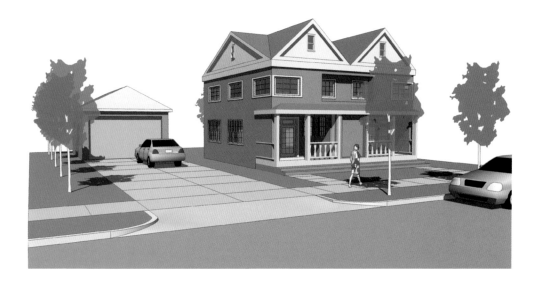

Slopes and Grades

This tutorial will teach you how to use arcs and edges drafted on a vertical surface to generate a series of gentle slopes and grades. Make sure the arcs are flush with vertical face of the walls.

Download from 3D Warehouse and open model: Slopes_Grades

1. Draw three connected arcs along the vertical surface of the wall as shown in the graphic at the top of page 234. Make sure to connect the first point of the first arc and the second point of the third arc to the bottom corner endpoints of the wall and Flatwork Base. Select the three drawn arcs and the arcs that compose the adjacent edge of the trail. With all the edges selected, activate the From Contour tool.

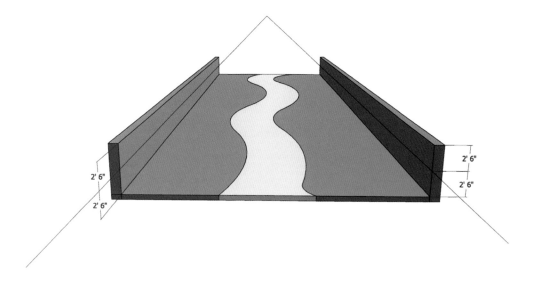

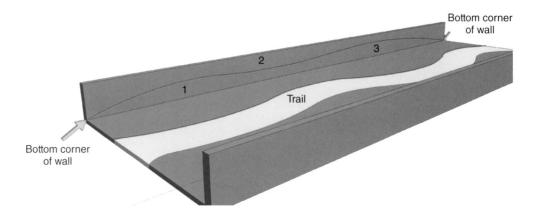

Bottom corner of wall

Bottom corner of wall

1

2

3

Trail

2. From Contour will generate a surface between the selected edges. Edit the generated Slope group and clean up and delete the artifact faces that overlap the trail. Make sure Hidden Geometry is toggled to visible when you erase the extra faces.

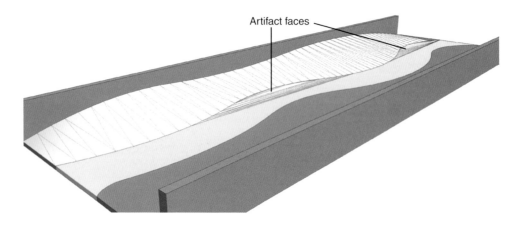

Artifact faces

3. Add a green lawn and plant color to the generated slope.

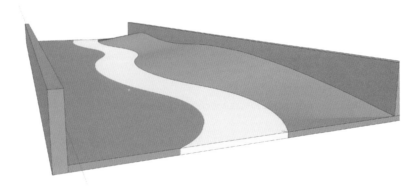

4. Repeat steps 1 through 3 on the opposite wall: draw three arcs, select the edges along the trail and drawn arcs, and activate the From Contour tool to generate a slope. Clean up any artifact geometry. Add color to the simulated terrain.

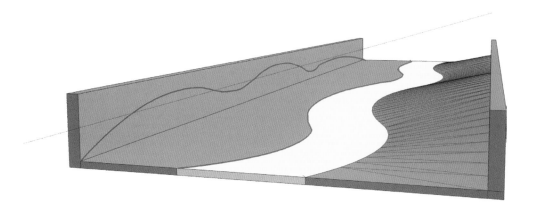

5. Add trees and vegetation to the simulated slopes. Include people, benches, and other amenities to complete the scene. Learn to snap trees and other objects to the sloping surfaces generated in the tutorial.

Building Entry Walk

The goal of this tutorial is to construct a walk and associated terrain leading up to a building entry. This tutorial is more complex than the previous examples using construction geometry. All the edges drafted will be used to define the various slopes and grades. The purpose of the tutorial is to demonstrate how simple edges can be used to generate specific elevations and grades.

Some of the steps for this tutorial can appear to be complex. Take your time and work through them. The method is relatively easy once complete, but it requires you to think three-dimensionally.

Download from 3D Warehouse and open model: Building_Entry_Walk

1. Identify the areas in the model reviewed in the diagram: the four arcs that compose the walk (two on each side) and the building entry and walk starting point. The building entry is located 8'-6" up along the vertical face of the building where the walk ends.

    You will use the arcs and walk endpoints as references to construct a framework to model the sloping walk and landscape.

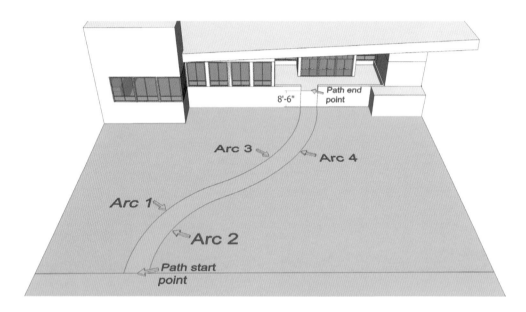

2. Draft three horizontal edges onto the walk, snapping to the arc endpoints and midpoints. These edges will be used in the next step to place vertical edges along the length of the walk.

    a. Draft Edge 1 between the approximate midpoints of Arc 1 and Arc 2. Make sure the edge is perpendicular (magenta when being drafted).

    b. Draft Edge 2 from the endpoint where Arc 1 and Arc 3 connect to the opposite endpoint where Arc 2 and Arc 4 connect.

    c. Draft Edge 3 at the approximate midpoint of Arc 3 to the midpoint of Arc 4. Make sure the edge is perpendicular.

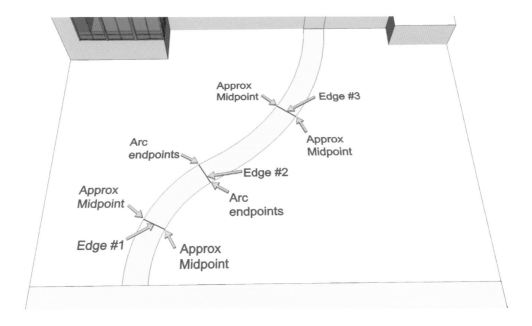

3. Select, copy, and paste (using Move/Copy) the 8′-6″ vertical edge at the building entry. Select one of the vertical edges that flank the building entry. Select the edge at its bottom endpoint. Paste the edge to both endpoints of Edges 1, 2, and 3 from the previous step.

The copied edges represent the highest point that the slope needs to reach to achieve the sloping walk.

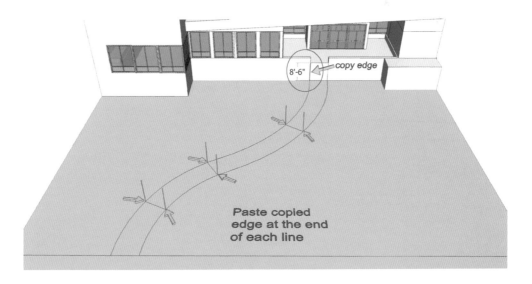

4. The arcs and edges added in the next steps (4 through 9) are called projected arcs and projected edges. They are the vertical projections of the lines that form the horizontal walk. In essence, you are building a sloping wireframe of the horizontal walk. The projected lines will be snapped to various points along the vertical edges added in step 3.

   Start with walk Arc 3.

   a. Using the Arc tool, snap the first point of projected Arc 3 to the top of the vertical edge at the building entry.

   b. Next, snap the second point to the midpoint of the vertical edge where Arc 1 connects to Arc 3. Snap the bulge (third point) of the arc approximately three-quarters of the way up on the vertical edge at the midpoint of horizontal Arc 3.

      The diagram shows the intended result. The arc is sloping from the building entry to the mid part of the walk. The projected arc should be located directly above the horizontal Arc 3.

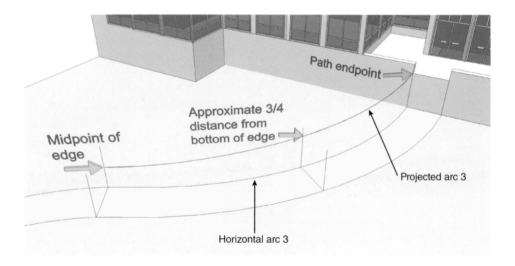

5. Copy the two horizontal edges added in step 2 that are connected to horizontal Arc 3 upward along the vertical edges. Move/Copy each edge separately. The edges should be snapped to the intersection point of projected Arc 3 and the vertical edge. Use the diagram as reference. These copied projected edges will be used as guides to snap to projected Arc 4.

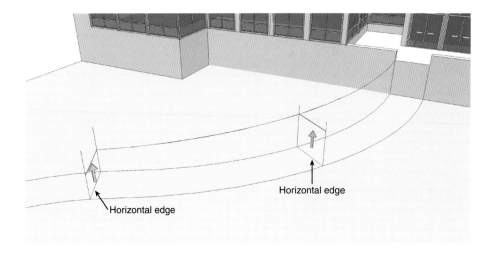

6. Add a second projected arc above horizontal Arc 4. Use the projected edges copied in step 5 as references for the arc snap points and bulge location. Snap the first point of the arc to the top of the building entry opposite projected Arc 3. Snap the second point to the endpoint of the projected edge copied upward in step 5 located at the intersection of Arc 2 and Arc 4.

Snap the bulge to the endpoint of the projected edge located at the midpoint of horizontal Arc 4.

The added projected Arc 4 should be parallel to projected Arc 3 and directly above horizontal Arc 4, as indicated in the diagram.

If done correctly, you will have created a simple wireframe composed of edges and arcs. There should now be two sloping arcs sloping from the building entry toward the middle of the walk. The first half of the walk is now complete.

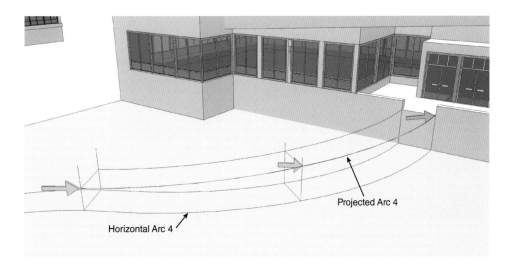

7. Repeat steps 4 through 6 on the lower part of the walk at horizontal Arcs 1 and 2, creating projected Arcs 1 and 2.

   a. Start with projected Arc 1. Draft an arc, snapping the first point to the endpoint of horizontal Arc 1 at the endpoint at ground. Snap the second arc point to the endpoint of the projected Arc 3.

   b. Snap the arc bulge approximately three-quarters of the way down from the top of the middle vertical edge located at the midpoint of horizontal Arc 1.

   With projected Arc 1 complete and connected to projected Arc 3, one side of the walk frame is complete.

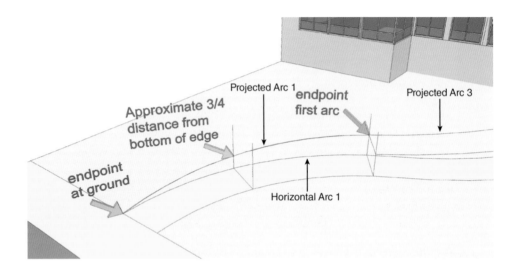

8. Move/Copy upward the horizontal edge located at the midpoints of horizontal Arcs 1 and 2. Snap the copied edge to the intersection of projected Arc 1 and the vertical edge to which the arc bulge was snapped.

   Add projected Arc 2. This is similar to step 7. Snap the first point of the arc to the endpoint of horizontal Arc 2 at the start of the walk. Snap the second point to the endpoint of projected Arc 4. Last, snap the bulge to the endpoint of the projected edge copied and placed in this step.

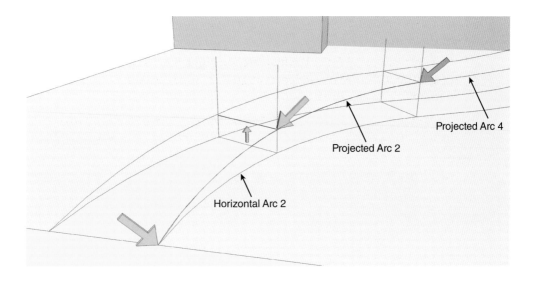

Projected Arc 4

Projected Arc 2

Horizontal Arc 2

9. Delete all the projected and vertical edges. Do not delete any of the arcs.

The resulting construction geometry consists of four connected, sloping arcs that parallel the walk underneath. The projected arcs now provide a realistic, sloping path from the start of the walk to the building entry.

The next steps are similar to the Slopes and Grades tutorial. A series of edges and arcs will be drafted on the vertical faces of the building. This will help further define the future grades that will define the Building Walk Entry.

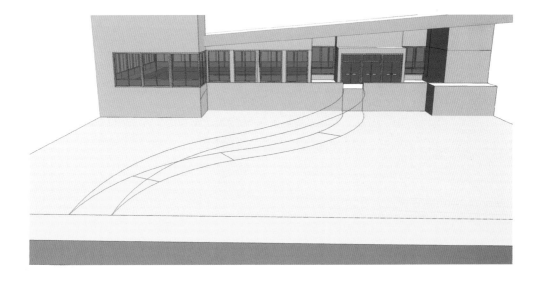

10. Draft a series of connected arcs on the vertical surfaces of the building. Starting with the surfaces to the left of the walk, begin at the location where projected Arc 3 connects to the building entry. There will be a total of three arcs on three faces. The last arc should connect to the bottom outside endpoint of the building (where it intersects the ground). Follow the diagram for the relative heights and placement of these arcs.

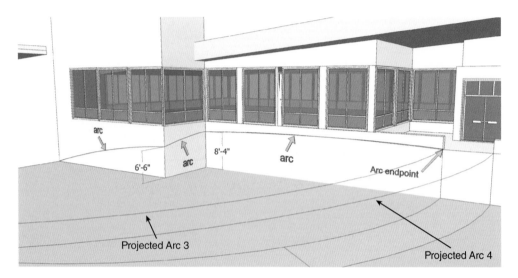

11. Next, starting at the intersection of projected Arc 4 at the building entry and moving to the right, draft another series of connected arcs on the vertical surface of the building. As with step 10, there are a total of three arcs, with the last arc connecting to the bottom of the building where it intersects the ground. Make sure to follow the diagram to achieve the heights and placement of the arcs.

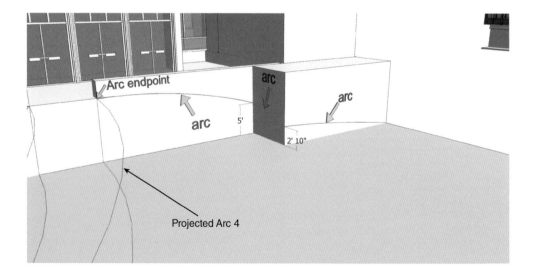

12. It's time to generate the walk and grade surfaces. Select all the edges drafted in steps 4 through 11, as indicated in the diagram. Include the outer bottom edges of the ground that runs parallel to the entry walk.

With all the edges selected, activate From Contour.

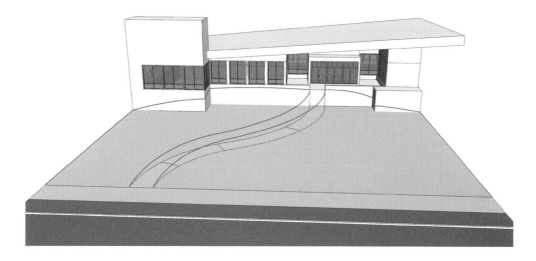

13. The From Contour tool will generate a sloped trail and terrain leading to the building entry. Toggle on Hidden Geometry (View ➤ Hidden Geometry).

You can see all the faces that From Contour generated to create the slopes and walk. However, color is needed to help define the walk surface and landscape. The next steps will demonstrate how to add color.

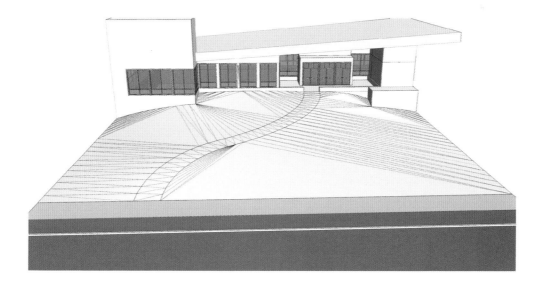

14. Enter the group instance of the generated slope creating by using From Contour. Select all the faces that compose the walk. The outside arcs of the walk will be clearly visible. Use the Select tool and hold Ctrl to create an additive selection. Try using the selection box to select the correct faces. Hidden Geometry must be toggled to visible for this work.

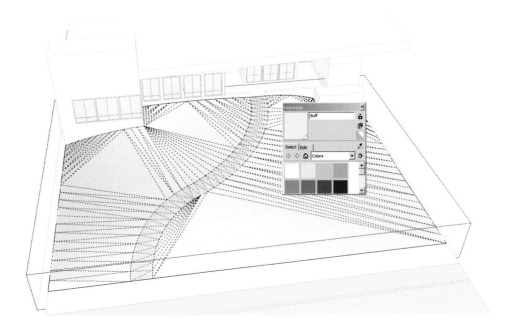

15. With the faces of the path selected, apply a Marker ➤ Beige color from the Materials palette to the faces. Exit the component instance and apply a lawn (green) color to the Slope group. This will paint the remaining surfaces. Toggle Hidden Geometry to off.

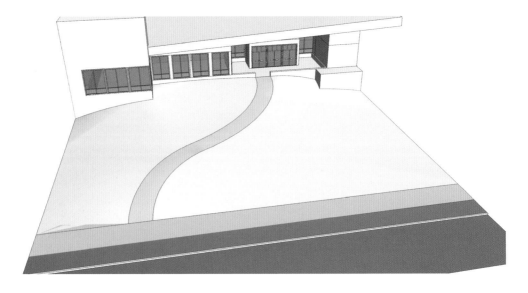

The sloping entry walk and terrain are completed. While there are other advanced methods to achieve the same goal, using construction geometry allows you to measure the rise and run of a particular walk, grade, or elevation to create greater precision. This is useful when designing accessible ramps or to gain an understanding of what specific slopes are part of a project model.

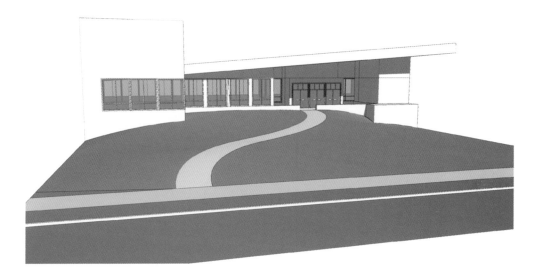

16. Add trees, cars, people, pedestrian lights, bike racks, and other amenities to the walk and grades to make the scene more realistic.

Park Landform

Now it's time to work on the park. In this tutorial, you will give the park a personality of its own. You will learn to generate terrain using three separate Sandbox tools: From Scratch, Drape, and Smoove. In combination, they allow you to generate smooth terrain fitting into a specific site plan location. The height or depth of the terrain is easily controlled, and you will learn to snap the terrain to the tops of walls and edges.

Download from 3D Warehouse and open model: Park_Landform

1. Review the base model. For this tutorial, you will apply From Scratch, Drape, and Smoove to Areas 1 and 2 to generate simulated terrain.

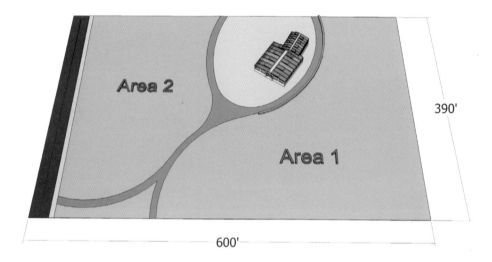

2. Directly adjacent to the park Flatwork Base model, draw a grid using From Scratch. The grid should be 400′ × 600′ with 10′ × 10′ grid spacing.

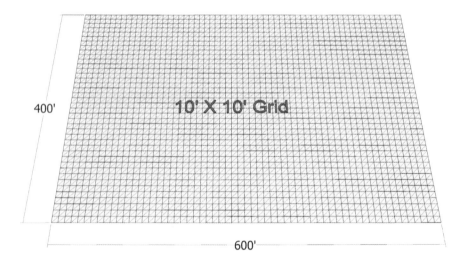

3. Select the surfaces of Area 1 and Area 2. With both surfaces selected, right-click and convert them into a single group. Move the group and place it over the From Scratch grid created in step 2. Ensure that the surface areas of Areas 1 and 2 fit within the bounds of the From Scratch grid.

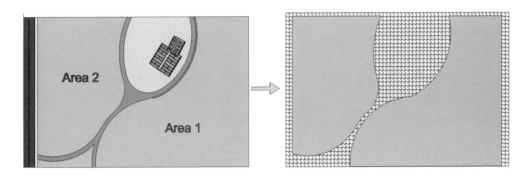

4. Move the Area 1 and 2 group that you placed on the grid upward on the vertical axis to sit directly above the grid.

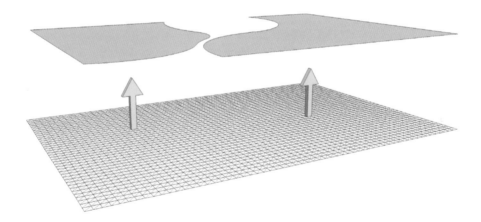

5. Select the From Scratch grid, right-click, and select Soften/Smooth Edges. Set the tab to the far right and check the Soften Coplaner box. This will cause the grid edges to be hidden.

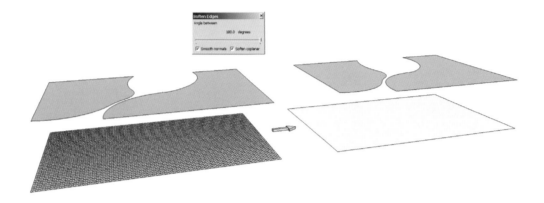

6. Select the Area 1 and 2 group and activate the Drape command. Select the grid below the group by hovering over it. This will drape the edges of the group onto the grid. Enter the From Scratch grid instance (it is a group). The draped edges should have subdivided the grid face.

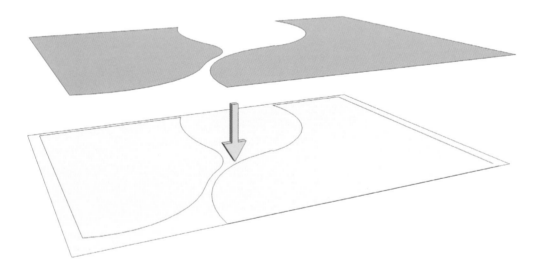

7. In some cases, the Drape command will not subdivide the grid face. A gap at the bottom-right corner in the edge work prevents the face from being subdivided. Enter the Grid group instance to fix the problem.

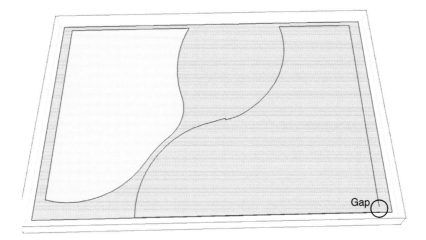

8. In the grid instance, add an edge connecting the endpoints where the gap is located. Make sure the added edge subdivides the face.

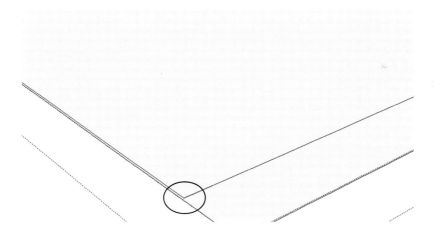

9. Delete the Area 1 and 2 group located above the From Scratch grid. Next, enter the grid instance and delete the edges and faces of the grid outside the surface areas that define Area 1 and Area 2. Once the extra faces are deleted, toggle on Hidden Geometry (View ➤ Hidden Geometry). With the hidden geometry visible, the grid lines are shown and

can now be manipulated. The form of the From Scratch grid conforms to that of the site plan.

10. Select the cut-out From Scratch grid and place it back into the Flatwork Base. Use the corners of the grid to snap to a known corner or location of the Flatwork Base.

    Once the grid is in place, you will be ready to manipulate the geometry to simulate terrain using the Smoove tool.

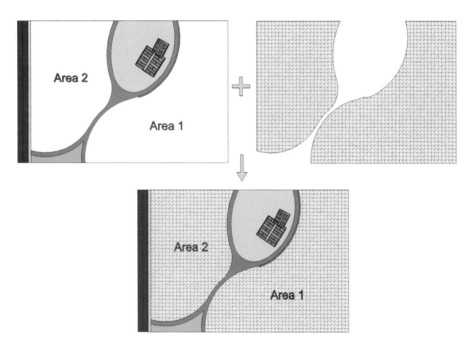

11. Enter the grid instance. Activate the Smoove tool and set the Smoove tool Radius to 60′. Start with Area 1 and reactivate the tool and pull the surface upward 10′ by entering the value in the Measurement window. With the Smoove tool circle active, hover over a location of the grid. Select the location by left-clicking. Pull the surface upward. Before

clicking again, enter a value in the Measurement window to generate a specific height. Using the Smoove tool to generate specific heights can take some practice to master.

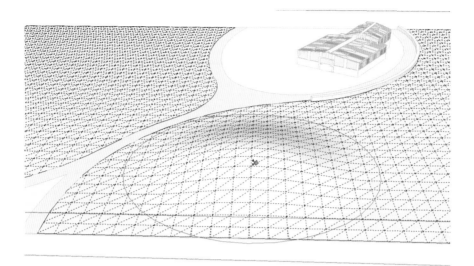

12. Move the Smoove tool to the approximate outer edge of the pulled-up faces and double-click. This will repeat the last Smoove command and raise another "mound" to the same height as the first one. This is one method of using the Smoove tool to create a constant and level grade.

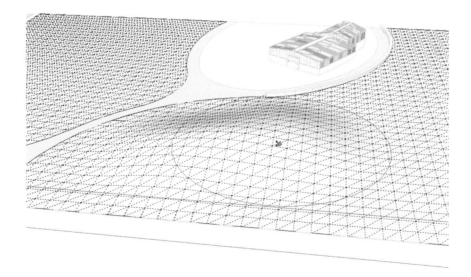

13. Continue to generate the mound started in steps 10 and 11. Repeat step 11 to create a series of mounds. To generate a smooth terrain, when repeating the Smoove command on the next set of faces, locate the Smoove tool circle so the outer edge of the Smoove

circle is located approximately over the highest part of the adjacent mound. Then repeat the command (double-click). This will elevate the top of the new faces to match the adjacent mound without creating a "saddle" or gap between the landforms.

Try to create a landform that snakes its way through Area 1 and maintains a regular height, without too many gaps or saddles.

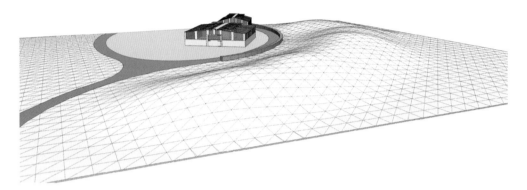

14. Next, you will use the Smoove tool to snap the grid surface to the top of a wall so that the wall "retains" the terrain.

    Locate the wall adjacent to the path and building in Area 1. Adjust the Smoove tool Radius to 30′. Place the Smoove tool over the faces directly adjacent to the wall. Activate the Smoove tool and pull the faces upward. The Smoove tool will allow you to snap to an inference point at the top of the wall. This will bring the grid surface up to match the wall height.

    Repeat this step, snapping the grid to the top of the wall face and creating a consistent grade along the top of the wall edge.

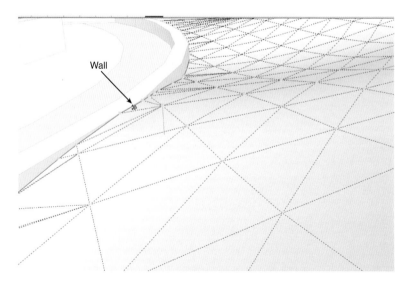

Wall

The grid surface is now contoured to the wall, creating a simulated retaining wall. This method can be adapted to be used to snap the grid to the vertical surfaces of buildings and other objects.

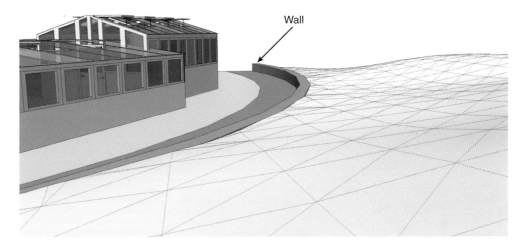

15. The Smoove tool can also be used to create swales.

   a. Set the Smoove tool to 55'. In a location adjacent to the trail in Area 2, indent the grid faces enough to make a gentle depression.

   b. Move the Smoove tool over to the edge of the depression and double-click to repeat the exact depth of the indent.

     This is identical to creating the landform in step 13. Like the landform, the depth of the indent can be assigned by entering a value in the Measurement window.

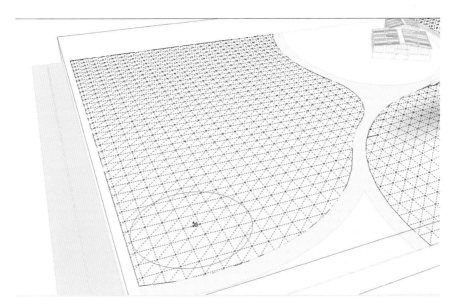

16. Continue to repeat step 14, creating a swale in the area adjacent to the path.

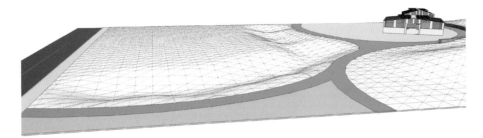

17. Adjacent to the swale in Area 2, practice creating some gently uplifting grades with the Smoove tool. Practice adjusting the size of the Smoove tool radius. The goal is to create gently sloping and smooth landforms simulating terrain.

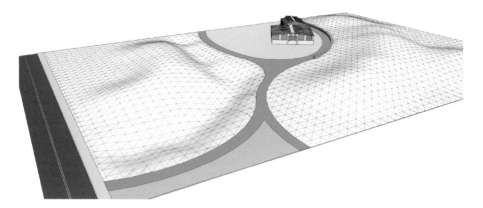

18. Once you've completed the simulated contour, turn off Hidden Geometry and add a green color to the surfaces.

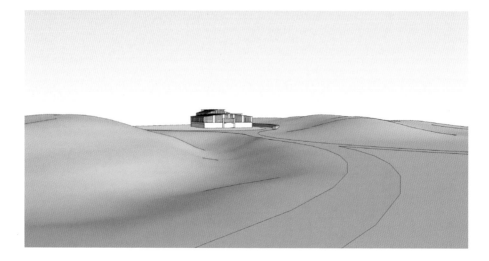

19. Add the site amenities (trees, people, benches, etc.) to the site plan.

By adding these simple and quick grades to the site and coupling them with a variety of site amenities, you have transformed the model to depict a specific program, form, and feeling.

Campus Quad—Area 1

The Campus Quad model is comprised of four areas. Using the methods outlined in the previous grading tutorials, you will add conceptual grades to each of these areas to create a holistic and graded site model. Some of the instructions are brief. Apply what you learned in the previous tutorials to complete the steps.

Download from 3D Warehouse and open model: Campus_Quad

1. Review the base model and note each area designation.

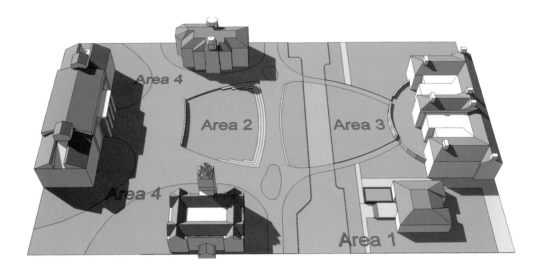

2. Identify Area 1. In this location, you will add a conceptual grade to incorporate the steps and building into the site.

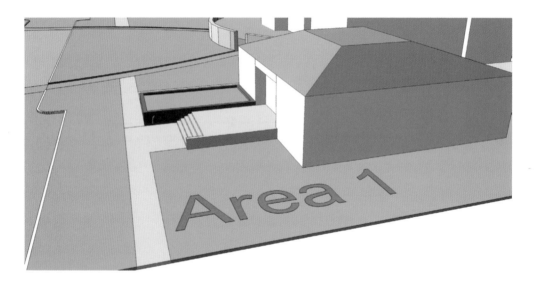

3. Draft a series of edges and arcs, as indicated in the image at the top of page 257.

   a. Approximate some of the edges on the ground plane as closely as possible.

   b. Add edges and arcs along the face of the step wall and the building surface.

   c. Select all the drafted edges as indicated.

   d. Activate the From Contour tool to stitch the faces together.

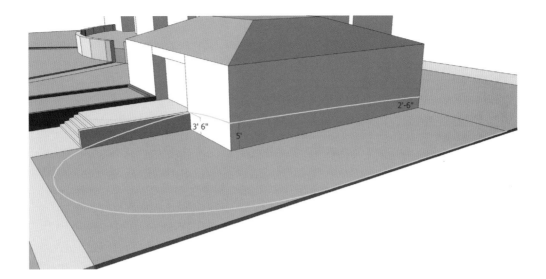

4. Enter the group instance of the generated From Contour faces and hide the outer edge (use the Eraser tool+Shift) as indicated by the arrows. After leaving the group instance, delete the original construction geometry around the outer edge. This will allow the simulated terrain to appear to be part of the landscape.

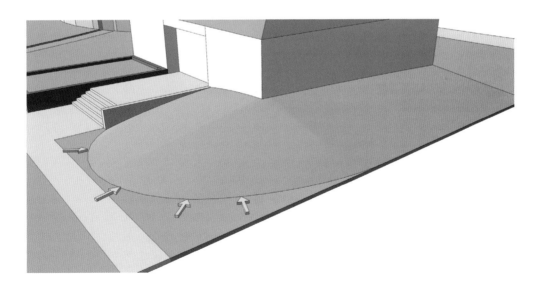

Now that you've finished Area 1 of the Quad, the steps and building are better integrated into the site landscape and aspect.

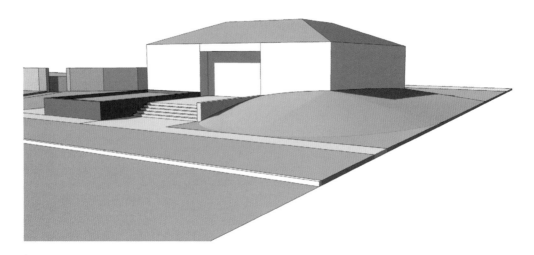

Campus Quad—Area 2

For this tutorial, locate Area 2. Carefully follow the diagrams for the drafting and placement of arcs and edges. You will need to create a wireframe that surrounds three sides of the Green to be able to generate the desired terrain.

1. Identify Area 2 in the example model. Pinpoint the areas described in Area 2 that will be referenced in the tutorial. You are going to add a subtle slope to the steps and landscape area. The idea is to simulate steps that tie into the landscape or the Green.

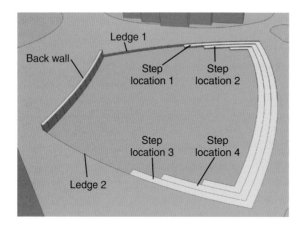

2. Starting with the Back Wall location, copy the top edges of the wall (facing toward the Green) downward, snapping the copied edges to the intersections of Ledges 1 and 2. This is the first set of edges that will be used to generate a simulated terrain.

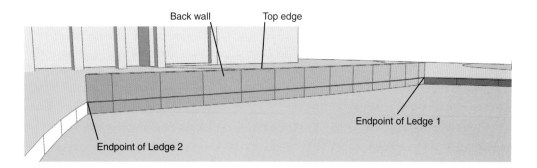

3. Draw an arc from the intersection of the wall and edge at the endpoint of Ledge 1 to the top of Step Location 1. Snap the midpoint of the arc to the vertical faces of Ledge 1. Do not snap the arc bulge to the top of the vertical surfaces but slightly below the lip of Ledge 1. The arc could be partially hidden behind the vertical faces. As long as the arc is selectable, this will not pose any problems when creating the slope.

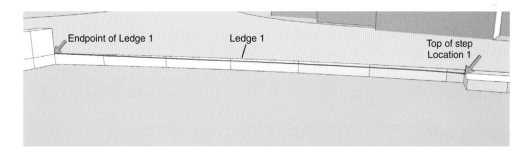

4. Copy the edges of Step Location 1 to the endpoint of Step Location 2. Draw a line from the endpoint of the copied line to the endpoint of the arc generated in the previous step. This is the small diagonal edge on the side of the step shown in the diagram.

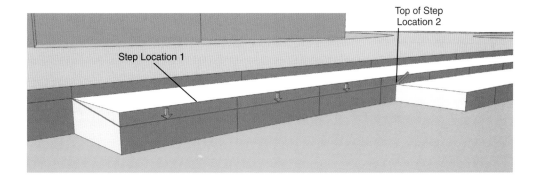

5. Copy the vertical edges of Step Location 2 downward and snap them to the top point of the lowest step. Connect the copied edge to the tops of the adjacent steps by adding diagonal lines at either end. One line should connect diagonally to the top of the step (at the endpoint of the edge copied in the previous step) and another edge should be placed diagonally to connect along the ground. Use the diagram for clarity.

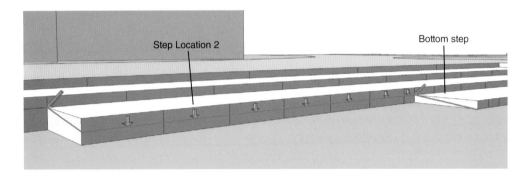

6. Repeat steps 3 through 5 on the opposite side of the Green. Repeat step 3 on the other side of the Green for Ledge 2 location, drafting an arc from the back of the wall to the top of Step Location 3.

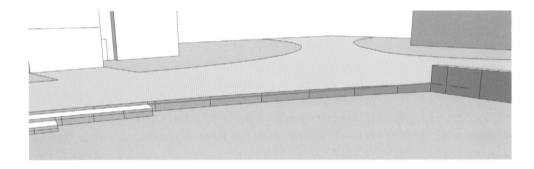

7. Repeat steps 4 and 5 on Step Locations 3 and 4 on the other side of the Green. This will complete the creation of the wireframe.

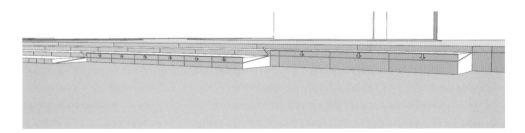

8. Select all the drafted and copied edges in steps 2 through 7. Activate the From Contour tool.

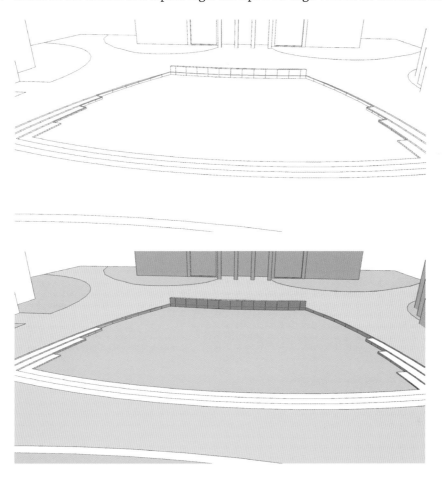

The From Contour tool will stitch the selected edges, generating a simulated slope.

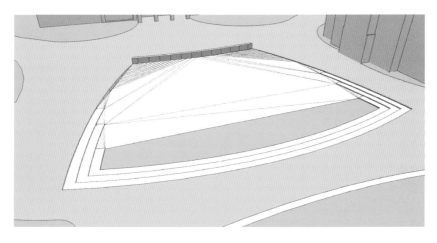

9. Add color to the generated surface. Using Shift+Erase, hide any lines that might distract from the surface.

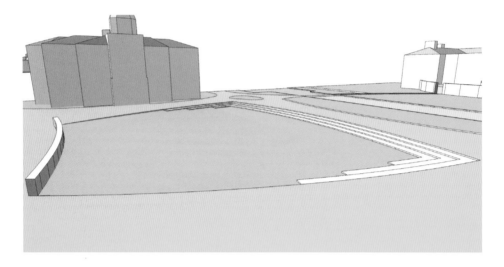

The back wall and steps are integrated into the site model. Although the generated surface created a very subtle grade, the viewer's eye will pick up the subtleties in the surface. The simulated grade depicts a more realistic and accurate representation of the Quad Green.

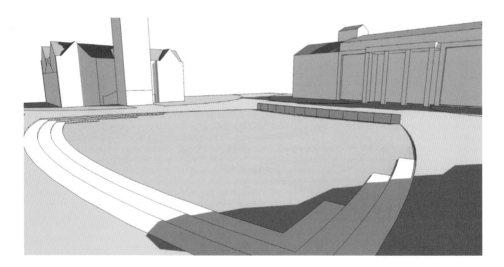

Campus Quad—Area 3

This tutorial uses the same model from Areas 1 and 2 to complete Area 3. Successful completion will require attention to detail and patience. Although the steps are quick, creating the desired surfaces is somewhat complex. The intent is to show how it is possible to create varied, yet connected elevations in multiple locations.

As with the previous tutorial, pay close attention to the diagrams for the locations to place, copy, and draft arcs and edges.

1. Identify Area 3 in the example model. Start with Path 1. Locate the vertical edge, as indicated in the following diagram (the edge is part of the landing to the building).

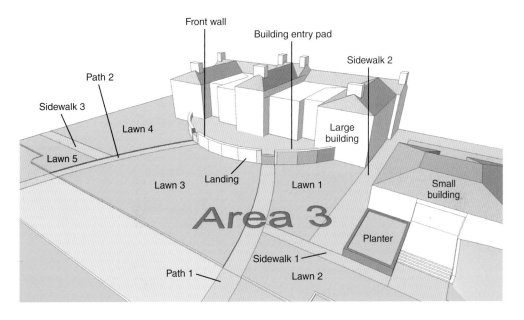

2. Copy and paste the edge at the front of the building entry pad to the indicated locations. These edges will serve as guides to snap the projected arcs. You will use these edges to lay out a series of projected arcs defining the walk in 3D space.

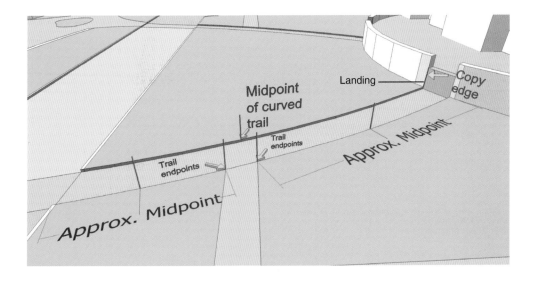

3. Draw an arc as indicated on the inside of Path 1. Snap the arc points to the start and end of the walk as indicated (end of path and end of walk). Snap the arc bulge to the midpoint of the vertical edge created in the previous step.

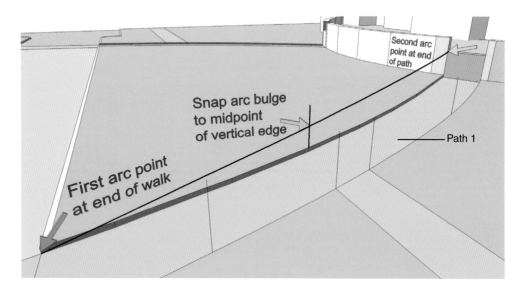

4. Continuing with the path:

   a. Draw an arc from the bottom corner of the walk to the midpoint of the vertical edge as indicated.

   b. Snap the bulge one-third of the way up along the vertical edge, as indicated in the diagram.

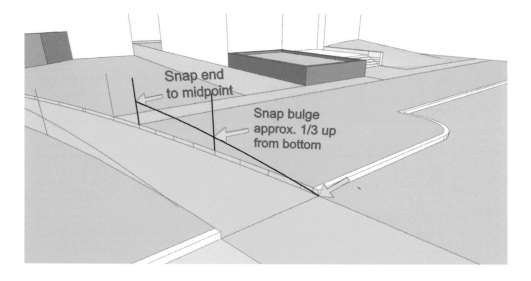

5. At the two vertical edges located where Path 1 intersects Sidewalk 1, draw a single edge from midpoint to midpoint of the vertical edges.

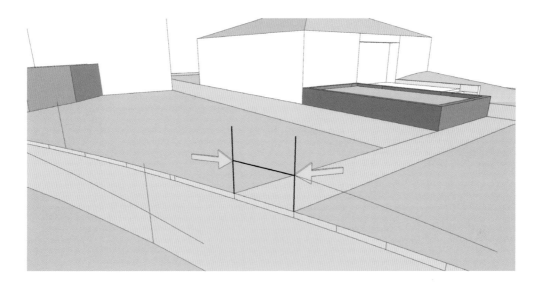

6. Draw a second arc to complete the outer edge of Path 1. Snap the arc points to the endpoint of the edge drawn in step 5. Snap the arc bulge as indicated.

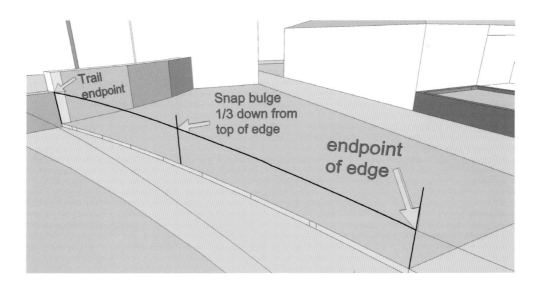

7. Repeat steps 2 through 6 to the Path 2 location. Copy and paste the vertical edge from the front of the Building Landing to the indicated locations. Repeat the steps completed for Path 1. Snap arcs to the appropriate locations to create a series of sloping arcs that lead from the edge of the walk by the road to the building landing.

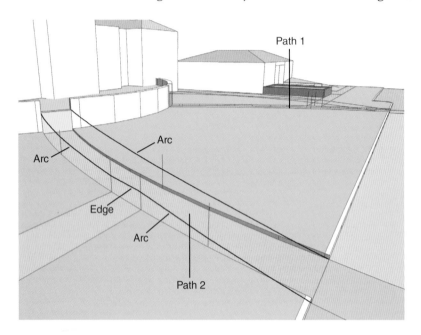

8. Add two sloping edges to the Sidewalk 1 location. Starting from the endpoint of the edge drafted in step 5, draw two edges to the end of the planter and the end of Sidewalk 1, as indicated in the diagram.

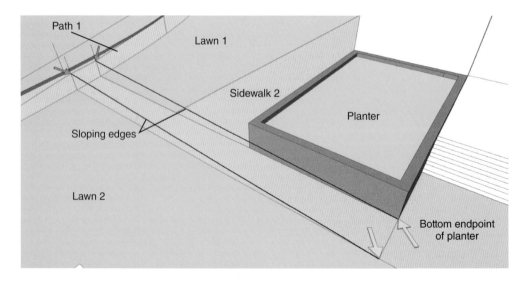

9. Draw two edges to define Sidewalk 2.

    a. Starting with the intersection of the edge and planter drawn in step 8, add an edge that extends to the end of the small building as indicated.

    b. Draw a vertical edge from the front part of Sidewalk 2 to intersect the sloping edge of Sidewalk 1 as drawn in step 8.

    c. From the endpoint of the drawn vertical edge/intersection, add an edge that parallels the edge drawn from the planter to the corner of the large building.

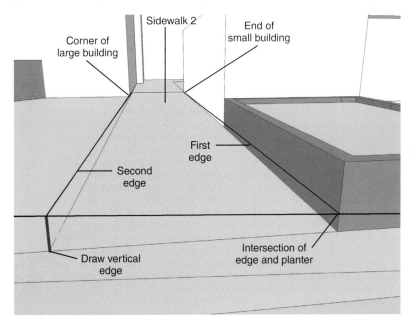

10. Add two sloping edges to define Sidewalk 3. Adding the edges is similar to the process in step 8.

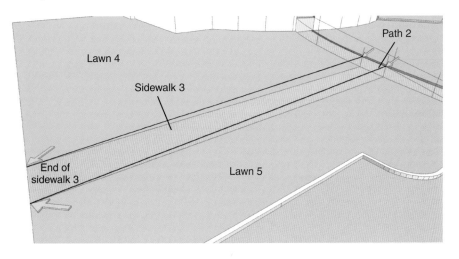

11. Select the edges that compose Path 1 (the arcs and edges drafted in steps 3 through 6). With the edges selected, activate the From Contour tool to stitch the edges to create a sloped path leading to the building entry pad.

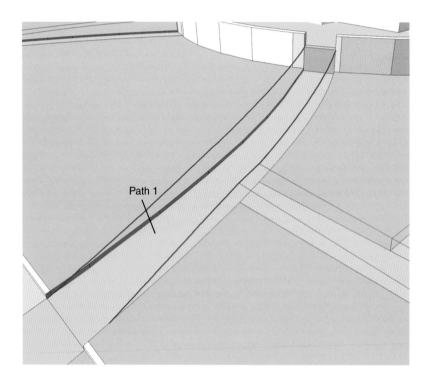

12. Select the sloping edges that define Sidewalk 1 (drafted in step 8). Activate the From Contour tool to stitch the selected edges to form an elevated walk for Sidewalk 1.

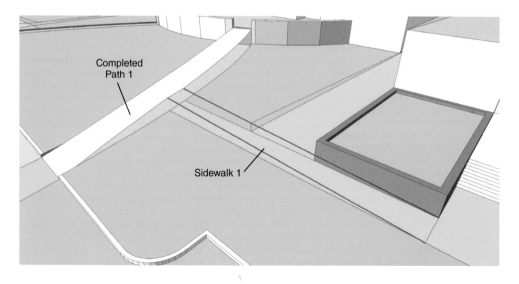

13. Select the edges that define Sidewalk 2 (created in step 9). Activate the From Contour tool to stitch the edges with faces.

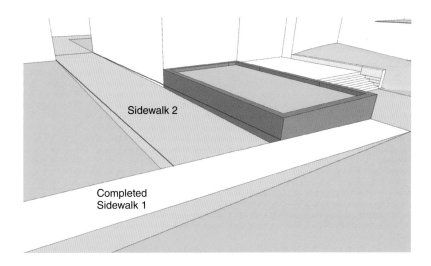

When Hidden Geometry is toggled to visible, the stitched faces for Path 1, Sidewalk 1, and Sidewalk 2 show the completed sloping walks.

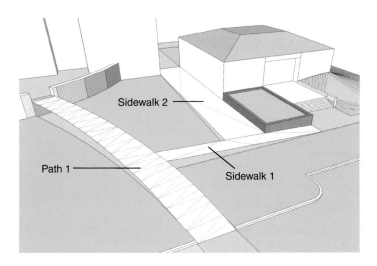

14. Create faces for the remaining paths. Select the arcs and edges for Path 2 and stitch the edges with faces using From Contour. Select the two edges for Sidewalk 3 and generate the faces using From Contour.

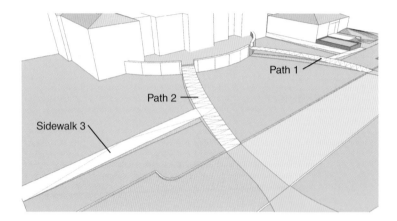

15. Add color to the sloping walks: Path 1, Path 2, Sidewalk 1, Sidewalk 2, and Sidewalk 3.

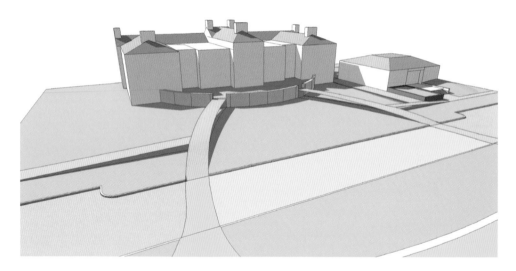

16. At the location for Lawn 1, draw two arcs that will be used to help construct a sloped surface. Draw Arc 1 as indicated. When you snap the bulge of the arc to the wall, make sure it has a slight upward bow.

Connect Arc 2 to the end of Arc 1 to the intersection of the large building and Sidewalk 2.

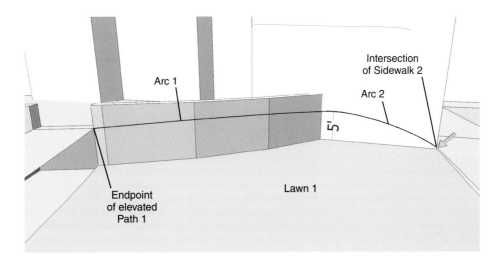

17. Select the edges as indicated by the diagram for the location of Lawn 1. Make sure to select the sloping edges for Path 1 and Sidewalks 1 and 2. Activate the From Contour tool to stitch the drafted faces to create a grade that connects to the wall and the generated walks.

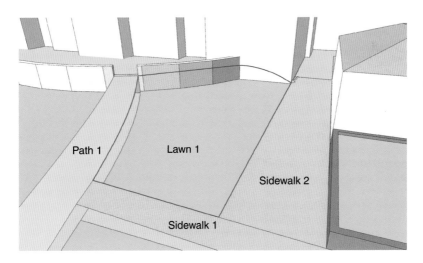

The From Contour tool will stitch faces connecting the paths and the wall. The generated geometry will simulate a gentle sloping grade.

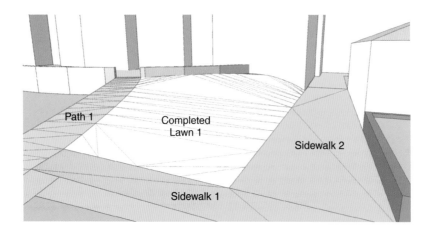

18. Select the edges that outline Lawn 2.
    a. Make sure the selected edges include the drafted construction geometry (sloping lines) used to define Path 1 and Sidewalk 1.
    b. Draw a perpendicular edge, as indicated, to define the end of Lawn 2 area. Include this edge in the selection.

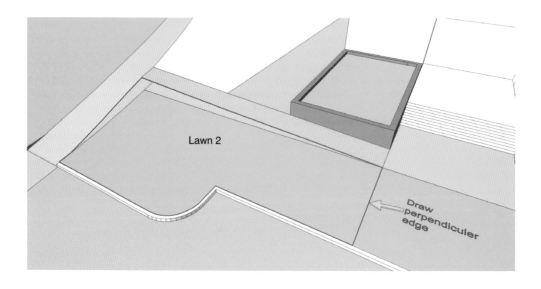

19. With the edges for Lawn 2 selected, activate From Contour to generate a slope. Clean up the artifact faces around the curb and overlapping faces found in the lawn. Enter the group instance for the slope and use the Eraser tool to delete edges, as indicated in the diagram.

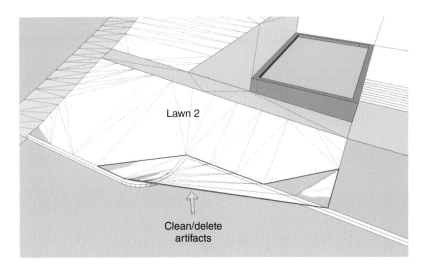

Lawn 2

Clean/delete
artifacts

When Lawn 2 is completed and Hidden Geometry is set to visible, the view starts to look like the final composed scene. Varying walks and slopes lead up to the large building and are integrated into the site plan with conceptual grades.

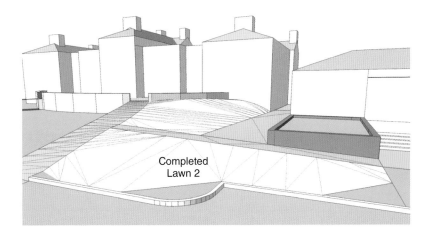

Completed
Lawn 2

20. Draft an arc on the Front Wall. Attach the arc endpoints to the inside endpoints of Path 1 and Path 2. Snap the arc bulge to the center edge of the front wall. Place the bulge 1'-5" below the top of the wall.

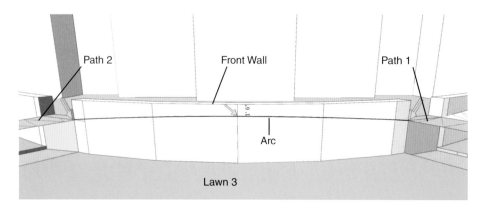

21. Select the edges that outline Lawn 3 (the inner arcs that define Paths 1 and 2, the inside curb edge at the bottom of Lawn 3, and the arc edge drafted in step 20). Once they are selected, activate From Contour to generate a slope to define Lawn 3.

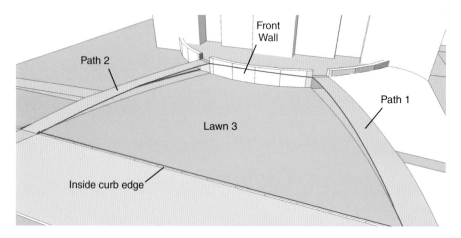

From Contour will define a gentle grade for Lawn 3.

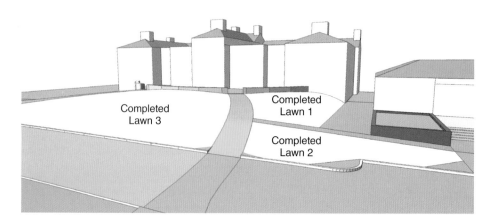

22. To define the location for Lawn 4, draft a series of arcs and edges on the side of the large building. Start with the intersection/endpoint of Path 2 and continue along the walls; use the indicated dimensions to specify the heights of arcs and edges. Connect the last arc (far left) back down to the ground plane.

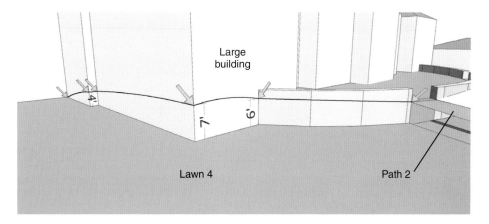

23. Select the edges that outline Lawn 4 and apply the From Contour tool to generate a slope. Select the edges that outline Lawn 5 and apply From Contour to that location.

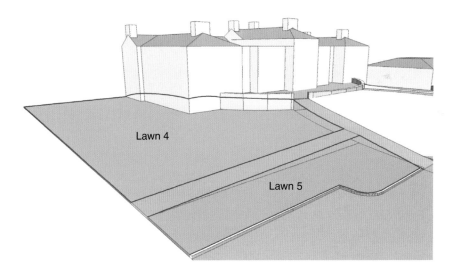

The following graphic shows the completed paths, walks, and lawns for the large building as viewed from across the street. The gentle slopes lead up to the building pad and help establish the building as a prominent feature. The gentle terrain leads the viewer's eye and helps define a specific concept to the grades and terrain of the site.

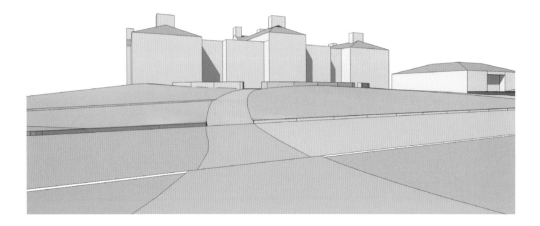

The following graphic shows the view from Area 2 to Area 1 and Area 3. The conceptual grades used to define all three areas create a subtle interplay of elevation visible across the site.

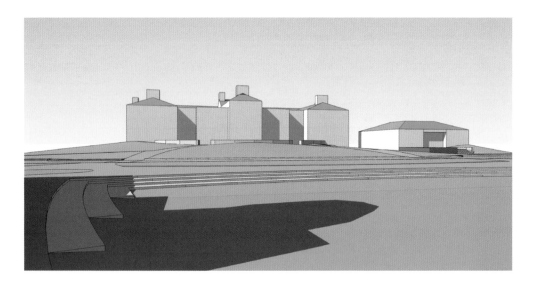

Campus Quad—Area 4

Use the same model from Areas 1, 2, and 3 to complete Area 4. This exercise will use the From Scratch, Drape, and Smoove tools to create subtle grades around the three buildings.

1. Identify the four locations that make up Area 4.

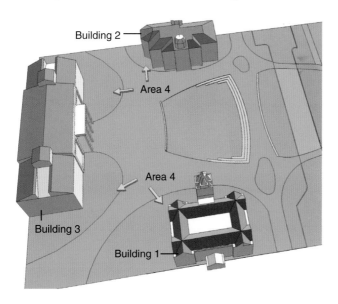

2. Select the surface areas of Lawns 1, 2, 3, and 4. With all four areas selected, right-click and select Make Group.

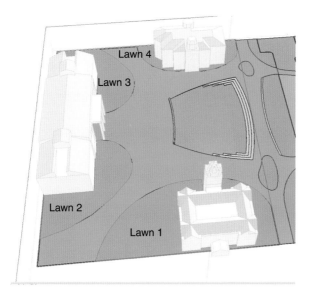

3. Copy the group you created in step 2 and place it directly adjacent to the base model. Make sure to leave enough room between the copied lawns and the original model to complete the next steps.

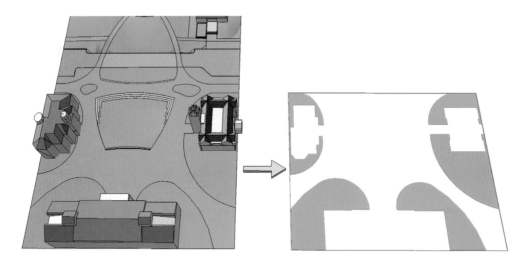

4. Adjacent to the copied lawn locations, use the From Scratch tool to create a grid that is 270′ in width and 395′ in length. The grid must be composed of 6′ × 6′ squares.

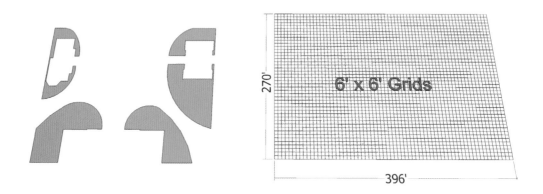

5. Place the Lawn group directly above the grid created in step 4. Ensure that the lawn grouping does not stretch nor is located beyond the bounds of the From Scratch grid.

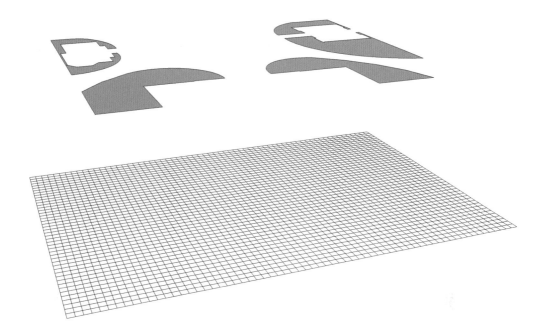

6. Select the From Scratch gird, right-click, and use Soften Smooth Edges to hide the grid lines.

7. Select the Lawn group and, using the Drape command, drape the Lawn group onto the grid below.

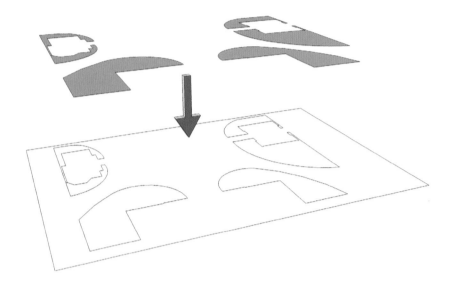

8. Enter the From Scratch grid instance and delete the extra faces and edges, leaving behind the identical form of the Lawn group. Add color to the grid cutout to represent the lawn areas. Once completed, toggle Hidden Geometry to visible. The grid faces will now be visible and ready to have Smoove applied to them. You can delete the original Lawn group located above that was used to drape onto the grid.

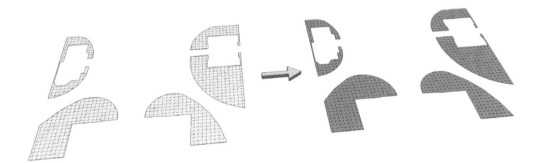

9. Place the From Scratch grid cutout back into the site plan: Select a common endpoint on the group and move it back to the common endpoint of the Campus_Quad model.

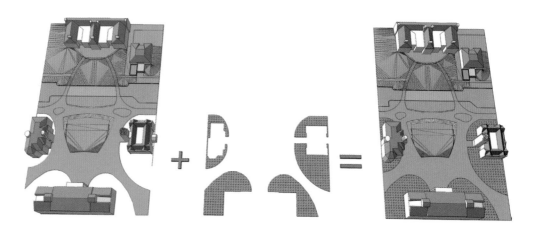

10. Starting with Building 1 (building labels shown in step 1), enter the From Scratch grid lawn instance and use the Smoove tool to gently lift the faces to simulate a sloping grade against the building. Do not exaggerate the terrain, but sculpt the simulated landform to create terrain that complements the building and site plan. You can snap the Smoove tool to the vertical faces of the building or add values into the Measurement window to generate a precise height to the landform.

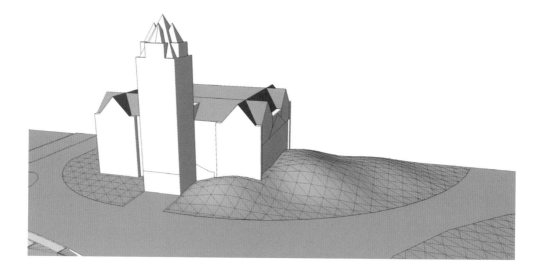

11. Repeat step 10 on Buildings 2 and 3.

Use the Smoove tool on Building 2. Create a very subtle and minimal slope with the grid.

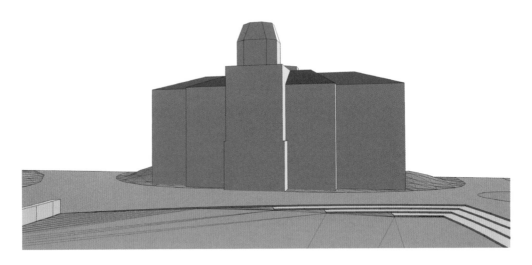

12. Use the Smoove tool around Building 3. As with Buildings 1 and 2, create a subtle slope with the Smoove tool.

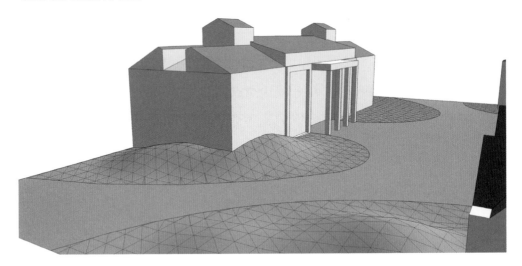

The following graphic shows the view of the Campus Quad once the grade has been Smooved around the three buildings. Hidden Geometry is toggled to visible.

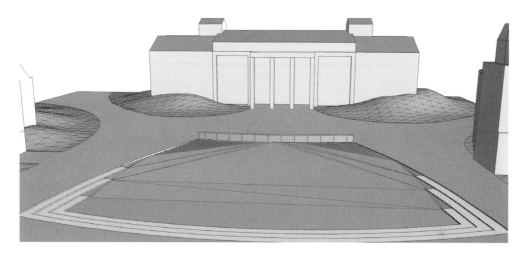

The following figure shows the view of the Quad with Hidden Geometry toggled to off. The site plan now incorporates subtle grades within the plaza areas.

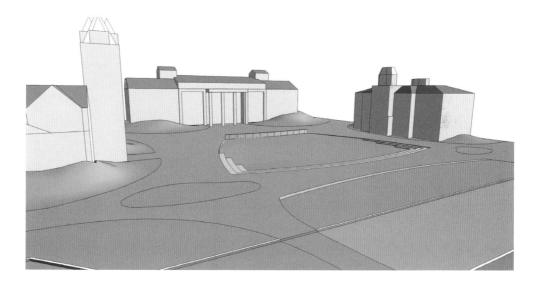

13. Add trees, people, bollards, benches, and other site amenities to the site plan. The buildings in these final images are clad with Material ➤ Stone ➤ Stone_Flagstone_Ashlar. The Window components were added from the SketchUp Architectural Bonus pack found at www.sketchup.com.

In this graphic, you can see the view looking out across the Quad and across the street.

In this graphic, you can see the view looking at the large building. This view includes vegetation, site amenities, and people. These site components help emphasize the conceptual terrain added to the site plan.

This is the view from the large building's entry pad, out across the site.

CHAPTER 14

Complex Canopies

The From Contour tool can be utilized to generate fluid, organic, and complex geometry. In combination with SketchUp's drawing and modification tools, this Sandbox tool can create whatever shapes you can imagine.

The tutorials in this chapter demonstrate the steps needed to create complex geometry. By starting with a 2D plan, drafting construction geometry, and then stitching edges and faces using the From Contour tool, you will learn the best approach to modeling a canopy and tensile structure.

2D Plan to 3D Form

As with the many other tutorials found in this book, drafting a 2D silhouette of an object, building, or site plan yields a three-dimensional object model. Modeling complex canopies entails drafting construction geometry using a 2D surface as a reference.

As with conceptual 3D grading, the complex forms are dependent on the creation of construction geometry to define a shape and form, which is then stitched together with From Contour to provide "skin" or faces.

As you work through the tutorials in this chapter, utilize the following general guidelines to create a wireframe for a 3D object.

▶ Make a top-down plan outline. Imagine and then draft what the object would look like from plan view. Use the 2D plan as a reference to place the construction geometry.

▶ The reference edges are used as follows:

▶ Vertical edges will be added to various points on the outline. They allow you to place arcs and edges at specified heights.

- ▶ The height of all the vertical edges should be equal to the tallest point the object will have when completed.
- ▶ Vertical edges will be added to the endpoints of all 2D plan endpoints and some midpoints.
- ▶ Add a vertical edge to the endpoints and midpoints of all 2D arcs on the plans. Two-dimensional arcs with vertical edges will be used to create projected arcs upward in 3D space.
- ▶ The vertical edge placed at the midpoint of the 2D arcs helps you determine the bulge (third point) of an arc in space.
- ▶ Arcs are the primary edges used to define organic, complex, and curved faces.
- ▶ When assessing the wireframe, do not hesitate to add additional edges that will help define the form. The more specific and detailed the wireframe, the more accurate the final model will be.
- ▶ Once the form is generated with From Contour, delete the 2D plan and vertical reference edges. Clean up any artifact faces generated by From Contours.

The tutorials outline two very specific structures that can be created using construction geometry. However, you can utilize the general methods outlined here and experiment to create your own forms, objects, and structures.

Simple Canopy Tutorial

In this tutorial, you will make a simple canopy.

Download Model: Simple_Canopy

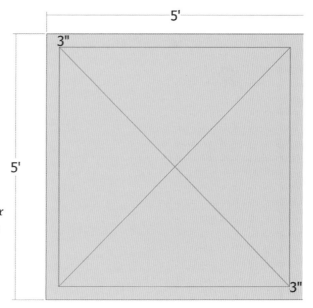

1. Draft a 5′ × 5′ rectangle. Offset the rectangle face 3″ inward. Then draw two diagonal edges from corner to corner of the offset face, as indicated by the diagram. This forms the 2D base that will be used to generate a 3D canopy.

2. Draft four arcs between the outer edges and the edges offset in the previous step. The arcs should be snapped from endpoint to endpoint of the square's outer edges. Snap the bulge of the arc to the midpoint of the interior edge that was offset in the previous step.

3. Delete the outside edges of the rectangle. The arcs should have subdivided the 3"-wide face. Deleting the edges will leave faces defined by the outer lines of the arcs. You can begin to see the basic form of the canopy.

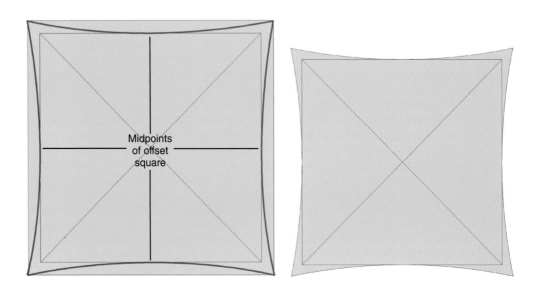

4. At the center of the surface (the point of intersection of the diagonal lines), draft a 1' vertical edge. This edge will define the highest point of the canopy.

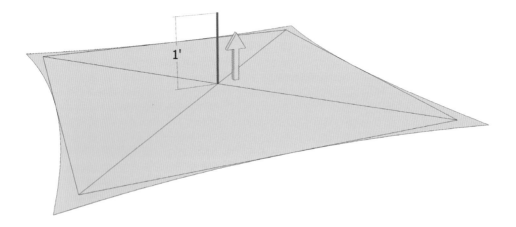

5. At the midpoint of two adjacent outer-edge arcs, draft a 3″-high vertical line. Only add the edges to these two arcs.

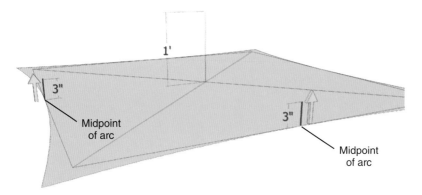

6. Draw two arcs. Start from opposite corners and snap the bulge of the arc to the top endpoint of the 1′ vertical edge drafted in step 4. Once these arcs are snapped to the top of the 1′ edge, the arc lines will be subdivided in half.

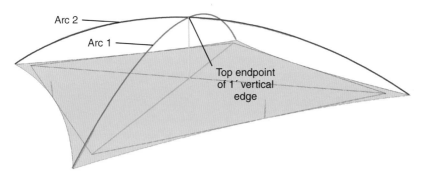

7. Add another arc, snapping to opposite corner endpoints. Snap the arc bulge to the top of the 3″ edge drafted in step 5.

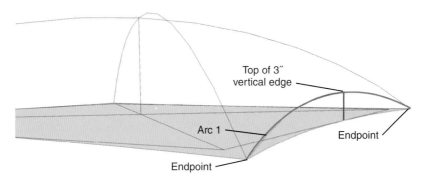

8. Select the edges as indicated in the diagram. Select the arc drawn in step 7. Next, select the two half arcs created in step 6. The two arcs should be the ones connected/adjacent to the arc from step 7. Activate the From Contour tool to stitch the edges with faces.

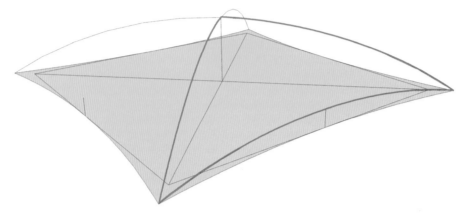

9. A series of faces creating an organic shape or canopy will be generated. Enter the group instance generated by From Contour and, with the hidden geometry visible, delete all the artifact faces below the arc from step 7.

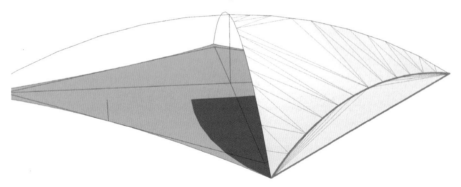

10. Apply a color to the canopy surface group.

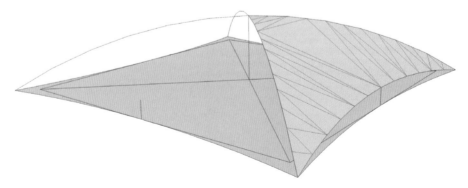

11. Use the Rotate tool and copy the Canopy group at 45 degrees:

    a. Select the Canopy group.

    b. Next, activate the Rotate tool. Snap the first rotate point to the bottom endpoint of the 1′ vertical edge.

    c. Snap the second rotate point to the bottom endpoint of the 3″ vertical Edge 1 connected to the Canopy group.

    d. Holding the Ctrl key, select the third rotate point. Snap the third point to the bottom endpoint of the adjacent 3″ vertical Edge 2.

    This will create a copy of the Canopy group at 45 degrees.

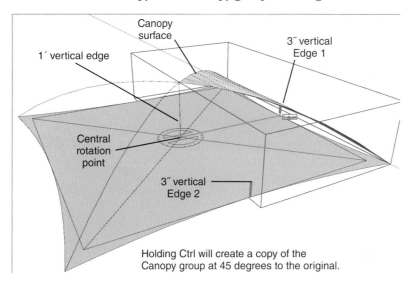

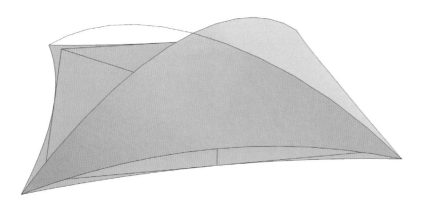

12. Immediately enter **3x** into the Measurement window. This will create two additional copies of the Canopy group rotated around the center axis at 45 degrees.

Select all four canopy surface groups and make them into a single component. Name the component **Small Canopy**. Delete the 2D base and vertical edges.

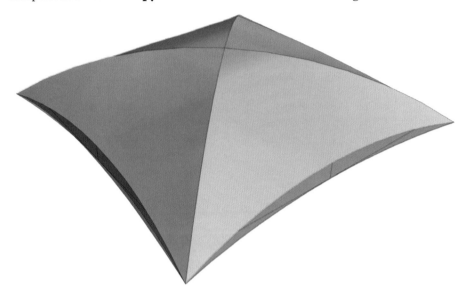

13. Elevate the Canopy component 8′. Directly below, draft a small circle with a 2″ radius. Push/Pull the face of the circle 8′ in height. Select the cylinder and make it a component called Tube. Select both the Small Canopy and the Tube and make them into a component called Sun Shade. Attempt to rotate each component within the Sun Shade to have a slight tilt as shown in the graphic.

Complex Canopy Tutorial

In this tutorial, you will make a more complex canopy. To perform this tutorial, please download the indicated model.

Download Model: Complex_Canopy

1. Review the 2D face base plan that will be used to construct the canopy. Note the five arc edges that compose the outline for the canopy.

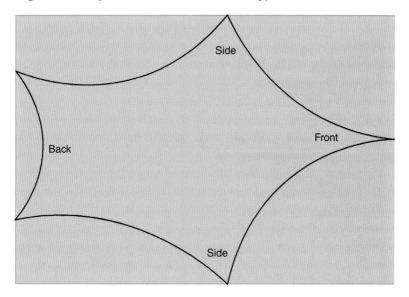

2. Push/Pull the central surface upward 35'. Toggle Hidden Geometry to Visible (View ➤ Hidden Geometry). The vertical dashed edges will be used for reference when you add and connect the arcs.

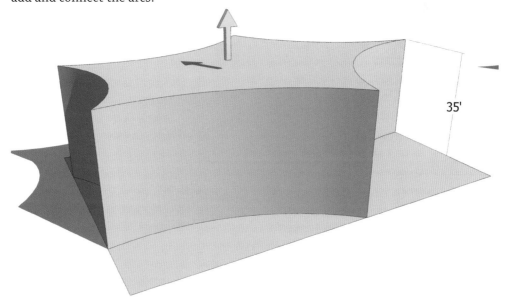

3. Select the Push/Pulled faces, right-click, and select Make Group. Make sure the 2D base from step 1 (the original download for the model) is not included in the base and remains its own separate geometry.

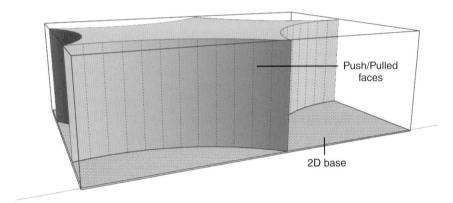

4. Starting with one side of the group, draft two arcs as indicated in the diagram.

   a. Draw one arc from the top endpoint at the front of the group to the bottom side endpoint. Snap the bulge to the face of the group so it dissects that side approximately in half.

   b. Draw a second arc, starting at the back side (where there are two endpoints to the object). The first arc point, at the back, should be 25′ upward along the back vertical edge.

   c. Snap the second point to the bottom side endpoint and the bulge to the group face, dissecting it approximately in half.

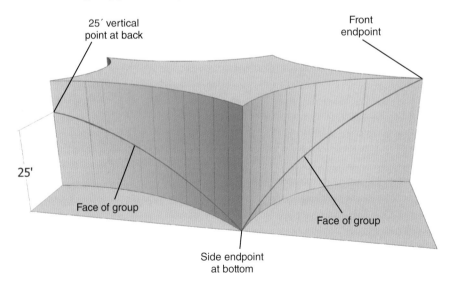

5. Repeat step 4 to the other side of the 35'-high group, drafting two arcs in the identical fashion to the same points and heights indicated in step 4. The arcs drawn in steps 4 and 5 start to define the frame and shape of the canopy.

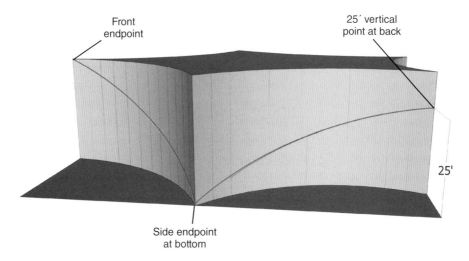

Front endpoint

25' vertical point at back

25'

Side endpoint at bottom

6. At the back end of the object, draft an arc that snaps to the endpoints of the arcs that have endpoints located 25' upward along the group face. Snap the bulge of the arc 30' upward along the back face. The bulge should be located 5' above the endpoints of the arc.

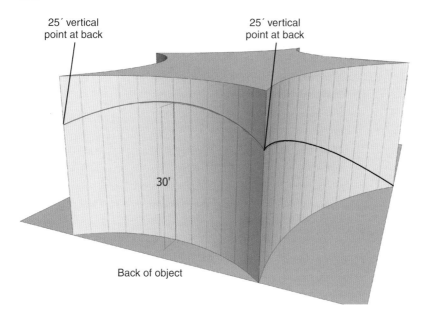

25' vertical point at back

25' vertical point at back

30'

Back of object

7. Delete the group created in step 3. Make sure the arcs drafted in steps 4, 5, and 6 and the original base are not deleted. The remaining edges form the construction geometry (wireframe) that will be used to generate the canopy.

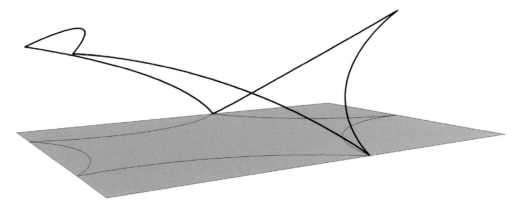

8. The wireframe for the canopy needs a "spine" to help support the canopy shape. Draft a horizontal edge from the midpoint of the back arc of the 2D surface to the endpoint at the front of the 2D surface. At the midpoint of the drafted line, draft a 24′ vertical edge.

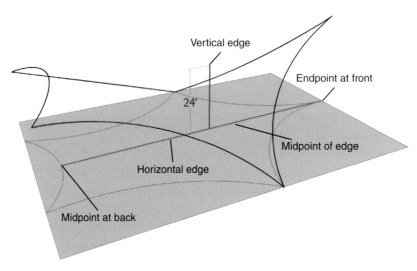

9. Add an arc to establish the spine of the canopy. Snap the first point of the arc to the midpoint of the arc drafted in step 6 that runs along the back. Snap the second point to the top endpoint at the front of the canopy frame. Snap the bulge to the top of the 24′ vertical edge added in step 8.

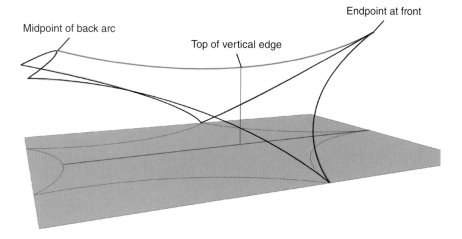

Midpoint of back arc

Top of vertical edge

Endpoint at front

10. Delete the 2D base and the vertical edge drawn in step 8. Select the wireframe construction geometry for the canopy as shown in the diagram and activate the From Contour tool to stitch the edges with faces.

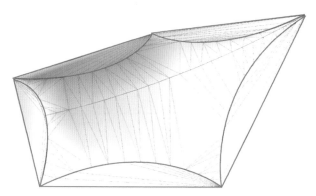

11. Delete the artifact geometry of the canopy, as shown in the diagram.

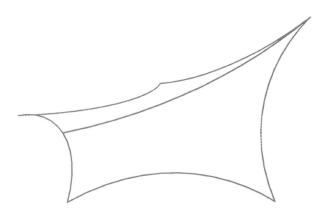

12. Add color to the canopy faces and toggle the hidden geometry to off.

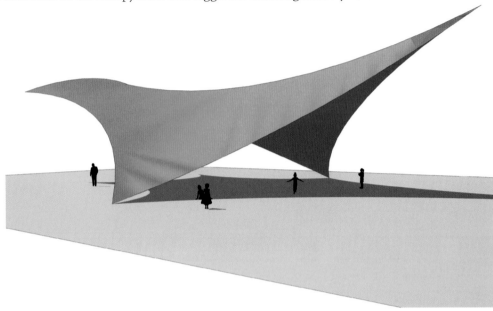

When viewed in context, the finished canopy serves as a playground shelter and a landmark for the park.

CHAPTER 15

Digital Elevation Modeling

Digital Elevation Modeling (DEM) refers to modeling a site plan and related amenities onto a 3D terrain surface. This chapter provides an overview of the entire process. The reviewed process can be applied to any size of terrain and site model, from residential lots to large-scale plans.

Skill Level

The following tutorial is an intermediate to advanced exercise. It requires a basic working knowledge of SketchUp. Make sure you have worked through and understand the previous parts of the book before trying to tackle the tutorial.

DanielTal.com has a complete, detailed, walk-through video tutorial for members. It reviews the process outlined in this chapter and includes supplemental materials showing alternative ways to sculpt and grade digital elevation models.

Terrain Extensions

Some of the terrain extensions outlined in previous chapters are used as part of the process. These include Tools on Surface, Artisan, and JointPushPull.

TopoShaper is an additional extension that you'll need to use. It can help generate a grid or mesh terrain, and it is available through the SketchUcation Plugin Store.

Dataset

The typical approach to generating a DEM starts with a CAD file that includes at minimum contour or point data with Z elevations or values. The chapter tutorial demonstrates the basic dataset and includes contours, a road, a house, walls, steps, and vegetation. The original CAD file used for the tutorial is organized around the principles reviewed in Part 4.

3D Terrain Types

Two general types of terrain can be created in SketchUp and other 3D modeling programs: a Triangulated Irregular Network (TIN) and *mesh,* a terrain surface composed of grids (Fig. 15-1, Fig. 15-2).

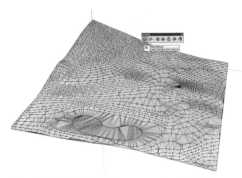

Fig. 15-1: With the hidden geometry visible, the triangulated edges and faces form a TIN.

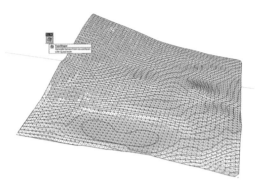

Fig. 15-2: The small, square surfaces seen on the terrain form a mesh.

The From Contour tool on the Sandbox menu is used to create TINs. These surfaces tend to be more accurate because From Contour creates faces connecting all the various edges. However, the more detailed or complex the terrain, the less accurately the From Contour tool functions. In addition, the Smoove tool and its improved extension, Artisan Sculpt Brush (see Chapter 12), function poorly on TINs and are more suited for meshes.

The From Contour tool works best when it is used in tandem with the Simplify Contours extension, which is found on the Extension Warehouse. When using imported CAD contour lines, use Simplify Contours first. This will make it considerably faster for From Contours to generate a terrain. From Contour is used extensively in the tutorial to create new, proposed grades merged into the mesh.

Meshes are the desired terrain surface. They are easier to sculpt and adjust than TINs. For most projects, start by creating a mesh terrain using the TopoShaper extension, which is used in this tutorial.

DEM Tutorial

The following tutorial demonstrates how to create a residential site plan modeled on a generated mesh terrain.

Importing the CAD File

The first thing you'll need to do is import the CAD file of the site plan (Fig. 15-3). Now just follow these steps:

1. You'll need to move all the linework, except the contours, directly above the terrain. Ensure that you maintain the alignment of these edges relative to the terrain (Fig. 15-4).

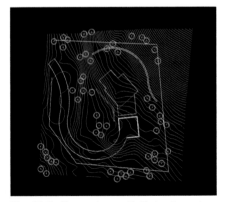

Fig. 15-3: The contours with Z elevation values

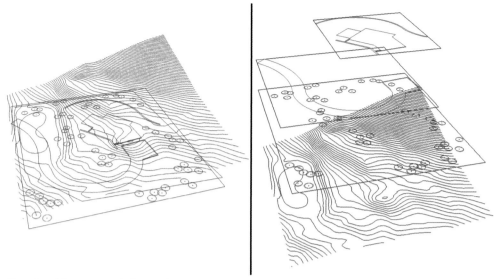

Fig. 15-4: The imported CAD file in SketchUp (left); the edges aligned relative to the terrain (right)

2. Turn off all the linework except the terrain (Fig. 15-5). This will make it easier to work. You can turn the linework back on when you need to work on the lines specifically. (To learn about organizing CAD files prior to importing them into SketchUp, see Part 4.)

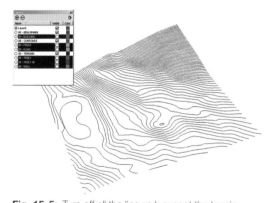

Fig. 15-5: Turn off all the linework except the terrain.

Generating Terrain with TopoShaper

Now it's time to generate the terrain by following these steps:

1. Select all the contour lines and activate TopoShaper (Fig. 15-6). TopoShaper has many options.

   This tutorial focuses on the quickest path to create a mesh. Feel free to experiment with some of the other functions.

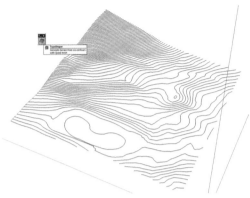

Fig. 15-6: Selecting the contour lines and activating TopoShaper

2. From the first TopoShaper screen, select Calculate Terrain at top (Fig. 15-7).

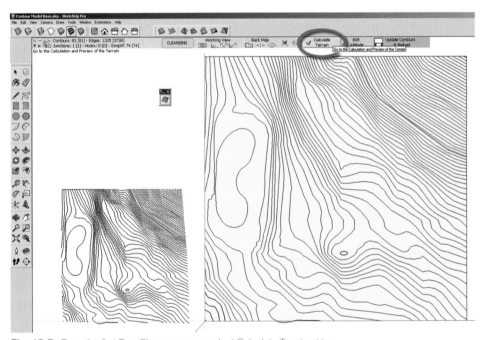

Fig. 15-7: From the first TopoShaper screen, select Calculate Terrain at top.

3. On the second screen, adjust the grid spacing to generate a tighter or larger mesh. Select the Grid option if you want to adjust the size. Once you are done, select Generate Terrain (Fig. 15-8).

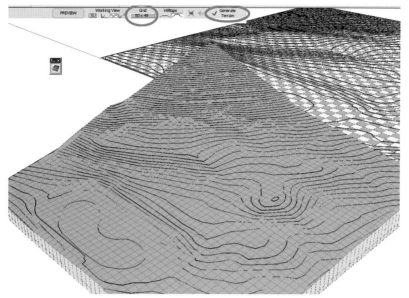

Fig. 15-8: Adjust the grid spacing to generate a tighter or larger mesh.

4.   Select the Exit Tool button at the top right. The mesh is completed (Fig. 15-9).

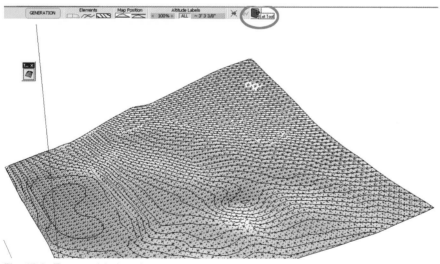

Fig. 15-9: The completed mesh

Draping the Road

Now use the Drape tool on the terrain.

1.   Turn on the Road layer. Select the Road group, and then select the Drape option in the Sandbox tools (Fig. 15-10).

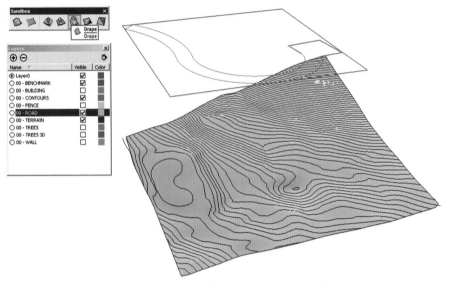

Fig. 15-10: Turn on the Road layer. Select the Road group and then the Drape option in the Sandbox tools.

2. Now that the road linework is draped onto the terrain, the next step is to select the surface and apply a color. If the faces do not subdivide correctly, use Tools on Surface's Line on Surface tool to try to correctly subdivide the face (Fig. 15-11).

    To help you better understand how to subdivide stubborn surfaces, follow the steps outlined in Chapter 18, under the "Healing with the Line Tool" section.

3. Add color to the road surface (Fig. 15-12).

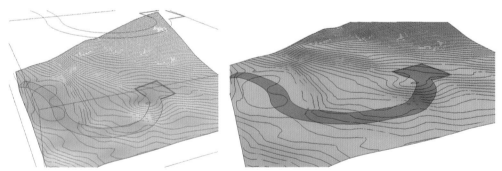

Fig. 15-11: Drape the Road linework onto the terrain.

Fig. 15-12: Add color to the road surface.

4. The terrain does not appear even enough to accommodate the road. Using the Artisan extension Sculpt Brush tool, flatten and equalize the grades on and around the road (Fig. 15-13) to complete the road (Fig. 15-14).

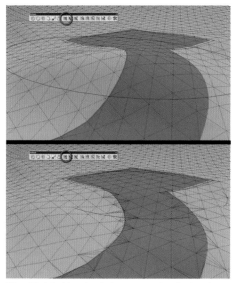

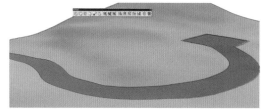

Fig. 15-13: Use the Artisan extension Sculpt Brush tool on and around the road.

Fig. 15-14: The completed road

As an alternative method to using the Drape tool, you can use the Instant Road extension by Vali Architecture.

Modeling the Home

Now model the home using these steps:

1. Turn on the Wall and Building layers. They will be modeled next (Fig. 15-15).
2. Create faces for the wall, steps, and building plans (Fig. 15-16).

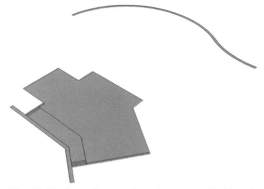

Fig. 15-15: Turn on the Wall and Building layers.

Fig. 15-16: Create faces for the wall, steps, and building plans.

3. Using the basic dimensions given in the diagram, extrude the house, steps, and walls with Push/Pull (Fig. 15-17).

    The InstantRoofNui extension by Chuck Vali was used to create the roof.

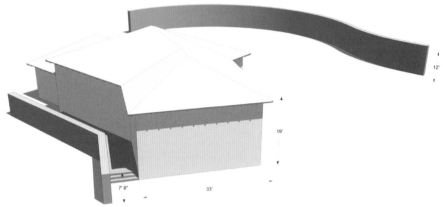

Fig. 15-17: Extrude the house, steps and walls with Push/Pull.

4. Add windows, doors, and textures to the models (Fig. 15-18).

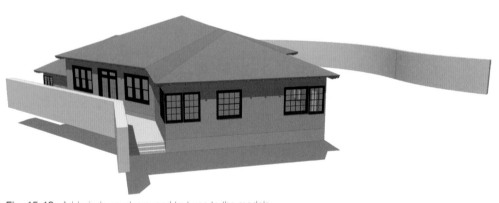

Fig. 15-18: Add windows, doors, and textures to the models.

Positioning the Home and Walls

Now it's time to position the home and walls in the grade.

1. Turn on the terrain again. The home and walls should be located above the terrain (Fig. 15-19).

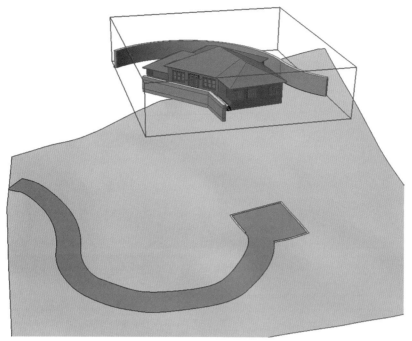

Fig. 15-19: Turn on the terrain again.

2. Use DropGC and the Move tool to place the home and walls into the terrain. Position them as well as you can based on the desired elevations (Fig. 15-20).

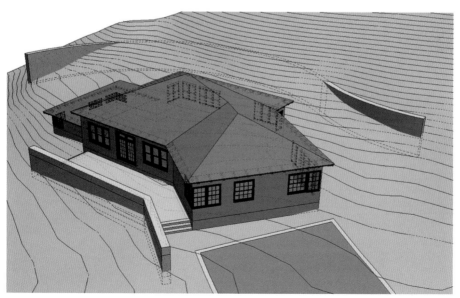

Fig. 15-20: Use DropGC and the Move tool to place the home and walls into the terrain.

3. Use the Tools on Surface Line tool to draw a line representing the grading extent. You should be able to select the area once it's complete (Fig. 15-21).

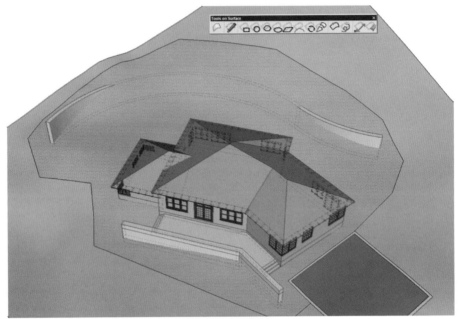

Fig. 15-21: Use Tools on Surface's Line tool to draw a line representing the grading extent.

4. Delete the surface that was subdivided by Tools on Surface (Fig. 15-22).

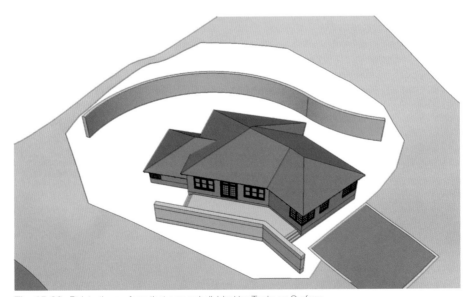

Fig. 15-22: Delete the surface that was subdivided by Tools on Surface.

Generating the Proposed Grades

When you draw the proposed grading profiles, do it one section at a time. The process is similar to the one described in Chapter 13.

1. Draw profile lines on the back of walls, the home, and the steps. The first proposed grade will be grading the back wall to the adjacent terrain (Fig. 15-23).

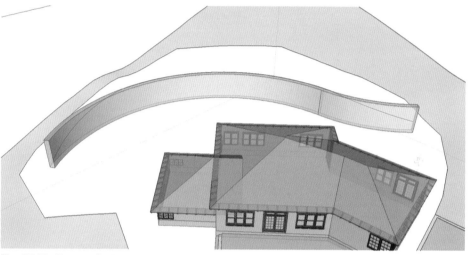

Fig. 15-23: Draw profile lines on the back of walls, the home, and the steps.

2. From Contours generates the proposed grade. Edit the proposed surface, deleting the extra faces (Fig. 15-24).

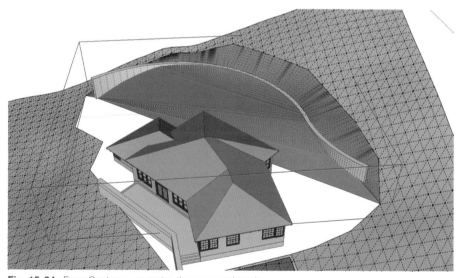

Fig. 15-24: From Contours generates the proposed grade.

3. The edited terrain now cleanly connects the back wall to the terrain (Fig. 15-25).

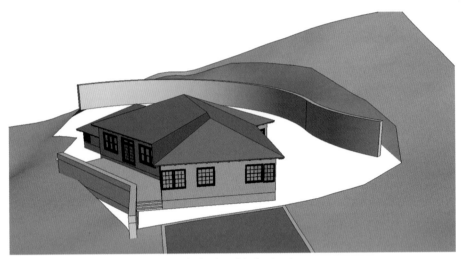

Fig. 15-25: The edited terrain connects the back wall to the terrain.

4. Draw the next profile and select the edges to generate the proposed grade (Fig. 15-26).

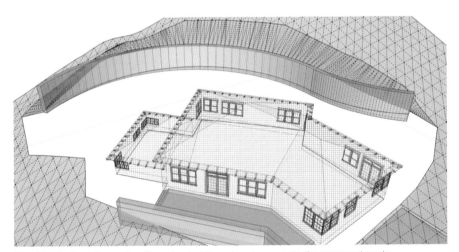

Fig. 15-26: Draw the next profile and select the edges to generate the proposed grade.

5. The next section is graded using From Contours (Fig. 15-27).

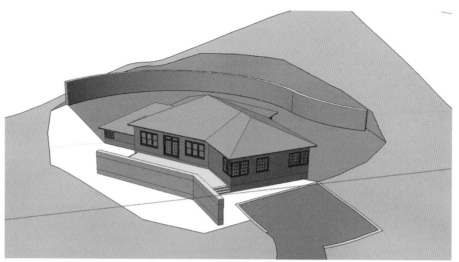

Fig. 15-27: The next section is graded using From Contours.

6. Select the last profile around the drive, front wall, and steps (Fig. 15-28).

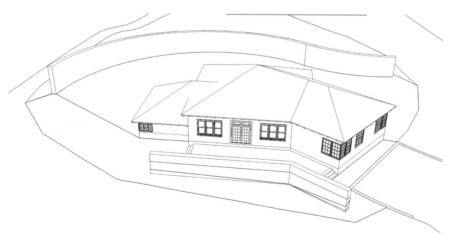

Fig. 15-28: The last profile around the drive, front wall, and steps is selected.

7. Add the proposed grades using From Contours (Fig. 15-29).

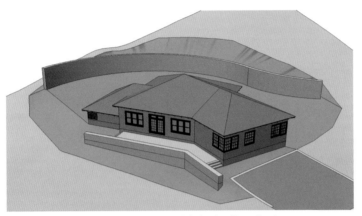

Fig. 15-29: The proposed grades are added using From Contours.

8. Texture the proposed grades to match (Fig. 15-30).

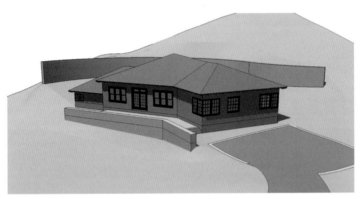

Fig. 15-30: The proposed grades are textured to match.

9. Using the Contours extension, which you can find on SketchUcation, generate new proposed contour lines (Fig. 15-31).

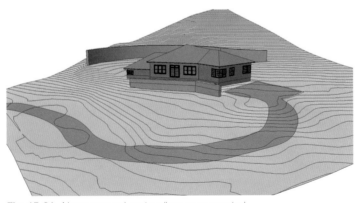

Fig. 15-31: New proposed contour lines are generated.

Depressing the Road

Use Tools on Surface's Offset tool to create a curb (Fig. 15-32), and use JointPushPull to depress the road (Fig. 15-33).

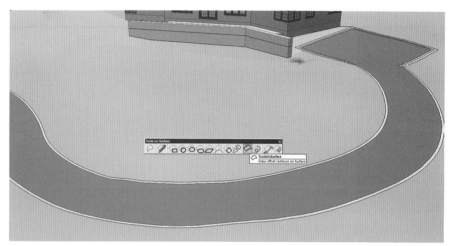

Fig. 15-32: Using Tools on Surface's Offset tool, select the road and offset a 6″ curb.

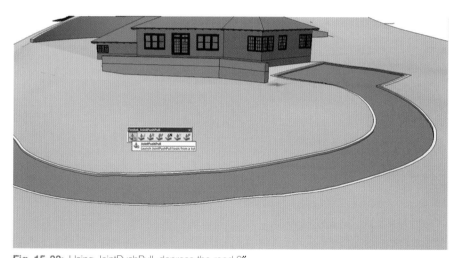

Fig. 15-33: Using JointPushPull, depress the road 6″.

Completing the Model

Add some trees to complete the model and give it a more realistic feel.

1. Turn on and select the CAD Tree blocks (Fig. 15-34).

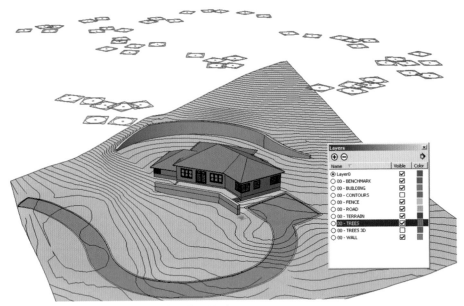

Fig. 15-34: Turn on and select the CAD Tree blocks.

2. Right-click one of the selected blocks and select DropGC. This will drop the Tree blocks directly downward onto the terrain (Fig. 15-35).

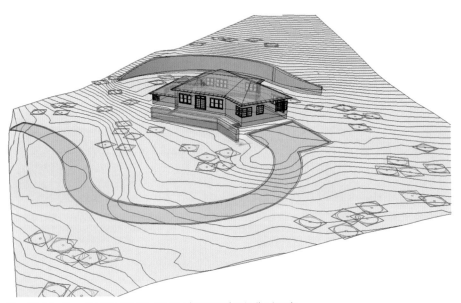

Fig. 15-35: Drop the Tree blocks directly downward onto the terrain.

3. Using the block-to-component replacement method outlined in Chapter 19, replace the 2D blocks with 3D trees. Use CLF Rotate and Scale Multiple on the vegetation. Turn on the shadows and export the scene (Fig. 15-36).

Fig. 15-36: Replace the 2D blocks with 3D trees. Use CLF Rotate and Scale Multiple on the vegetation. Turn on the shadows and export the scene.

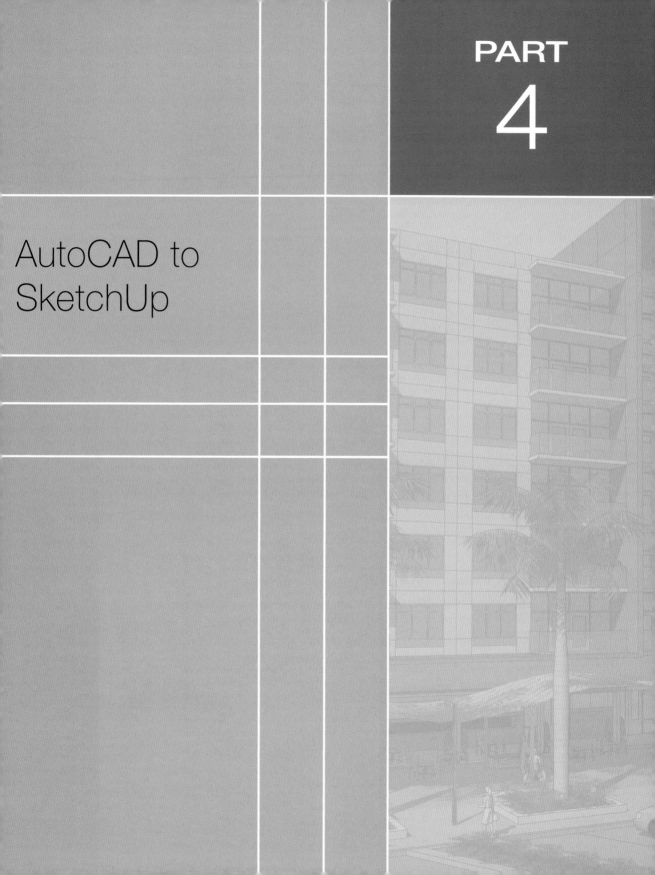

AutoCAD to SketchUp

Overview of AutoCAD to SketchUp

SketchUp and AutoCAD can be used synergistically to generate detailed site models. The programs are highly compatible; AutoCAD lines can be transformed into SketchUp geometry. Utilizing 2D AutoCAD plans as a starting point for SketchUp geometry is arguably the fastest way to generate a detailed site plan model.

This chapter provides a quick overview of the general method for integrating SketchUp and AutoCAD platforms while using SketchUp Process Modeling. This chapter reviews

- ▶ How to organize and then import an AutoCAD file into SketchUp
- ▶ How to transform an imported AutoCAD file into SketchUp geometry
- ▶ The limitations when working with AutoCAD and SketchUp
- ▶ The importance of using extensions to help convert AutoCAD drawings into SketchUp geometry

Part of the method relies on five custom extensions that are essential when working in tandem with both software platforms. You should download the outlined extensions, which are described in Chapter 17.

General Overview

To create a model from AutoCAD linework in SketchUp, you'll utilize the same steps outlined for SketchUp Process Modeling, with some minor variations that take into account the origin of the linework. The conversion process has three general steps:

1. Organize the AutoCAD file.
2. Generate the geometry.
3. Convert site objects from AutoCAD blocks into SketchUp components.

Organizing the AutoCAD File

You'll need to identify the information in AutoCAD that you need for SketchUp and discard the rest (Fig. 16-1). The useful AutoCAD linework will be reorganized on appropriate layers. Other linework will be isolated and discarded. This includes organizing and including linework from AutoCAD Xref files.

Fig. 16-1: An AutoCAD base file filled with the relevant project information: architecture, civil, utility, survey info, and the site plan

When they are imported, the AutoCAD layers and the information on those layers will directly transfer into SketchUp. All of the AutoCAD information will be organized on specific layers to establish layer organization in SketchUp (Fig. 16-2, Fig. 16-3). Therefore, the basic organization of layers as outlined in SketchUp Process Modeling is accomplished in AutoCAD prior to importing a model into SketchUp.

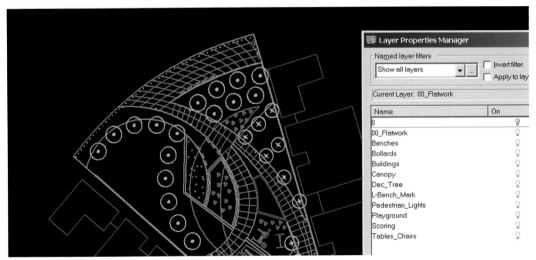

Fig. 16-2: The AutoCAD site plan and layers

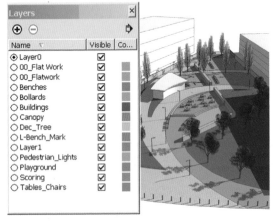

Fig. 16-3: When AutoCAD layers are imported into SketchUp, they retain their layer names and information.

The organized CAD linework (Fig. 16-4) will be broken into two categories:

▶ Linework that defines the surfaces of the site plan and creates the Flatwork Base (Fig. 16-5)

▶ AutoCAD blocks that define individual objects, site elements, and vegetation (Fig. 16-6)

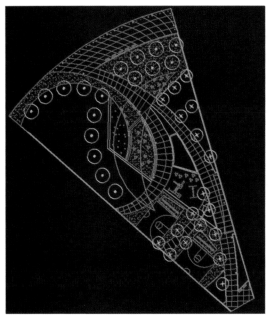

Fig. 16-4: The organized AutoCAD file containing only the linework needed to create a SketchUp file

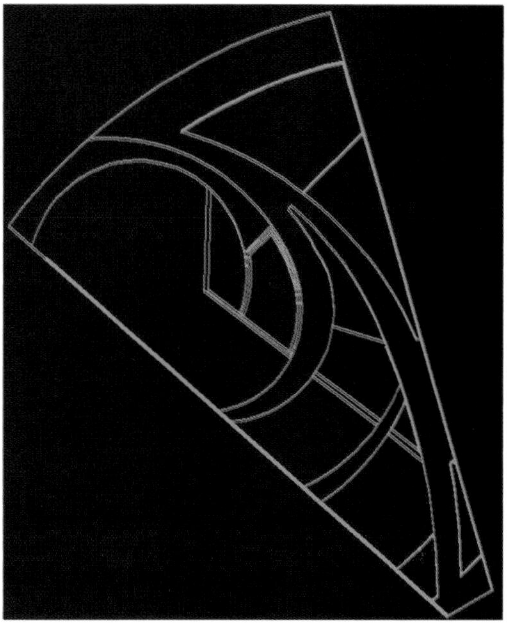

Fig. 16-5: The Flatwork Base linework is organized into an AutoCAD base file. This is the first file with lines that is imported into SketchUp.

The two categories of information will be broken up into two separate AutoCAD files. These files are then imported into SketchUp.

- One file contains the linework that defines the Flatwork Base (Fig. 16-5).
- The second file contains the AutoCAD blocks (Fig. 16-6).

For more information about organizing the AutoCAD files, see Chapter 17.

Generating the Geometry

The AutoCAD linework that composes the Flatwork Base is imported into SketchUp first. The imported linework is then used to generate faces and surfaces (Fig. 16-7).

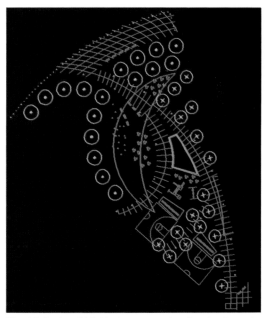

Fig. 16-6: AutoCAD blocks representing the site elements, furnishings, and vegetation. This is the second file imported into SketchUp.

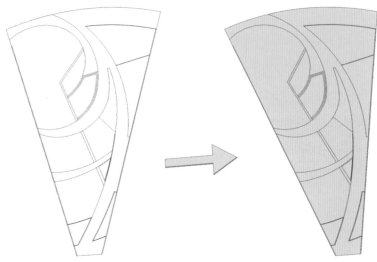

Fig. 16-7 AutoCAD linework is imported into SketchUp (left) and used to generate faces (right) to create a SketchUp Flatwork Base.

There are two different methods you can use to heal the bases to create faces:

► Use the Line tool to heal faces.

► Use five custom extensions, known as AutoCAD Cleanup scripts, to create geometry from the AutoCAD linework.

After you create the base geometry, you can add color and Push/Pull surfaces to create the volumes and add detail (Fig. 16-8). Generating the geometry is reviewed in detail in Chapter 18, where you will learn to organize the AutoCAD Flatwork Base.

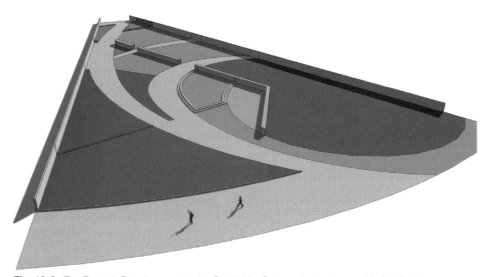

Fig. 16-8: The Flatwork Base is completed in SketchUp. Color and volume are added to the base.

Arranging the Objects

The last step is to import the second AutoCAD file that contains the blocks of site elements, furnishings, and vegetation (Fig. 16-9).

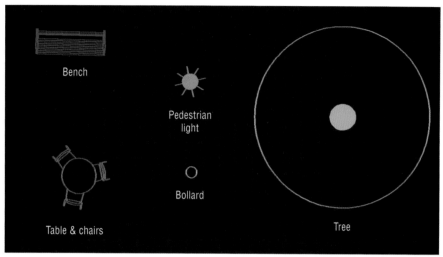

Fig. 16-9: AutoCAD blocks that represent a bench, a table and chairs, a pedestrian light, a bollard, and a tree

As with layers, AutoCAD blocks import directly into SketchUp. Once they are imported, AutoCAD *blocks* instantly become SketchUp *components* (Fig. 16-10). This means that all versions of the block are now components; they can be edited to affect all the other similar blocks/components in the model.

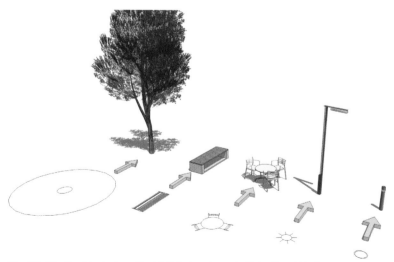

Fig. 16-10: The blocks from Fig.16-9 that are imported into SketchUp become editable components that are replaced with 3D SketchUp component models.

The last step of the conversion process simply replaces the 2D linework of the imported CAD blocks (Fig. 16-11) with 3D SketchUp components. This allows you to instantaneously and accurately arrange many types of site objects in a model (Fig. 16-12 through Fig. 16-14). Converting blocks into components and arranging the objects is reviewed in detail in Chapter 19.

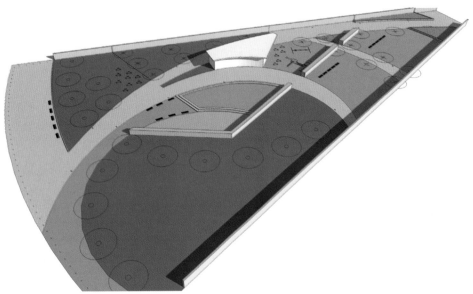

Fig. 16-11: An Imported AutoCAD file containing blocks placed onto a SketchUp Flatwork Base

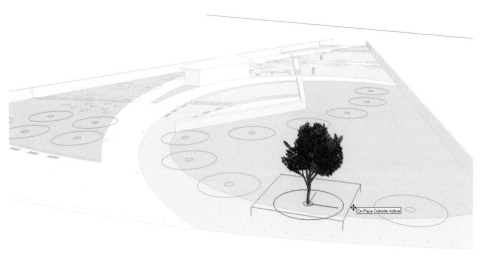

Fig. 16-12: Editing the 2D block/component and pasting a 3D component into the block is a quick way to add detailed elements to a model.

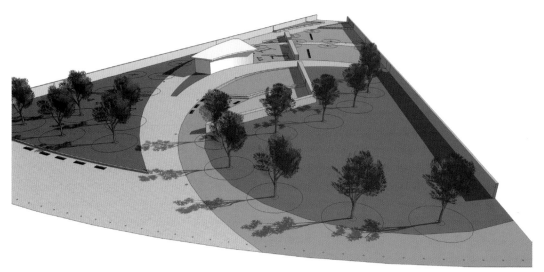

Fig. 16-13: A 3D component is placed into the 2D block. All versions of the former AutoCAD block now contain a 3D component.

Fig. 16-14: The final model view, with components copied into blocks to create a quick 3D detailed site model

Organizing AutoCAD

When you are working with AutoCAD files, your first step should be to reorganize the information so you can work with it efficiently in SketchUp. Your goal is to utilize SketchUp Process Modeling on an adjusted AutoCAD base file so that you can create a 3D model. This chapter uses the following general approach to reorganization:

1. Apply a comprehensive file and folder organization to convert efficiently from AutoCAD to SketchUp.

2. Identify information: linework, blocks, and associated layers. You will need them to create a usable Flatwork Base composed of *surfaces* and *objects* from the AutoCAD file.

3. Filter and remove any information that is not needed or that is redundant.

4. Organize the identified information onto new layers.

5. Use existing blocks or create new blocks to represent *objects* in the site plan.

To help follow along with the contents of this chapter, you will need to download four AutoCAD files from Wiley's website. Go to www.wiley.com/go/sketchupforsites to download the following AutoCAD files:

Park Base Plan.dwg (the main AutoCAD file)

CS_Park_BaseFile.dwg (the completed file)

Flatwork.dwg (an AutoCAD insert file)

Objects.dwg (an AutoCAD insert file)

The files will download as ZIP files (.zip). After they have finished downloading, unzip the files to an appropriate location.

✳ In this chapter, AutoCAD information refers to the linework, blocks, and layers that compose a site plan in AutoCAD.

AutoCAD Reorganization

When you are creating 3D models from AutoCAD information, file reorganization is the most time-consuming part of the process. AutoCAD files can be complex multilayered files in which only a small portion of the information is needed to create models. The process of identifying and reorganizing the information to create a usable base requires patience and attention to detail. The better organized the AutoCAD Flatwork Base file is, the easier and faster the model will be to create.

Once file reorganization is complete and the files are imported into SketchUp, the task of modeling is quick and efficient. This process will become much faster with practice, as you learn to quickly identify and separate the available information.

Folder and File Structure

So that you can efficiently work between the two software platforms and keep the various files well organized, you should establish a folder and file structure.

Choose a location for the folders, either on the local hard drive or on a project server. If you are working with an existing project file structure, you will probably want to keep the folders and files with the associated project.

Create a new folder named 3D. This will be the main folder containing all the AutoCAD and SketchUp folders and files. Within the 3D folder, create three additional subfolders (Fig. 17-1):

- ► CAD
- ► Images
- ► SU

You will use the CAD file to store the AutoCAD files you want to use in SketchUp. You will export the SketchUp model images to the Images folder. SU is the folder location for the SketchUp files.

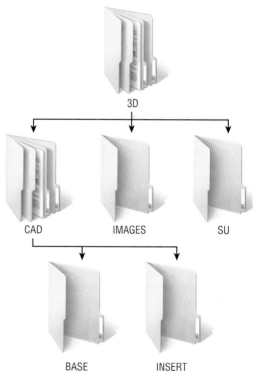

Fig. 17-1: An organizational folder structure for AutoCAD and SketchUp files

In the newly created CAD folder, create two additional subfolders:

- ▶ Base
- ▶ Insert

You will save a copy of the original base file in the Base folder. You will save edited AutoCAD files in the Insert folder.

AutoCAD Base Files

After you create the folder structure, your next step is to create a copy of the original project AutoCAD file. The original file refers to the AutoCAD base that is being used for the layout of the project. Typically (and in professional terms), these are schematic design, design development, or construction document base files that are used by an individual or the project team to delineate a site or building design.

Because you will significantly alter the AutoCAD project file, you need to use a copy. That way, you'll still have the original structure and information in the original project file. Project AutoCAD files are set up for specific needs and should not be altered. For these reasons, save a separate file to use to create a SketchUp model.

Save a copy of the main project file in the CAD/Base folder. You should save it as CAD_SU_BASE: this is short for AutoCAD_SketchUp_Base. Remember to save often when you're reorganizing the AutoCAD information.

 Never use the original main project AutoCAD files when you create a SketchUp model.

Sift through the CAD_SU_BASE file and identify the linework and blocks you need for the model. Your goal is to edit and generate an AutoCAD file that is composed of linework that represents *surfaces* and *objects*. To successfully complete the exercises in this chapter, you need to have a working knowledge of AutoCAD and the ability to identify this information.

Fig. 17-2 identifies some typical surfaces and objects on the Flatwork Base. Fig. 17-3 identifies some typical objects and site elements.

External Reference Files

At first glance, identifying and organizing the information in the AutoCAD files may seem like a daunting task—especially when External Reference AutoCAD files (Xrefs) are present. However, you can use a systematic approach to organize the linework and blocks into coherent and usable information. By using a systematic approach, you can divide your overall task into smaller tasks that you can easily handle. This approach starts with editing and then deleting all of the Xref files. Fig. 17-4 illustrates a complete AutoCAD file that includes associated Xref information. Examples of Xref files are illustrated in diagrams Fig. 17-5 through Fig. 17-7.

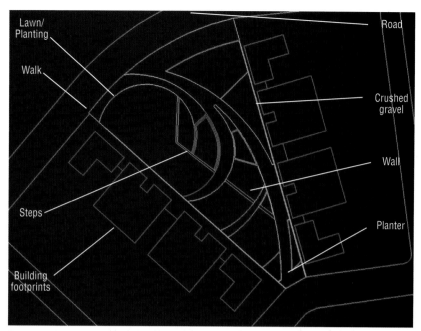

Fig. 17-2: Typical AutoCAD linework that creates surfaces

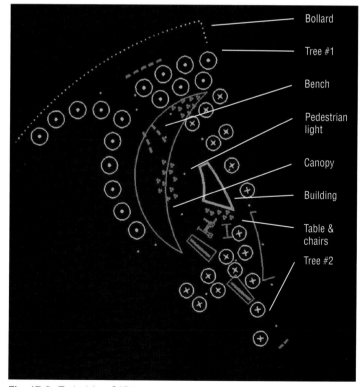

Fig. 17-3: Typical AutoCAD linework composing objects and site elements

Xref files for the purpose of reorganization fall into three categories:

Category 1 Xrefs that do not contain any relevant information

Category 2 Xrefs that have necessary linework and some irrelevant information

Category 3 Xrefs in which all the linework is needed for the Flatwork Base

1. Identify any Xref that falls under Category 1.
2. Simply detach those Xrefs from the CAD_SketchUp_BASE.

    a. To detach the Xrefs, type **Xref** at the AutoCAD command prompt. This will bring up the External Reference menu listing all the Xref files (Fig. 17-4).

    b. Select the files that will be removed (Fig. 17-8).

    c. At the right of the menu, with the files selected, choose Detach (Fig. 17-8). This will remove the selected Xrefs from the file.

Fig. 17-4: The AutoCAD Xref menu and Xref files. To the left of the menu is the overall site plan file with all the Xref information visible.

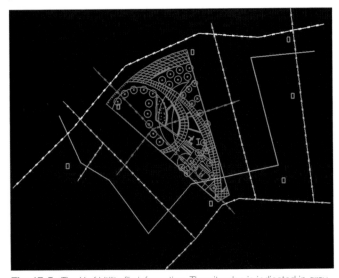

Fig. 17-5: The Xref Utility file information. The site plan is indicated in gray.

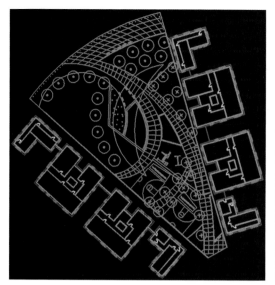

Fig. 17-6: The Xref Architectural file shows the building floorplans and footprint.

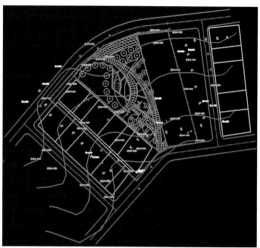

Fig. 17-7: The Xref Civil Engineering file shows the roads, plats, spot elevations, and grades.

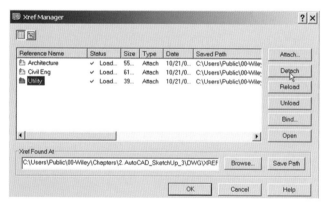

Fig. 17-8: Detaching an Xref within Xref menu. The Detach command option is on the right.

3. Identify any Xrefs that fall under Categories 2 and 3. You will handle them the same way, as detailed in the next step.

4. Bind/Insert them to the CAD_SU_BASE. When you Bind/Insert an Xref, it will be embedded in the base file instead of being externally referenced. The bound Xref, which becomes part of the drawing and not linked as a separate file, can be edited easily. To bind an Xref (Fig. 17-9), follow these steps:

   a. Enter **Xref** at the command prompt, bringing up the Xref menu.

   b. Select the Xrefs to bind into the drawing.

c. Select the Bind tab and check the Insert box. Press the OK button.

d. Press OK on the Xref menu.

Bind/Insert converts Xrefed information in a single block embedded in the AutoCAD file.

5. Select the Xref information after it is bound and explode it. Type **explode** in the AutoCAD command prompt and select the linework that composes the Xref(s).

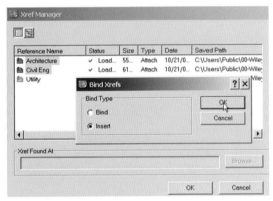

Fig. 17-9: Bind/Insert an Xref with the needed information into the CAD_SU_Base drawing.

Once the Xref information has been removed or inserted into the CAD_SU_BASE, the file is ready to be further organized. By performing the remainder of the exercises in the order they are presented, you will generate two separate pieces of information: the flatwork linework that defines the surfaces and a series of AutoCAD blocks that define the objects.

Isolating Surfaces

Using the AutoCAD Express Tools or the Layer menu, turn off any layers with linework that does not define surfaces. This includes turning off the layers that include site furnishings, elements, and vegetation (Fig. 17-10).

Carefully review the remaining information and make sure the surfaces (including the building footprints) you need to create a Flatwork Base are visible.

Once you have carefully reviewed the linework, create a new layer called 01 – Flatwork Base. Select all the linework for the surfaces and place the information on the newly created layers (Fig. 17-11).

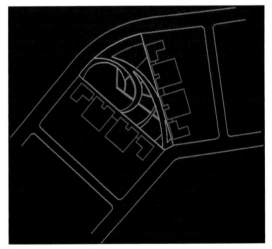

Fig. 17-10: AutoCAD plan drawing with all information, except the linework representing surfaces, turned off

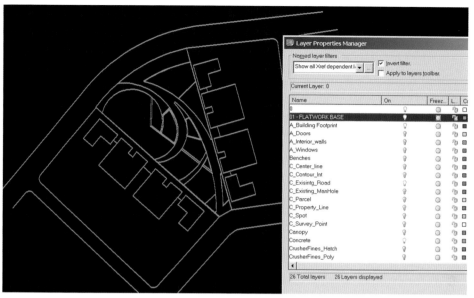

Fig. 17-11: Place all the surface linework onto a single layer (01 – Flatwork Base).

There are several ways to place linework onto a different layer. You can select all the linework and then, from the Layers dialog box, select the 01 - Flatwork Base layer—or you can use AutoCAD Express Tools (integrated as part of AutoCAD 2008 and 2009). Make sure that 01 - Flatwork Base is the current layer, and use the Change to Current Layer option.

Closing Perimeters

To successfully create faces in SketchUp, all of the edges must be connected to create a closed perimeter. Notice that the building footprint (not the interior plans) is included as part of the surface areas.

You will need to draft additional lines to close surfaces in most AutoCAD files. The following locations typically require additional edges:

► Streets and roads (Fig. 17-12)

► Walks and trails

► Overall site perimeter

► Building footprints

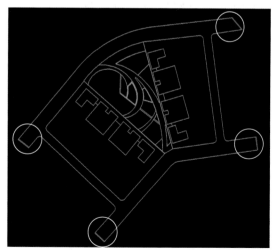

Fig. 17-12: Make sure to close perimeter areas with additional linework. In order to create faces for surfaces in SketchUp, surface areas need to be closed perimeters. The lines in magenta in the diagram are areas where another line was drafted to close a surface (the road).

This is easier to accomplish in AutoCAD than in SketchUp. Add lines as needed to create closed perimeters around surfaces. Draft all the lines on the 01 – Flatwork Base layer.

Organizing Site Objects

The second set of information that you will need to organize includes the site elements and objects.

All site objects should be composed as AutoCAD blocks. AutoCAD blocks are like SketchUp components; they are a bundle of linework composed as a single entity of information. Editing a block affects all similar blocks. As reviewed in Chapter 16, AutoCAD blocks automatically convert to components when they are imported into SketchUp. This allows the previous 2D block to be swapped with a 3D SketchUp representation of the object, quickly populating a model with site elements and vegetation.

If an object (or set of objects) is not a block, redraft it as a block. For example, if there is linework that represents pedestrian lights but they are not blocks, create a new block to represent the pedestrian light. Then copy the new block over the current linework that symbolizes the pedestrian lights. See the following section, "Creating AutoCAD Blocks," for how to generate new blocks.

Identifying the Objects

Sift through the plan and identify any site elements to be included in the SketchUp model (Fig. 17-13). Turn off all the other layers. Create new blocks to represent objects if necessary.

Creating AutoCAD Blocks

Identify any object that needs to be a block. Follow these standard steps to create a block. Copy and paste the generated block in the appropriate site plan locations.

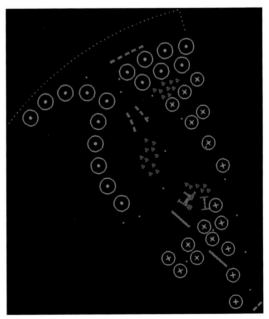

Fig. 17-13: Turn off all the linework except the site objects and site elements.

1. Draft the linework for the block on Layer 0 (make Layer 0 current).

2. In the CAD menu, type **block**. This will bring up the Blocks menu.

3. Choose the Select Object button.

4. Select the linework composing the object.

5. Check the Convert Selected to Block box.

6. Provide a name for the block at the top of the menu.

7. Select OK.

8. Place the block on the appropriate object layer.

9. Copy and replace as needed.

Placing Object Blocks on Layers

Once all the desired objects have been identified, sort and place each object block on a corresponding layer (Fig. 17-14). Each site object type should be on its own layer. If any are not, place the site objects on the appropriate layer.

Each individual object type, such as a tree or pedestrian light, has its own corresponding layer for that particular object. All pedestrian light blocks should be on the Pedestrian Light layer, all Tree blocks should be on the Tree layers, benches should be on a Bench layer, etc. If organized correctly, the imported AutoCAD blocks will arrive in SketchUp organized and easy to manage.

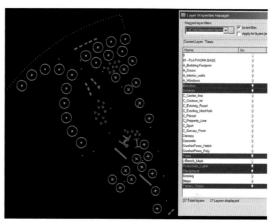

Fig. 17-14: Tree blocks should be on Tree layers, pedestrian lights on a Pedestrian Light layer, etc.

Once the blocks are swapped with 3D components, those components will still remain on the same layer they were placed on in AutoCAD.

Write Block Surfaces and Objects

Once the surface information has been compiled onto the 01 – Flatwork Base layer and objects have been identified and placed on the appropriate layers, the CAD_SU_BASE is complete.

The file information is now ready to be write blocked. Write Block (or WBlock) allows AutoCAD users to isolate specific information and export it out of AutoCAD, generating a new and separate AutoCAD file containing only the selected linework.

Two Write Block files will be exported from the CAD_SU_BASE: one file that represents the flatwork information and another file that contains object blocks.

Flatwork File

In AutoCAD, use Express Tools ➤ Isolate Layers to isolate the 01 – Flatwork Base linework. Alternatively, in the Layer menu, you can turn off all the layers except the 01 – Flatwork Base. The linework that represents the surfaces should be the only information that is visible.

Use the Write Block command to export the visible linework.

1. In the AutoCAD command window, type **wblock**. The Write Block menu will appear.

2. Select the surface linework and save the WBlock file into the 3D/CAD/Insert folder.

3. Name the exported information **Flatwork** (Fig. 17-15).

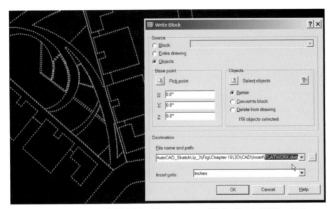

Fig. 17-15: The AutoCAD Write Block menu. Write Block (WBlock) the flatwork information to its own file called Flatwork. Save the file in the 3D CAD/Insert folder.

Object Blocks

Repeat the steps for all the object blocks. Isolate all of the object layers at once. Write Block the information and save it in the 3D/CAD/Insert folder. Name the exported information **Objects** (Fig. 17-16). The object blocks should all be saved out as a single file.

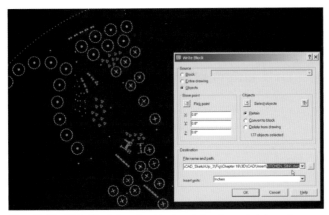

Fig. 17-16: Write Block the site object and site elements information.

Convert to Blocks

When both sets of information have been write blocked, close out of the CAD_SU_BASE. Navigate to and open both of the write blocked files: Flatwork.dwg and Objects.dwg.

Convert the information in each file into a single block (see "Creating AutoCAD Blocks"). Save the files and close. This step will help make the AutoCAD information easier to work with once it is imported into SketchUp. This is elaborated further in the next chapters. It should be noted that skipping this step can cause complications when trying to model the Flatwork Base in AutoCAD.

Importing the Flatwork File

The information is now ready to be imported and modeled in SketchUp.

AutoCAD and SketchUp Units

Before you import the AutoCAD files into SketchUp, you need to make sure the drafting units of the AutoCAD file match in SketchUp.

Check and note the drawing units for the AutoCAD file. In AutoCAD, you can find them under Format menu ➤ Units (Fig. 17-17).

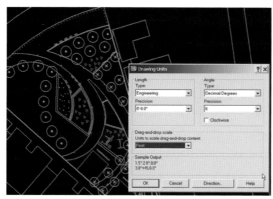

Fig. 17-17: The Drawing Units menu in AutoCAD. Before you import a file into SketchUp, the SketchUp units must match the drawing units in AutoCAD.

Prior to importing the file, in SketchUp, go to Window ➤ Model Info ➤ Units (Fig. 17-18). Change the SketchUp units to match those of the AutoCAD file.

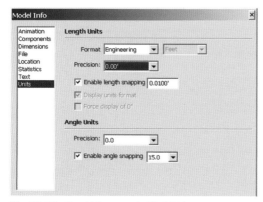

Fig. 17-18: The Units menu in SketchUp

This is one of the two locations where the model units need to be set in SketchUp. The second location is described in the following text.

The Flatwork Drawing File

The Flatwork CAD file will be imported first. Do not import both files into SketchUp. The Objects drawing file will be imported only after the Flatwork Base is completed in SketchUp, once the faces and volume have been created.

To import the file in SketchUp, go to File ➤ Import and navigate to the CAD/Insert folder. Set the file extensions to AutoCAD (.dwg). Next, select Options at the right of the import screen. The AutoCAD Import File Options menu will appear (Fig. 17-19).

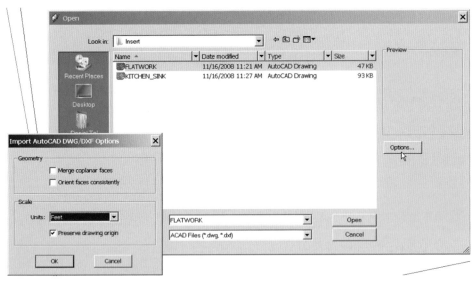

Fig. 17-19: When you import an AutoCAD file into SketchUp, you must set the units for the file.

1. Select the correct units from the Units pull-down menu.

2. Check the Preserve Drawing Origin box. Checking this option ensures that the file retains the same coordinate reference (i.e., site location) as drafted in AutoCAD.

3. Select the Flatwork file and choose Open. SketchUp will import the AutoCAD file into its work environment.

4. If the linework is not visible after the import, choose View ➤ Toolbars ➤ Camera and select Zoom Extents. SketchUp will adjust the view and show the imported CAD linework.

The AutoCAD surface information in SketchUp constitutes the information you need to create a Flatwork Base. The next chapter explains how to model the imported information. Chapter 19 deals with importing and converting the object's .dwg.

CHAPTER 18

Modeling the AutoCAD Flatwork Base

This chapter details two specific methods for healing and generating faces to define surfaces using imported AutoCAD linework. Once imported into SketchUp, the AutoCAD flatwork lines are converted into edges but not faces. The imported edges will be used to create faces.

The process of modeling the Flatwork Base originating from AutoCAD differs from the process outlined in Part 2. Typically, faces are produced when edges are drafted and connected to form a closed perimeter; SketchUp clearly understands where a face is desired.

Imported edges of predrafted closed perimeters and boundaries pose a challenge in SketchUp. Because they were not drafted in SketchUp, it is not clear where a face belongs and, in some cases, which edges are connected to which. SketchUp needs to be directed, so that it will understand where to create the faces.

Exploding the Flatwork Base

Download File: AutoCAD to SketchUp Flatwork

As indicated, after the AutoCAD information is write blocked from the CAD_SU_Base, the flatwork information will enter SketchUp as a component. Before you work with either method, the base needs to be exploded (Fig. 18-1).

In some cases, the Flatwork Base will need to be exploded twice because it imports as a component within a component. Regardless, make sure that the linework is not a component when you start to heal the faces.

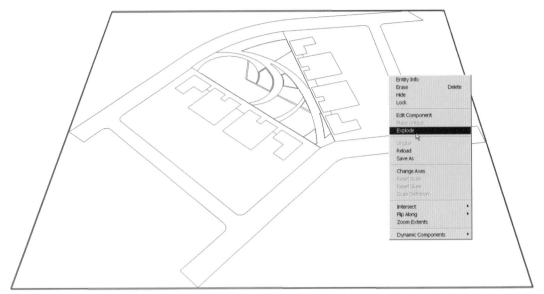

Fig. 18-1: Select the imported edges. They should be a single component. Explode the component.

The obvious question is, Why was the information made into a block in the first place? There is a bug in the conversion process from AutoCAD to SketchUp. Edges will have fewer anomalies if they are imported as a block (component) than if they are exploded.

Furthermore, SketchUp sometimes imports the AutoCAD information without converting it into a component. Making it a block in AutoCAD ensures that it will be a component in SketchUp.

Problematic AutoCAD Lines

When linework is imported from AutoCAD to SketchUp, some edges will enter SketchUp with distortions and anomalies. These anomalies are due to the basic differences between SketchUp and AutoCAD. AutoCAD works in two dimensions and, as such, can create finer and more precise linework. SketchUp, being a 3D drafting program, is optimized to display three-dimensional geometry. Some of the edges get garbled in translation. These distortions can make it difficult to heal faces.

Overlapping and Short Lines

Lines that are connected in AutoCAD, once in SketchUp, can overlap or fall short of the intended endpoint. For example, when two lines connected at 90 degrees are imported into SketchUp, a close inspection of the lines might show that one of the lines is either extended beyond the endpoint or falls short, creating a gap.

These overlaps and short lines are difficult to notice, but they affect how faces are created. With overlapping lines, the tiny amount of extra edge beyond the intersection of the lines will affect the healing of a face. The extra edge, by simply occupying the area of a possible future face, will prevent the face from being created (Fig. 18-2, Fig. 18-3).

Similarly, short lines create a gap causing what was formerly a closed perimeter to be open, thereby preventing a face from being generated (Fig. 18-2, Fig 18-4).

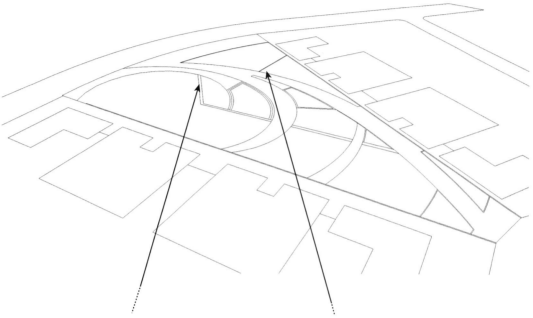

Fig. 18-2: Flatwork information in SketchUp after being imported from AutoCAD

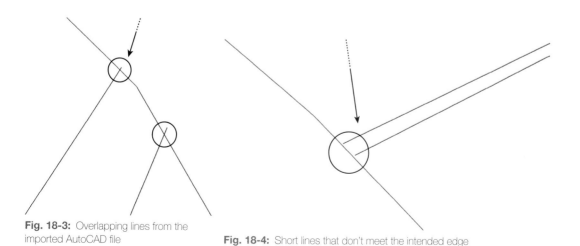

Fig. 18-3: Overlapping lines from the imported AutoCAD file

Fig. 18-4: Short lines that don't meet the intended edge

Arcs

SketchUp does not display true arcs. As outlined in Chapter 11, SketchUp arcs are composed of a series of edges faceted together.

Conversely, AutoCAD does generate "true" arcs. SketchUp reinterprets any imported arcs with faceted edges. The formerly smooth arc in AutoCAD becomes a series of lines that distort the overall shape and form of the arc in SketchUp (Fig. 18-5).

Imported arcs are the primary culprit in creating difficulties when you are healing faces. The reinterpretation of a smooth arc into a series of edges causes the arcs to either overextend or fall short of adjacent linework.

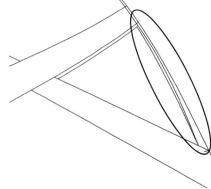

Fig. 18-5: Review the arc edges first.

Random Anomalies

No matter how well an AutoCAD plan was drafted, random anomalies will occur, even in straight edges. Imported lines can be broken in half. Minuscule gaps can appear in a single solid line in AutoCAD. In some instances, SketchUp will refuse to generate a face, even with a closed perimeter that does not have gaps or overlaps.

In most of these instances, you should look for very small edges that are hard to see. Selecting a location of these stubborn edges and then applying the Delete Short Lines extension (discussed in the following text) can help find and erase these micro edges that prevent the generation of a face.

On the DanielTal.com website (www.danieltal.com), the "Modeling from a Hand Drawn Plan" tutorial further reviews how to troubleshoot modeling faces and edges in SketchUp.

Healing the AutoCAD Flatwork Base

Considering all the problems that can occur with imported AutoCAD linework, generating faces seems to be a daunting task. There are two completely different methods you can use to heal the Flatwork Base. The biggest difference between them is the amount of time it takes to complete them. The Line Tool method (Method 1) takes considerably longer to complete than the CAD Clean-Up Extensions method (Method 2).

Method 2 is so fast that it allows a well-organized AutoCAD file to be developed and fully articulated in less than an hour. This has been demonstrated time and again, including at workshops and at live demonstrations at conventions of the American Society for Landscape Architecture.

So why show Method 1? Until recently, Method 1 was the only way to model imported AutoCAD lines. By trying this method, you will learn a great deal about how SketchUp generates geometry. The problems that arise when you use Method 1 are not exclusive to AutoCAD imported linework; they can crop up even when you are performing simple modeling. Learning how to problem solve the generation of faces in SketchUp is a useful skill.

Method 2 is practical and simple to use. To perform it, you will need to purchase three custom extensions and download a fourth one that is free. However, the small expenditure is worth it because of the ease of use. In addition, the new DynaSCAPE Cleanup extension can simplify the process further.

Healing with the Line Tool

Method 1 is simple and involves using the Line tool (View ➤ Toolbars ➤ Drawing ➤ Line Tool). Its drawback is that it can take hours—if not days, depending on the size of the file—to complete the base.

The basic premise of this method is to create faces. Instead of adding edges to create faces, the Line tool is used to identify imported edges by sampling points along an edge. Ideally, you select the endpoint of an edge and select (draw) another endpoint on the same edge.

For example, a surface area is defined by the perimeter of four edges. To heal the face with the Line tool, select an endpoint of one of the edges, travel along the same edge, and select another point (on the edge, midpoint, or endpoint). If the perimeter is closed and contains no anomalous edges, a face will be created.

However, it will become apparent rather quickly that this does not work so cleanly with all the edges in a drawing. Distortions in the imported linework will prevent some (or many) areas from healing faces.

Here are some tips and tricks to make this method work:

Sample the same edge. The idea is to identify the endpoints of existing edges, not to draft a new line. This mistake is easy to identify if a new edge is created (Fig. 18-6 through Fig. 18-10).

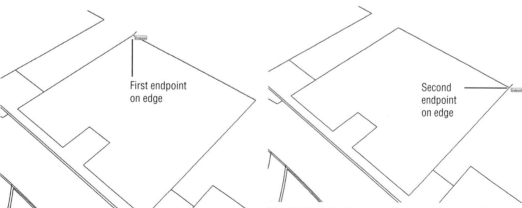

First endpoint on edge

Second endpoint on edge

Fig. 18-6: Using the Line tool, select the endpoint of an edge.

Fig. 18-7: Select the second point on the edge. Identifying the two points along a straight edge will heal the face.

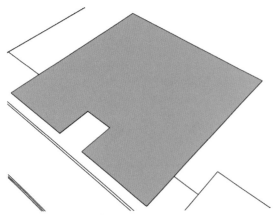

Fig. 18-8: The healed face

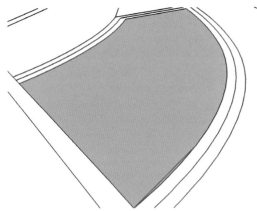

Fig. 18-9: Avoid drawing new edges. Identify only the endpoints along the same edge.

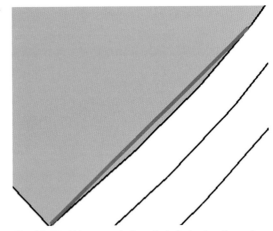

Fig. 18-10: Enlargement of small drafted edge. If an edge is drawn and a face is created, simply delete the extra edge and the face should remain.

Start with arcs. Locate any arcs and attempt to heal the surface area perimeter. If that fails, zoom in as close as possible to the intersection of an arc and an edge (or an arc and an arc). Look for the overlapping line and delete it—or use the Line tool to connect the endpoint of the arc to the adjacent and intended edge.

Heal the large areas first. Try to heal the faces of large, well-defined areas first. Select the endpoints and see if a face is healed (Fig. 18-11). Work with the smaller areas next.

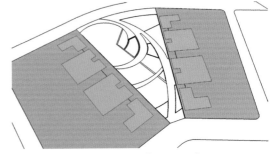

Fig. 18-11: Heal the larger surface areas first.

Hunt down the problem edges. If selecting the edge points fails, the next approach is to "hunt down" the problem edges. Starting at the endpoint of a line, draft another strategic edge and connect it to the midpoint of an adjacent line.

One of three things will happen:

▶ The entire face will be healed. If that is the case, delete or hide the strategic edge used to heal the face.

▶ No face will be generated. Try again by drafting a line from different areas or try to heal a small area of the perimeter surface.

▶ A face will be generated on one side of the drafted edge. This is the most common result. The opposite side without a face reveals where an anomaly might exist.

Continue to add more edges. Draft another line sampling another edge (endpoint, midpoint, or on edge). The result will be one of the three results detailed previously.

The goal is to narrow down the possible location of the problem edge. When enough edges are added, the location of a problem becomes more apparent. By zooming into the area where the faces will not generate, you will highlight the anomaly, typically a short line or an overlap (Fig. 18-12 through Fig. 18-15).

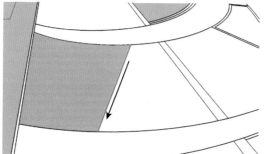

Fig. 18-12: When edges will not heal by identifying endpoints, use strategic edges within a surface perimeter.

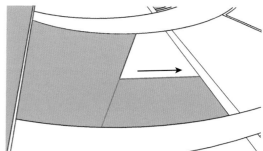

Fig. 18-13: Continue to add edges to narrow down the location.

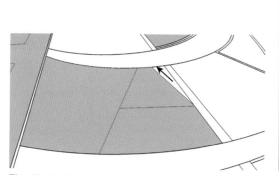

Fig. 18-14: The area should get smaller with each added edge.

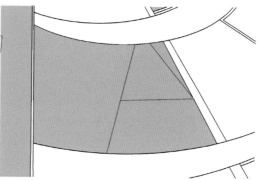

Fig. 18-15: Add edges until the face is healed. You may need to zoom in close to find the anomalies.

Redraft the edges. Perhaps the most effective way to heal faces is to delete and then redraw the edges. This ensures that the edges are connected at the endpoints. Because drafting new edges in SketchUp can be quick, you do not need to find the exact location of a distorted edge.

Deleting and redrafting the edges at intersections is the best approach; these are the prime locations where anomalies reside (Fig. 18-16 through Fig. 18-18).

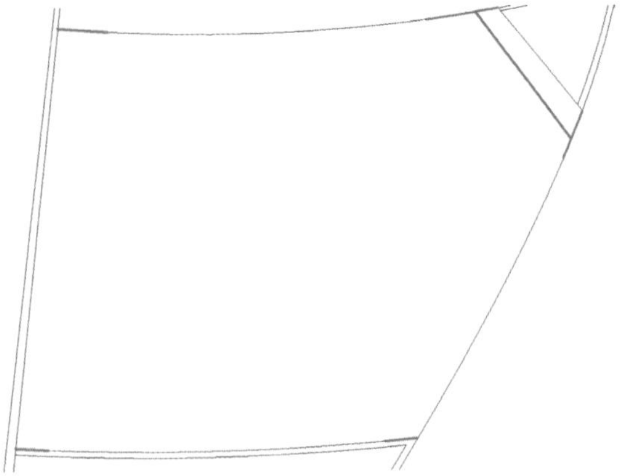

This technique is particularly useful with arcs. Imported arcs are broken into single faceted edges. Selecting the edge adjacent to an endpoint, and then deleting it and redrafting it, is the best place to start.

Fig. 18-16: Delete the edges at the line intersection and then redraft the lines. This ensures that the edges are connected efficiently.

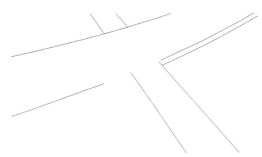

Fig. 18-17: In this instance, the top-right intersection contained the anomalous edge. Deleting the edge revealed that it was not correctly attached to adjacent edges.

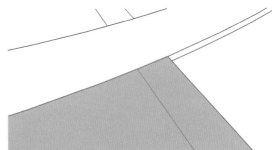

Fig. 18-18: Drafting the new edges to the connecting endpoints heals the entire face.

CAD Clean-Up Extensions

Method 2 centers on four custom tools collectively known as CAD Clean-Up extensions. These four extensions allow you to fix almost all the distortions in an imported AutoCAD base and then generate all the surface area faces with a simple click of the mouse. A fifth extension is useful when you are problem solving specific situations that arise with stubborn linework.

With almost any site plan, the process is the same. Although there are some limitations and problems that go along with this method, the results yield a Flatwork Base with minimal effort.

All the extensions are available at www.smustard.com (Fig. 18-19). These exceptional and extremely useful extensions were created by Todd Burch.

Fig. 18-19: The extensions are available at **www.smustard.com**.

With the exception of Make Faces, all the extensions cost between $10 and $20 (USD). They are worth the investment. Once they are installed into SketchUp, most of the extensions are located under the Extensions pull-down menu (Fig. 18-20). The Make Faces extension is located under the Tools pull-down menu (Fig. 18-21).

Fig. 18-20: The CAD Clean-Up extensions are located in the Plugins pull-down menu.

If you really want to work with AutoCAD files, these extensions are a must. The design professions are driven by contract and billable hours. Most site plans and other drawings are drafted in AutoCAD or a similar compatible DWG program as part of a widely accepted design process. Using this method and extensions allows you to quickly create site plans and building models. In some cases, you can create a Flatwork Base in a matter of minutes.

The basic premise of using these extensions is to select all the edges of the imported CAD file and apply the extensions in order.

Extend Close Lines This extension will extend lines to connect to the adjacent

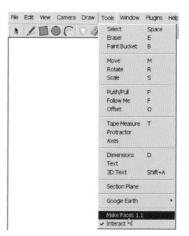

Fig. 18-21: The Make Faces extension is located under the Tools menu.

and intended edge. This solves the problems with gaps between edges in imported AutoCAD lines.

Delete Short Lines This extension will delete all overlapping and minuscule edges that prevent faces from being healed. The extension helps remove the overlaps found in imported AutoCAD lines.

Close Open Line Segments This extension helps generate an edge between two points where a gap is present. Although similar to Extend Close Lines, it is different. Extend Close Lines only extends a single edge (makes it longer).

Make Faces This extension will generate faces from the selected linework. Instead of using the Line tool to heal faces, selecting the entire base and running this extension will heal faces for an entire site plan.

Intersect Overlapping Lines This is the supplemental fifth extension. It will sift through all the selected edges and convert any overlapping edges or intersections into endpoints.

Working with Extensions

Download File: AutoCAD to SketchUp Flatwork

The following procedure outlines the process for using combined extensions on the imported AutoCAD edges. Sometimes the extensions run differently on different computer systems. Due to these inconsistencies, **make sure you save your work after each step**.

1. Select all the edges. From the Extensions menu, select Extend Close Lines. A dialog window will appear, indicating how many edges were extended by the extension. Save the file (Fig. 18-22, Fig. 18-23).

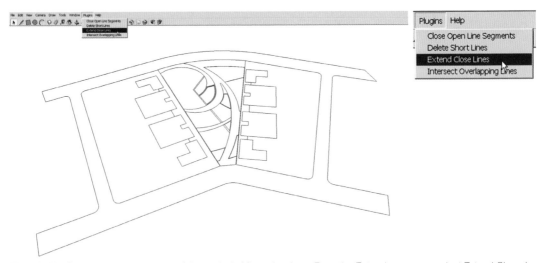

Fig. 18-22: Select the all the linework of the exploded flatwork edges. From the Extensions menu, select Extend Closed Lines.

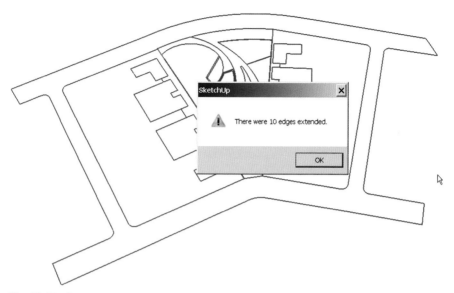

Fig. 18-23: Select all the linework of the exploded flatwork edges. From the Extensions menu, select Extend Closed Lines.

2. Reselect all the edges. From the Extensions menu, select Delete Short Lines. This extension runs inconsistently. One of two things will happen:

   ▶ After the extension runs the operation, all the edges will appear to be deselected. However, all of the selected but hard-to-see short lines will be selected. Immediately press the Delete key. All of the short lines will be deleted. Save the file.

   ▶ A pop-up menu will appear and indicate how many lines were deleted (Fig. 18-24). If this happens, you won't need to do anything else.

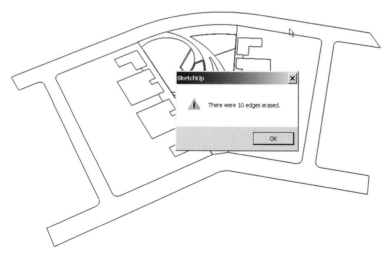

Fig. 18-24: From the Extensions menu, select Delete Short Lines. One of two things will happen.

3. Select all of the edges. From the Extensions menu, select Close Open Line Segments. You will be asked if you want to save a copy of the file. Select No (you should already be saving the file in each step anyway). Press OK.

The Close Open Line Segments extension takes longer to run than the other two extensions. Once the extension is completed, a pop-up window will appear indicating how many edges were closed. Save the file (Fig. 18-25).

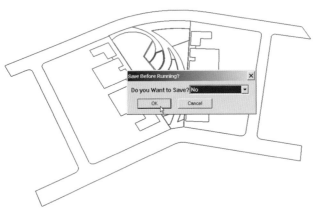

Fig. 18-25: The Close Open Line Segments extension will allow you to save the file before you run the extension.

4. Select all of the edges. Under the Tools menu, select Make Faces. A progress bar will run at the bottom left. Once the extension finishes running, faces will be generated from the edges (Fig. 18-26, Fig. 8-27).

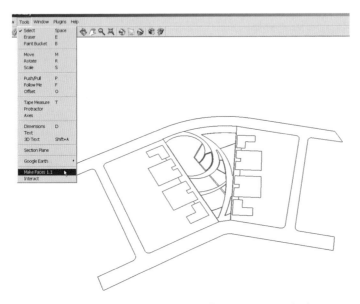

Fig. 18-26: Select all of the edges. From the Tools menu, go to the bottom and select Make Faces.

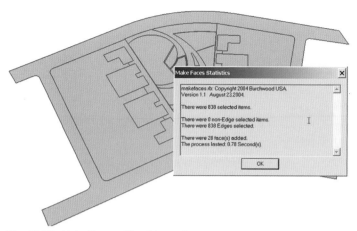

Fig. 18-27: Make Faces will heal the surface locations.

In most cases, faces will be generated at all closed perimeters. Begin to select the faces and make sure they are correctly subdivided. None of the faces should extend beyond a surface edge.

Troubleshooting Extensions

Running these extensions is not always a perfect science. Given the variation and complexity that is part of any AutoCAD file or site plan, you are likely to run into some of the following common problems.

Size Limitations

Running the Close Open Line Segments and Make Faces extensions can take time. The more edges you select, the longer it will take the extension to process.

The solution is to select the edges of the site plan in manageable chunks and apply the extension selectively area by area. If the system seems to freeze or takes too long, close SketchUp and reload the file. This is why you should save the file after each step.

In most situations, Close Open Line Segments is more limited in application than Make Faces. However, both extensions were able to run successfully on a large 500-acre site plan, although doing so took time.

As a general rule, the smaller an area is (i.e., the fewer its edges), the better the tools will work.

Incomplete Faces

In some instances, in particular with large-area site plans, not all faces will be generated. The first thing to do is to try to reapply the extensions with a fresh file. In many cases, the second time around will heal all the faces.

If the extension is rerun a second time and not all the faces are healed, then use the Hunting approach outlined in Method 1 and add edges between the lines until all the faces are complete.

Or, select the edges of the missing area. You do not need to be precise about the selection and can use a selection box. You should ensure the edges that compose the missing faces are included. Then rerun the AutoCAD clean-up extensions on the selected location. This has proven to be very effective.

DynaSCAPE CAD Cleanup

The DynaSCAPE Sketch3D subscription includes the download of the DynaSCAPE CAD extension that can also clean and prepare CAD line work.

The extension works in the same fashion as the extensions mentioned in the previous section. It has two important differences:

▶ The DynaSCAPE extension performs all the functions of the other extensions combined at once and in the correct order.

▶ The extension is considerably faster to process through the CAD linework.

This extension can quicken the workflow for users who need to model from imported CAD linework. It is important to note that the method used to adjust linework after applying CAD Clean-Up extensions is still relevant to this tool.

Method Summaries

Using the Line tool (Method 1) is a tedious approach to healing faces on an AutoCAD base plan. It is simple to apply, but the results can vary. If you have a very large site plan with a lot of distorted edges, modeling a Flatwork Base can be very difficult.

Although learning how to use the Line tool is valuable, using AutoCAD Clean-Up extensions to model a base plan in SketchUp is the preferred method.

Using extensions (Method 2) offers the fastest approach to healing AutoCAD linework to generate a Flatwork Base. The speed and efficiency with which this method generates faces greatly enhances the modeling process.

Even though Method 2 does requires some problem solving, this disadvantage is minor compared to the time it takes to model a site plan base without using these extensions.

After being applied to over a hundred site plans on various computer systems, Method 2 has been shown to work more than 95 percent of the time with only minor problems.

Next Steps

Download File: AutoCAD to SketchUp – Flatwork with Faces

After the face geometry is healed, your next modeling steps should follow the process outlined in Chapter 6.

1. Add color to the faces to better represent the intent of the surfaces (Fig. 18-28 through Fig. 18-30).

2. Use Push/Pull to add volumes to walls, steps, buildings, and any other relevant locations (Fig. 18-31, Fig. 18-32).

3. Adjust the volumes to provide the desired detail (Fig. 18-33).

4. Once complete, select the entire Flatwork Base geometry and make it into a group. Place the group on the 01 – Flatwork Base layer by using the Entity Info menu: select the Flatwork Base group, right-click, and select Entity Info.

5. To complete the model, add the site objects and elements to the base (Fig. 18-34). This is reviewed in the next chapter.

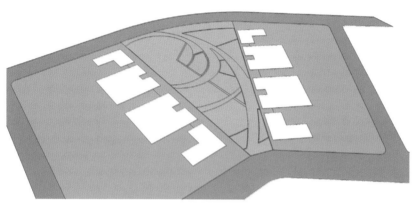

Fig. 18-28: Add color to the roads, lawn area, and buildings.

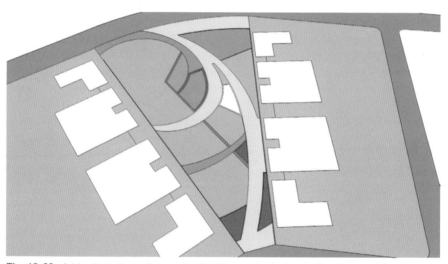

Fig. 18-29: Add color to the walks, planting locations, water feature, walls, steps, and structure.

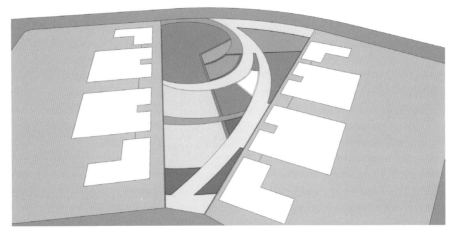

Fig. 18-30: The base with all the surface areas applied with colors and materials

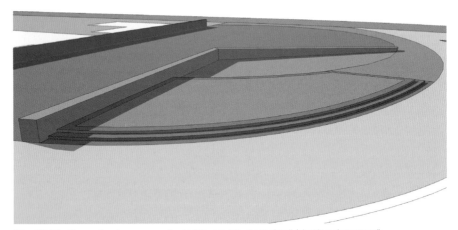

Fig. 18-31: The wall volume was adjusted to provide more detail (slanting downward).

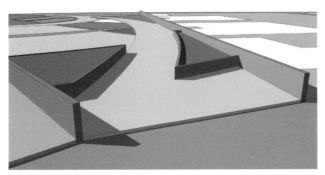

Fig. 18-32; The perimeter wall and planting areas are Push/Pulled upward and provide volume.

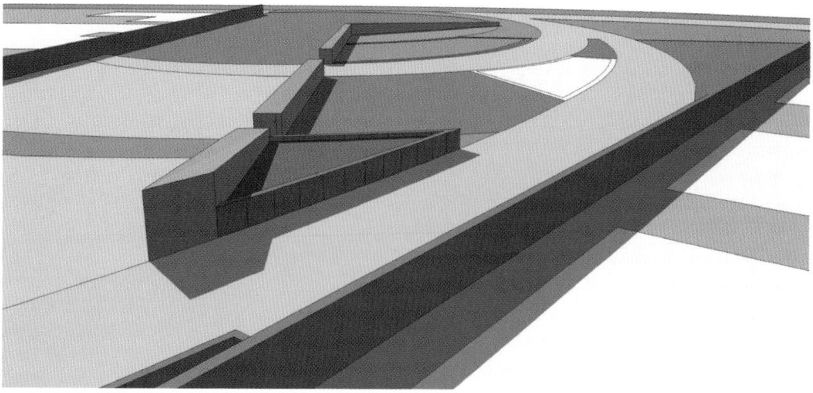

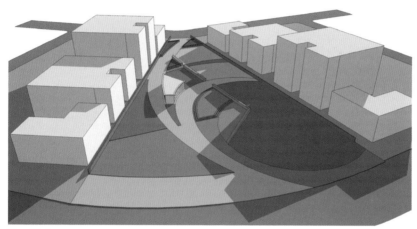

Fig. 18-33: The planter areas are raised. The decorative detail is added to the gray wall.

Fig. 18-34: The completed Flatwork Base. Select all the geometry and convert the base into a group. Place the group on the Flatwork layer.

Two flatwork models can be downloaded from 3D Warehouse. SPM Part 4: AutoCAD to SketchUp Flatwork with Color is the completed Flatwork Base with colors applied. AutoCAD to SketchUp – Completed Flatwork is the Flatwork Base with color and volumes added.

CHAPTER 19

Arranging
the Model

Now that the Flatwork Base is completed, your last step is to arrange the site element components on the base. Choose File ➤ Import and select the AutoCAD file Objects.dwg from the CAD/Insert folder. Make sure that the units and Preserve drawing origin are correct in the Option window, and then select Open.

Populating the Flatwork Base

SketchUp will import all the AutoCAD blocks and their associated layers into the drawing file. In some cases, the imported blocks and edges will not appear in the right location and will need to be aligned with the Flatwork Base.

Frequently, the imported Objects.dwg blocks will appear under or in the Flatwork Base. This will probably be the case if a volume (such as a 6″ curb or thickness) was added to the flatwork (Fig. 19-1).

Before you explode the Objects information, move it upward (vertically) to sit on top of the Flatwork Base's lowest volume, typically the walks and lawns (Fig. 19-2).

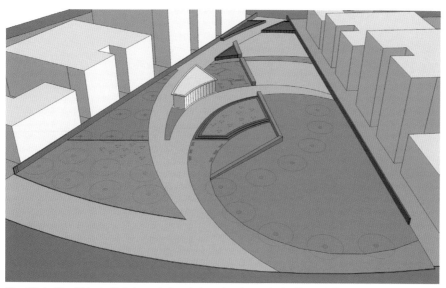

Fig. 19-1: The Objects file is imported and placed underneath the Flatwork Base.

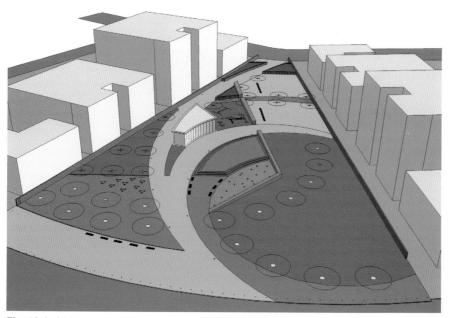

Fig. 19-2: Make sure the Objects component sits on top of the lowest flatwork surface.

Occasionally, the inserted Objects.dwg file will not insert correctly and will be misaligned with the Flatwork Base. If that is the case, realign the inserted blocks manually; select all the inserted blocks and move them to the correct locations with the Move/Copy tool. Do this before you explode the Objects information. This will make moving the information easier because it will be a single component (Fig. 19-3).

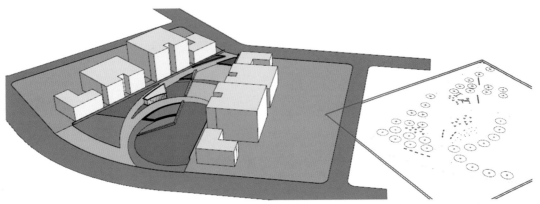

Fig. 19-3: On some occasions, the imported file will be misaligned with the Flatwork Base. Select the inserted component and place it in the correct location on the base.

Exploding the Objects

As with the flatwork linework, the imported blocks will enter SketchUp as a single component (Fig. 19-4). Select the imported Objects component, right-click, and explode it.

Fig. 19-4: Explode the imported Objects block/component.

If it is exploded, but the information was a component within a component, explode it again. The goal is for each block/component to be individually selectable. Ensure that no individual component is exploded (Fig. 19-5).

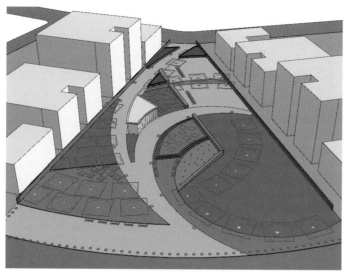

Fig. 19-5: The individual block/components should remain after the larger component is exploded.

Importing Layers

As previously illustrated, a 2D block imported from AutoCAD is easily replaced with a 3D component version in SketchUp. If the site elements were organized on layers, these layers will import into SketchUp. Replacing the block with a component does not remove the object from the layer. For example, editing the single Tree block/component with a 3D version will place trees wherever that component is present. The 3D versions will still be on the Tree layer.

Furthermore, the Tree layer can be toggled on or off to hide or make the tree visible; the AutoCAD layer structure will be preserved (Fig. 19-6).

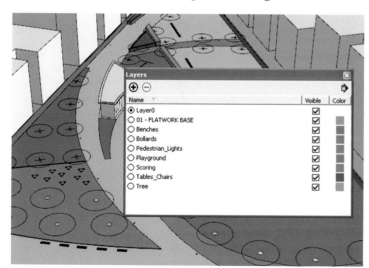

Fig. 19-6: The AutoCAD layer structure stays intact. Each component type is on its own layer, just as in AutoCAD.

Replacing the Components

Replace all the 2D imported block/components with 3D pre-made or custom components. This process is simple. Double-click any given component (Fig. 19-7). Once in the component instance, directly insert the desired 3D component into the component instance (Fig. 19-8).

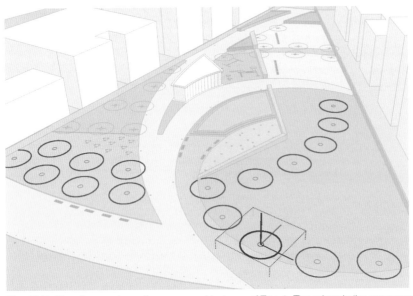

Fig. 19-7: The diagram shows the component instance of Tree 1. The edges in the component are selected; all instances of the edited component will be edited through this single component.

Fig. 19-8: The 3D Tree component is inserted directly into the edited block/component.

Adjust the imported 3D component to sit correctly (on center) within the block. Once adjusted, delete all the 2D edges and keep only the 3D component (Fig. 19-9).

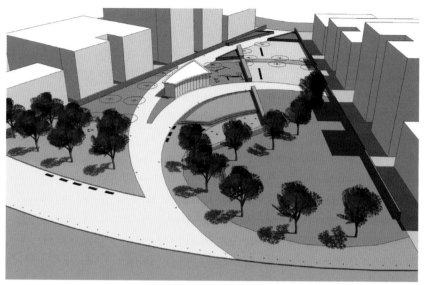

Fig. 19-9: The 2D edges are deleted and only the 3D trees remain, instantly populating the site plan with trees.

Continue to replace the 2D component blocks with 3D SketchUp components, as demonstrated in Fig. 19-10 through Fig. 19-24. Bollards (Fig. 19-10, Fig. 19-11), pedestrian lights (Fig. 19-12, Fig. 19-13), benches (Fig. 19-14 through Fig. 19-16), fountain heads (Fig. 19-17, Fig. 19-18), tables and chairs (Fig. 19-19, Fig. 19-20) and additional trees (Fig. 19-21 through 19-24) are swapped.

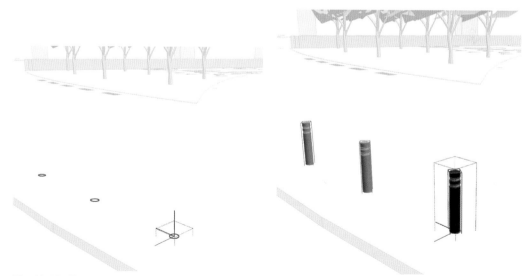

Fig. 19-10: Editing the 2D Bollard block/component

Fig. 19-11: The 3D bollard being inserted into the 2D component instance of the imported AutoCAD block/component

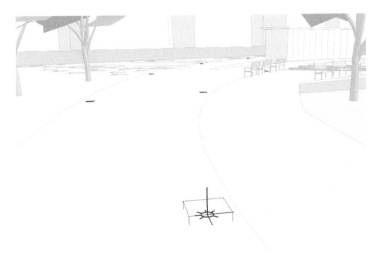

Fig. 19-12: A component instance of the 2D Pedestrian Light block/component

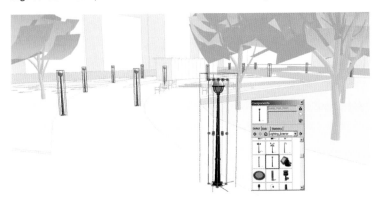

Fig. 19-13: The 3D Pedestrian Light component is inserted directly into the imported Pedestrian Light block.

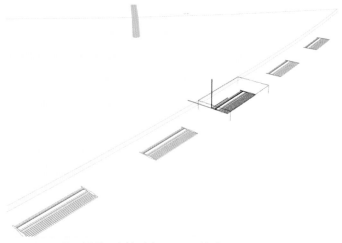

Fig. 19-14: The 2D Bench block/component instance

Part 4: AutoCAD to SketchUp

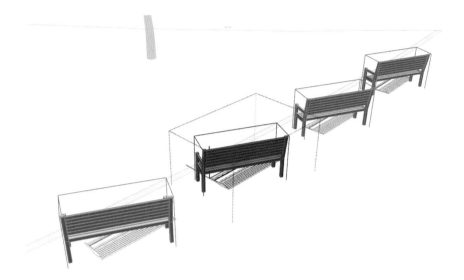

Fig. 19-15: The inserted 3D Bench component. The 3D component needs to be rotated and adjusted to face the correct direction. To universally adjust all of the benches, do this while you are working in the component instance.

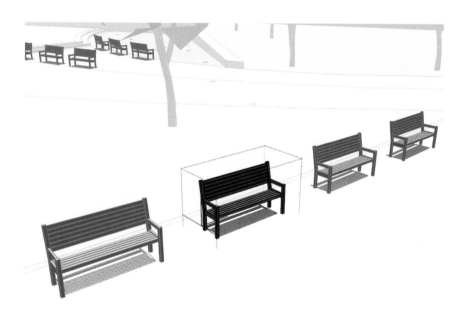

Fig. 19-16: The adjusted 3D Bench component

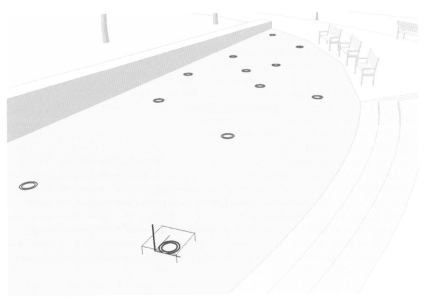

Fig. 19-17: The Water Fountain Spouts component instance

Fig. 19-18: The fountain jets replaced with the representative 3D component

You may want to toggle off the high face-count component layers, such as trees and shrubs, after they are replaced. This will make working with the model easier. Some of the inserted components will need to be moved, rotated, or scaled to better fit their context. Remember to adjust the components within the component instance; doing so will affect all similar components of the same type.

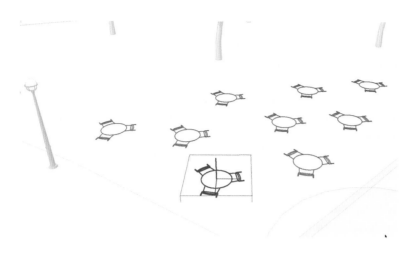

Fig. 19-19: Working in the 2D Table and Chairs component instance

Fig. 19-20: The 3D Table and Chair component inserted directly into the 2D component equivalent

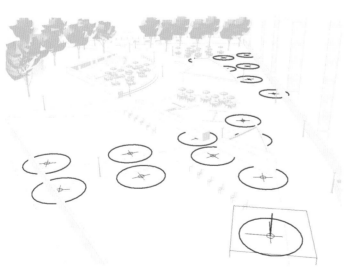

Fig. 19-21: Replacing the second Tree component

Fig. 19-22: A 3D Palm Tree component inserted directly into the Tree 2 component instance

Fig. 19-23: The palm trees populate the base.

Fig. 19-24: All of the 3D AutoCAD components are inserted into the 2D block/ components in the model.

Finishing Touches

The final elements and details that you add to the model are intended to give it depth and further convey the design intent. The following steps are common ones that add flourish to a site plan model.

Articulating the Buildings

Buildings provide context. You can add pre-made or custom Window and Door components to the buildings. Then you can further adjust and manipulate the volume of the building mass (Fig. 19-25 through Fig. 19-27). There are three types of buildings that should be included in a site plan:

▶ Any proposed building or structure that has been designed and modeled.

▶ Existing buildings adjacent to the site plan or proposed architecture. Google Earth and 3D Warehouse contain many pre-made existing buildings that can be downloaded and included in a site model.

▶ Any neighboring buildings that are not adjacent to the site plan or proposed structure. These can be included as volumes instead of articulated massings.

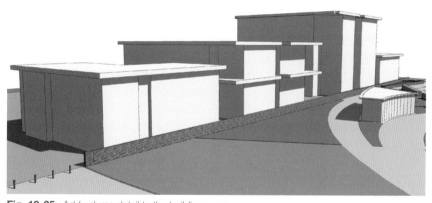

Fig. 19-25: Add volume detail to the building mass.

Fig. 19-26: Construct Window and Door components and place them on the buildings.

Fig. 19-27: The Building component details

Exchanging 3D Components

You can readjust the 3D components that you inserted into the imported block/components. When you enter the component instance, you can delete the inserted 3D component and exchange it with a different version.

Because the elements within the model can be edited easily, SketchUp is very versatile; this versatility can be utilized to convey design intent (Fig. 19-28 through Fig. 19-31).

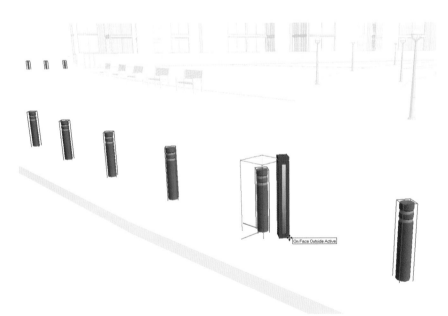

Fig. 19-28: Three-dimensional site elements can be easily replaced with other versions. The bollard is being exchanged for another.

Fig. 19-29: By replacing 3D components, you can exercise SketchUp's versatility.

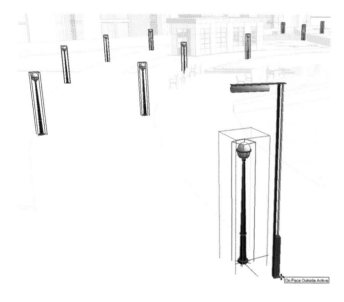

Fig. 19-30: The 3D pedestrian lights are replaced with a more contemporary version.

On Face Outside Active

Fig. 19-31: The 3D pedestrian lights

Conceptual Grading

You can easily add conceptual slopes and elevation to your models. By adding grade and elevation, you help communicate the spatial relationships and design intent (Fig. 19-32 through Fig. 19-37). For a review of conceptual grading, see Chapter 13. You should add conceptual grades, even minute slopes, where possible. Ideally, adding conceptual grade should be done before the Flatwork Base is populated with site elements.

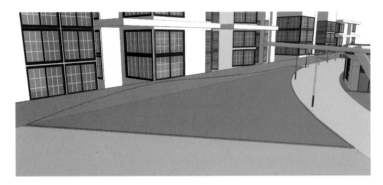

Fig. 19-32: Three arcs are drafted along the wall surface. With the three edges and perimeter lines selected, use the From Contours tool to generate a conceptual slope.

Fig. 19-33: Added slope with trees

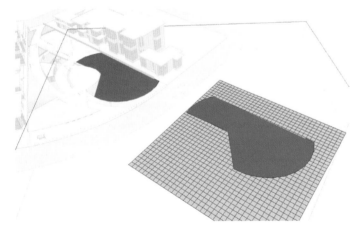

Fig. 19-34: The From Scratch tool is used to copy and align the large lawn area on the grid.

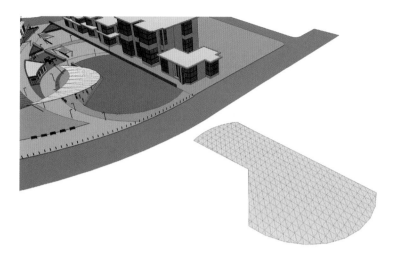

Fig. 19-35: The copied lawn area is draped onto the From Scratch grid. The grid is then trimmed to conform to the shape of the lawn area.

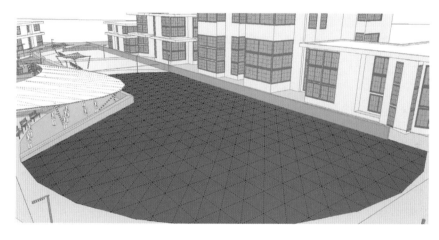

Fig. 19-36: The trimmed From Scratch grid outline is then placed into the site model.

Fig. 19-37: The Smoove tool is then applied to the grid to generate slopes and contours. In this case, the slopes were snapped to the back of the wall adjacent to the water feature. Trees were dropped onto the slope using the Drop extensions.

Adding More Components

Examine the model and determine whether it would benefit from more site elements. Although they were not drafted and included in the AutoCAD site plan, you can still add benches, bike racks, fountain heads, water fountains, canopies, etc. You can use pre-made or custom components to further populate the model and to articulate detail (Fig. 19-38 through Fig. 19-41).

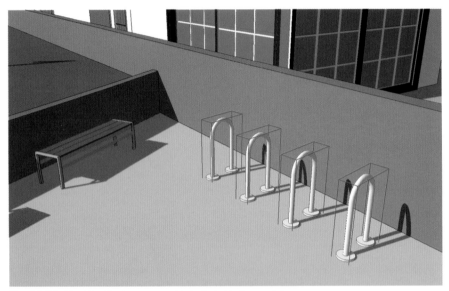

Fig. 19-38: The Bike Rack component is included in the model.

Fig. 19-39: A transportation kiosk

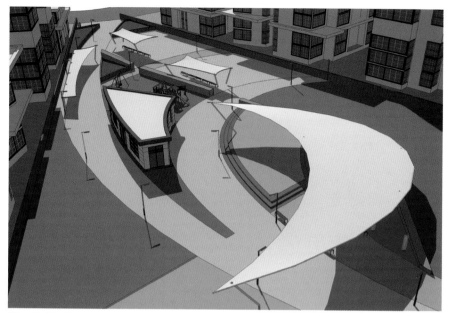

Fig. 19-40: Custom canopies (reviewed in Chapter 14)

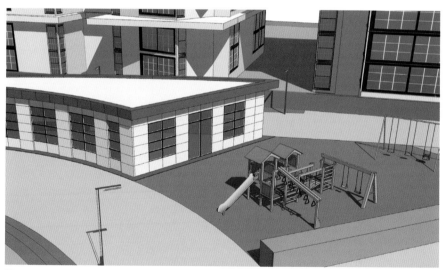

Fig. 19-41: Playground equipment

Making Adjustments

Material colors can be adjusted. They can be reapplied or tweaked in the Materials menu. Using the eyedropper in the Materials palette, you can select colors directly from the model. Then, using the Edit tab, you can change colors using the slider bars or by entering specific color tone values (Fig. 19-42, Fig. 19-43).

Furthermore, materials that utilize a texture image can be tweaked in Photoshop or other photo editors. With the material selected, select the Edit option in the Materials menu. Under Texture and to the right of the image name are two buttons; the one further to the right, when selected, will open the texture image in an external editor. You can then apply filters or any other adjustments to the texture image. Saving the image (keeping the same filename) will automatically update it in SketchUp. This option is only available in SketchUp Pro.

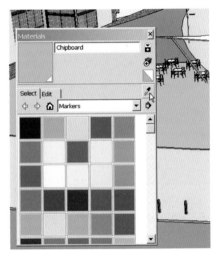

Fig. 19-42: You can adjust colors in the Materials Edit menu.

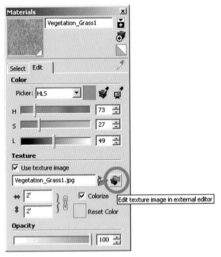

Fig. 19-43: Once the color is selected, select Edit. You can adjust the color by using the sliders or by entering numeric values.

Components can be adjusted to achieve specific results. For example, you can select the tree and other 3D vegetation components and apply Chris Fullmer's Scale and Rotate Multiple extension, creating a more natural tree habitat (Fig. 19-44, Fig. 19-45). The extension can be found at the Extension Warehouse (see Chapter 5).

Fig. 19-44: Inserted trees before Scale and Rotate Multiple is applied

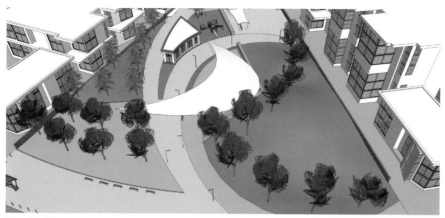

Fig. 19-45: Inserted trees after Scale and Rotate Multiple is applied

Adding New Details

The Flatwork Base can still be adjusted and modeled. In the example images, the lawn area adjacent to the site building is further subdivided with the Line tool to create a small planting area (Fig. 19-46).

The planting surface is offset to create a wall. The wall and planter are then given color and volume (Fig. 19-47, Fig. 19-48).

Small flower components are placed in the planter. Each type is placed on its own layer (Fig. 19-49).

Fig. 19-46: The lawn area near the building will be adjusted to add more detail to the model.

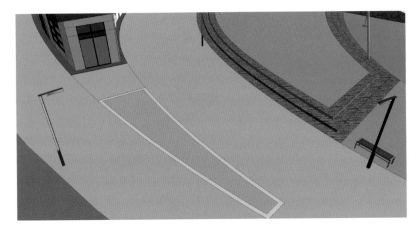

Fig. 19-47: The lawn area is further subdivided into smaller areas. Then the interior of the lawn is offset by 8″ to create a wall surface. Colors are adjusted for the wall and the interior planting surface.

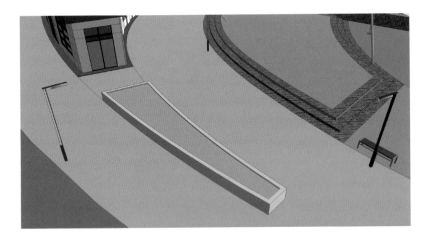

Fig. 19-48: The wall and planting surface are Push/Pulled to create volume.

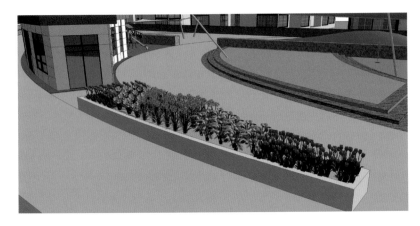

Fig. 19-49: Flower components are placed in the planter. Each flower type is on its own layer.

The flower massings are then randomized using the Scale and Rotate Multiple extension (you can install the extension from the Extension Warehouse) (Fig. 19-50).

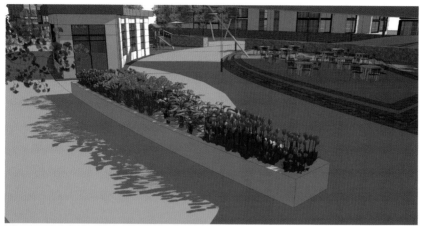

Fig. 19-50: To create a more natural-looking habitat, Scale and Rotate Multiple is applied to the Flower components. The flowers used here are from FormFonts.

Similarly, traffic and road striping can be included. Draft the appropriate shapes onto the Flatwork Base (Fig. 19-51). Convert them into components, add color, copy, and arrange the components to simulate a road or pedestrian crossing (Fig. 19-52 through 19-54).

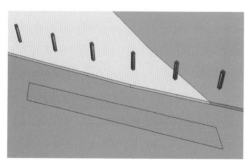

Fig. 19-51: Using the Line tool, subdivide a surface on the road.

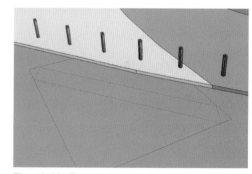

Fig. 19-52: The subdivided surface is then converted into a component.

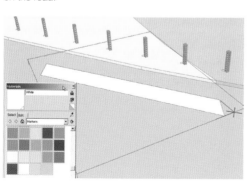

Fig. 19-53: Color is added to the component. In this example, the white color creates a pedestrian crossing stripe.

Fig. 19-54: The Pedestrian Crossing Stripe component is then copied and arranged to simulate a pedestrian crossing.

There are many ways to add detail to the Flatwork Base. Typically, they are added through drafting, offsetting lines, providing color, and adding volume (Fig. 19-55, Fig. 19-56).

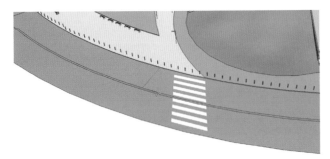

Fig. 19-55: The entire road surface is offset with the Offset tool. The offset lines are brought closer together to create a traffic dividing line in the center. The offset face needs to be further subdivided and "cleaned up" (not shown) to make sure it is a separate face from the road.

Fig. 19-56: Color is added to the subdivided face to simulate a center road stripe.

Adding People and Cars

People and cars are usually the last details you add to a model. They help create a sense of life and activate space. By carefully adding people and cars and placing them in specific locations, you can create well-composed scenes (Fig. 19-57 through Fig. 19-60).

Download File: AutoCAD to SketchUp – Completed Site Plan

Fig. 19-57: Adding People components to a model helps provide scale, context, and activity.

Fig. 19-58: A site program can be depicted or reinforced by placing People components into specific scenes like this outdoor café.

Fig. 19-59: By including people, you provide important scale that helps define the sizes, shapes, and relationships of the various site details and objects.

Fig. 19-60: Include cars and other vehicles to provide context, scale, and activity. Do not add too many vehicles because they can distract from a scene.

Index

line tool, 16
  healing faces, 343–46
Look Arounds, 174. *See also* Walk Through
    menu

M

Make Faces Extension, *see* AutoCAD
    Extensions
Make unique, *see* Components
materials palate, *see* Paint Bucket
Materials tools, *see* Paint Buckett
Midpoint, *see* Inference System
mirroring, *see* Scale tool,
Model organization and arrangement, 69,
    165–75. *See also* layers
  AutoCAD, 356–369
  Arrangement methods, 166–72
    Accuracy method, 166
    Speed method, 166
  finishing touches, 367
  order of component placement, 167–73
    Adjusting components, 167–73
Move/Copy tools, 18, 75
  arraying, 28, 75
    Use, 77
  array-divide, 75
  rotate, 64
  tutorial, 114–16
mouse, *see* navigation

N

Navigation, 21
numbers, entering values, *see* Measurements

O

Objects, 69
Offset tool, 18
  Offset arc, 65, 95
  creating curbs, 96
On edge, *see* Inference System
On face, *see* Inference System

online Help, *see* Support sites
Opacity, *see* Paint Bucket tool
Orbit tool, *see* navigation
overlapping lines, *see* AutoCAD problems and
    issues

P

Paint Bucket, 69–70
  applying color/material, 70, 98–99
    applying to hidden geometry, 121, 244
  editing colors/materials, 88, 374
  making transparent, 88
  textures, 99
  transparent materials, 146
Pan tool, *see* Navigation
Parallel Projection, *see* Camera menu
parapets, *see* Architecture
Path Copy Extension, 77
perimeter, 91
Perspective view, *see* Camera menu
Perpendicular to Edge, *see* Inference System
plan view 174. *See also* Camera menu and
    Views menu
Point inference, *see* Inference System
Position Camera, *see* Walk Through menu
pre-made components, *see* Components
profile edges, 20
Problem solving, 43–46
  SketchUp, 44–46
  tutorials, 44
Push/Pull tool, 19
  adding volumes, 70–73
  curved surfaces, *see* Joint PushPull
  deleting faces, 122
  facets, 182

R

Rectangle tool, 18
  layout a site plan with, 91–92
Red axes, *see* Inference System
Rotate tool, 76
  Rotate copy, 131–32, 291